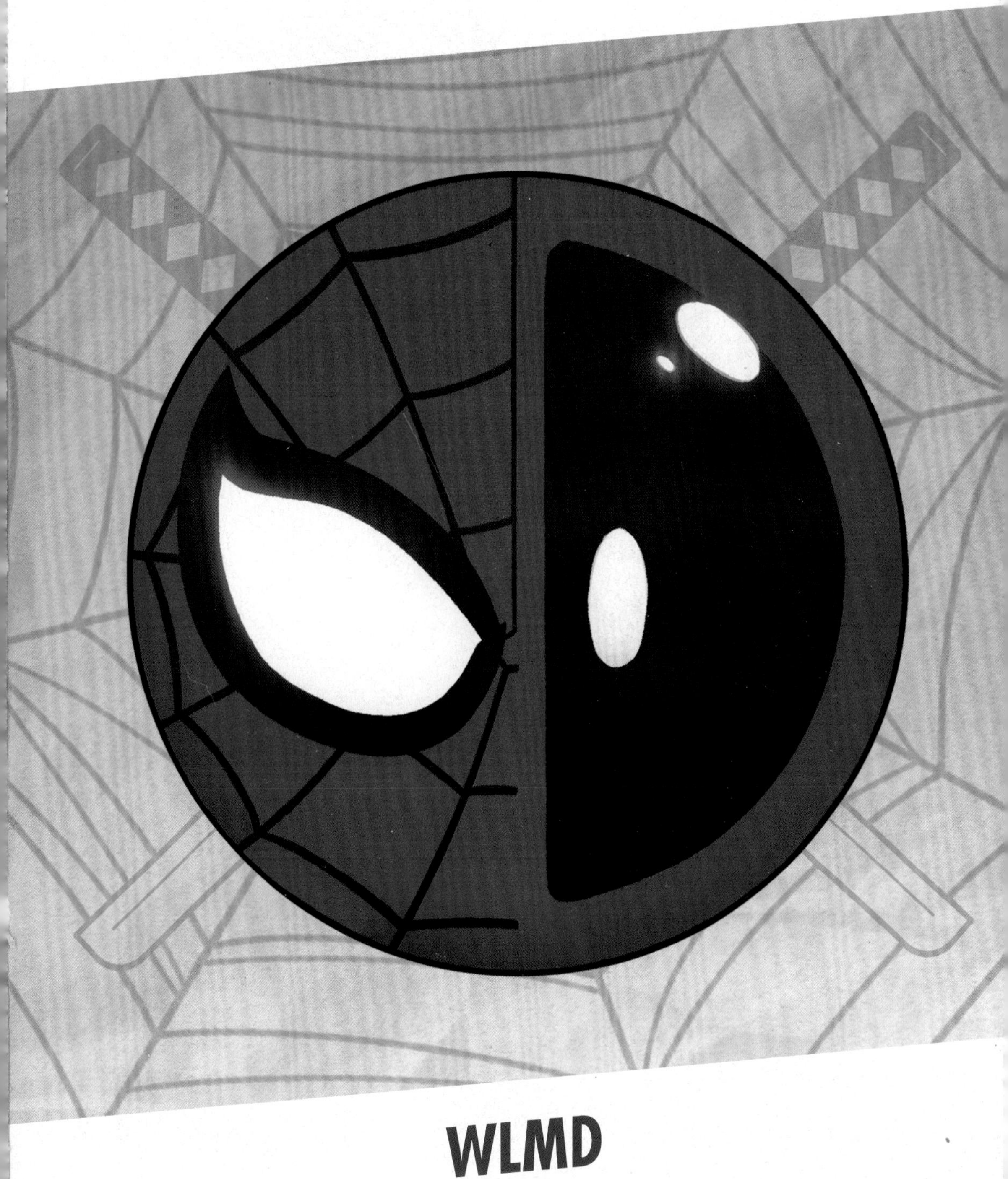

WLMD

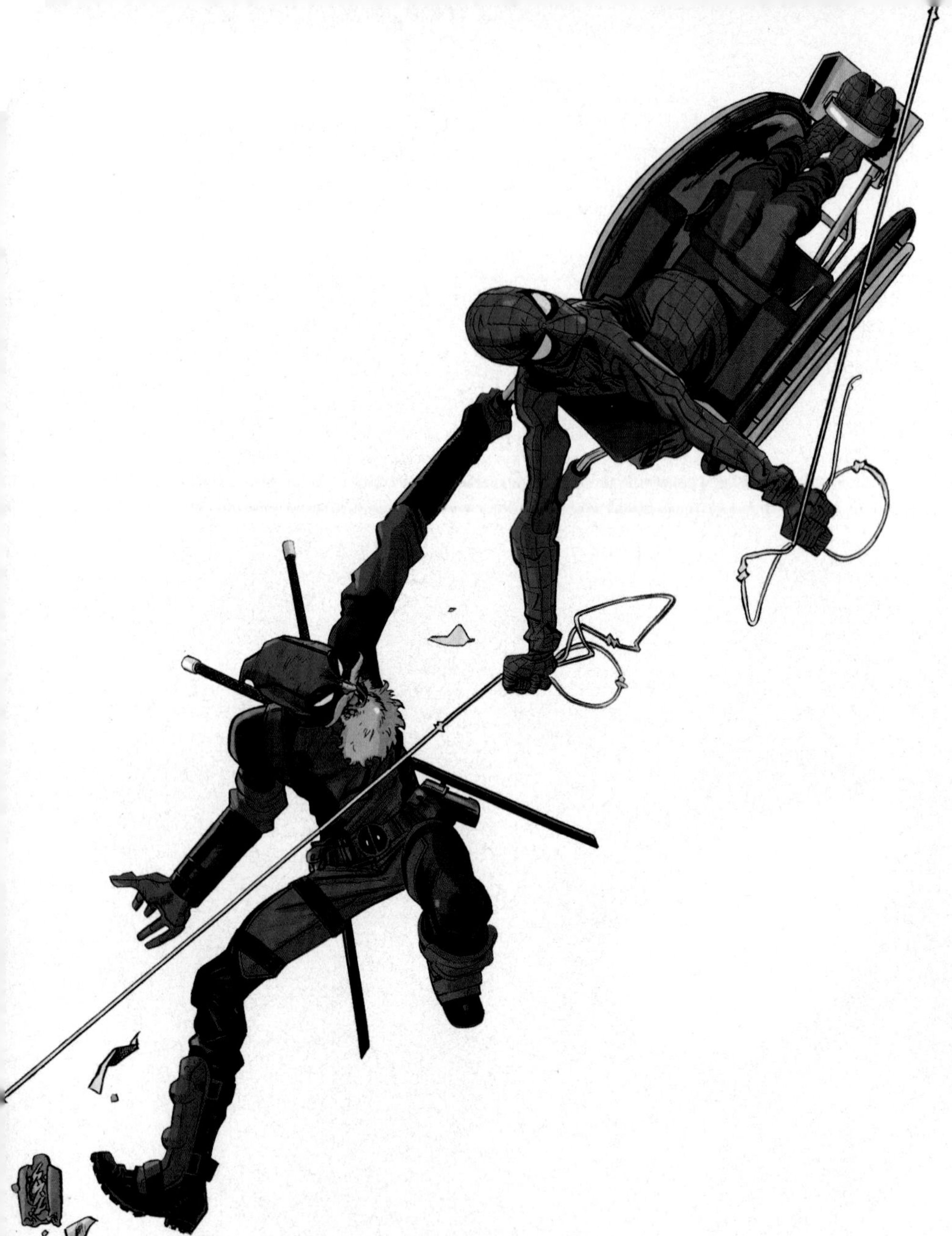



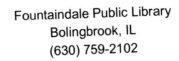

Collection Editor **JENNIFER GRÜNWALD**
Assistant Editor **CAITLIN O'CONNELL**
Associate Managing Editor **KATERI WOODY**
Editor, Special Projects **MARK D. BEAZLEY**

VP Production & Special Projects **JEFF YOUNGQUIST**
SVP Print, Sales & Marketing **DAVID GABRIEL**
Book Designer **ADAM DEL RE**

Editor In Chief **C.B. CEBULSKI**
Chief Creative Officer **JOE QUESADA**
President **DAN BUCKLEY**
Executive Producer **ALAN FINE**

**SPIDER-MAN/DEADPOOL VOL. 6: WLMD.** Contains material originally published in magazine form as SPIDER-MAN/DEADPOOL #29-33. First printing 2018. ISBN 978-1-302-91048-8. Published by MARVEL WORLDWIDE, INC., a subsidiary of MARVEL ENTERTAINMENT, LLC. OFFICE OF PUBLICATION: 135 West 50th Street, New York, NY 10020.  **Printed in Canada.** DAN BUCKLEY, President, Marvel Entertainment; JOHN NEE, Publisher; JOE QUESADA, Chief Creative Officer; TOM BREVOORT, SVP of Publishing; DAVID BOGART, SVP of Business Affairs & Operations, Publishing & Partnership; DAVID GABRIEL, SVP of Sales & Marketing, Publishing; JEFF YOUNGQUIST, VP of Production & Special Projects; DAN CARR, Executive Director of Publishing Technology; ALEX MORALES, Director of Publishing Operations; DAN EDINGTON, Managing Editor; SUSAN CRESPI, Production Manager; STAN LEE, Chairman Emeritus. For information regarding advertising in Marvel Comics or on Marvel.com, please contact Vit DeBellis, Custom Solutions & Integrated Advertising Manager, at vdebellis@marvel.com. For Marvel subscription inquiries, please call 888-511-5480. **Manufactured between 5/25/2018 and 6/26/2018 by SOLISCO PRINTERS, SCOTT, QC, CANADA.**

10 9 8 7 6 5 4 3 2 1

**MARVEL COMICS**
BEGRUDGINGLY PRESENTS...

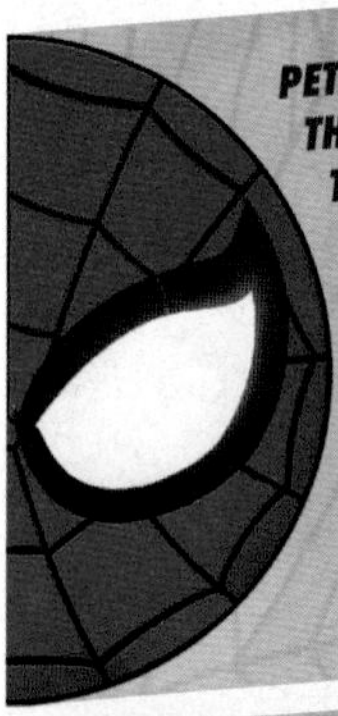

PETER PARKER WAS BITTEN BY AN IRRADIATED SPIDER, GRANTING HIM AMAZING ABILITIES, INCLUDING THE PROPORTIONAL SPEED, STRENGTH AND AGILITY OF A SPIDER, AS WELL AS ADHESIVE FINGERTIPS AND TOES. AFTER LEARNING THAT WITH GREAT POWER, THERE MUST ALSO COME GREAT RESPONSIBILITY, HE BECAME THE WORLD'S GREATEST SUPER HERO! HE'S...

THE WORLD'S GREATEST SUPER HERO!
# The AMAZING SPIDER-MAN

AVENGER...ASSASSIN...SUPERSTAR! WADE WILSON WAS CHOSEN FOR A TOP-SECRET GOVERNMENT PROGRAM THAT GAVE HIM A HEALING FACTOR THAT ALLOWS HIM TO HEAL FROM ANY WOUND. DESPITE EARNING A SMALL FORTUNE AS A GUN FOR HIRE, WADE HAS BECOME THE WORLD'S MOST BELOVED HERO, AND IS THE STAR OF THE WORLD'S GREATEST COMICS MAGAZINE (NO MATTER WHAT THAT JERK IN THE WEBS MAY THINK). CALL HIM THE MERC WITH THE MOUTH...CALL HIM THE REGENERATIN' DEGENERATE...CALL HIM...

# DEADPOOL

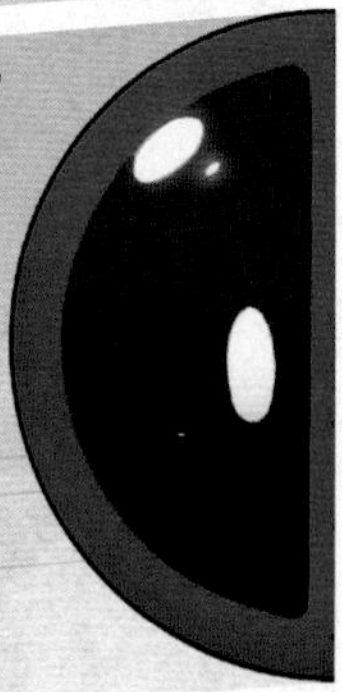

PETER PARKER WAS TRYING TO SETTLE INTO A QUIET RETIREMENT IN AN ASSISTED LIVING FACILITY, BUT FELLOW RESIDENT WADE WILSON NEVER COULD TAKE A HINT. WHEN THE DAILY BUGLE REPORTED THAT A YOUTHFUL DEADPOOL WAS BACK ON THE PROWL, WILSON PLEADED WITH PARKER TO DUST OFF HIS OLD WEB-SHOOTERS AND HELP HIM TAKE DOWN THE IMPOSTER, AGAINST WHOM THEY HOLD AN OLD, DEEP GRUDGE, BUT PETER REFUSED... UNTIL WADE HIRED SOME FOLKS TO STAGE A CRIME FOR PETER TO FOIL, AND HE GOT A TASTE OF HIS OLD HEROICS. AT LAST, THEY SUITED UP, SNUCK PAST RECEPTION AND HIT THE STREETS.

## WLMD


**ROBBIE THOMPSON**
Writer

**SCOTT HEPBURN** (#29 & #32),
**ELMO BONDOC** (#30-31) WITH **MATT HORAK** (#31) & **FLAVIANO** (#32) &
**MATT HORAK** (#33)
Artists

**IAN HERRING** (#29 & #32) & **BRIAN REBER** (#30-31 & #33)
Color Artists

**CHRIS BACHALO** (#29 & #32) WITH **MORRY HOLLOWELL** (#29) & **IAN HERRING** (#32);
**CHRIS BACHALO** & **AL VEY** (#30); **DAVE JOHNSON** (#31 & #33)
Cover Artists

**VC's JOE SABINO**
Letterer

**KATHLEEN WISNESKI**
Assistant Editor

**NICK LOWE** & **JORDAN D. WHITE**
Editors

**SPIDER-MAN** created by **STAN LEE** & **STEVE DITKO**

**DEADPOOL** created by **ROB LIEFELD** & **FABIAN NICIEZA**

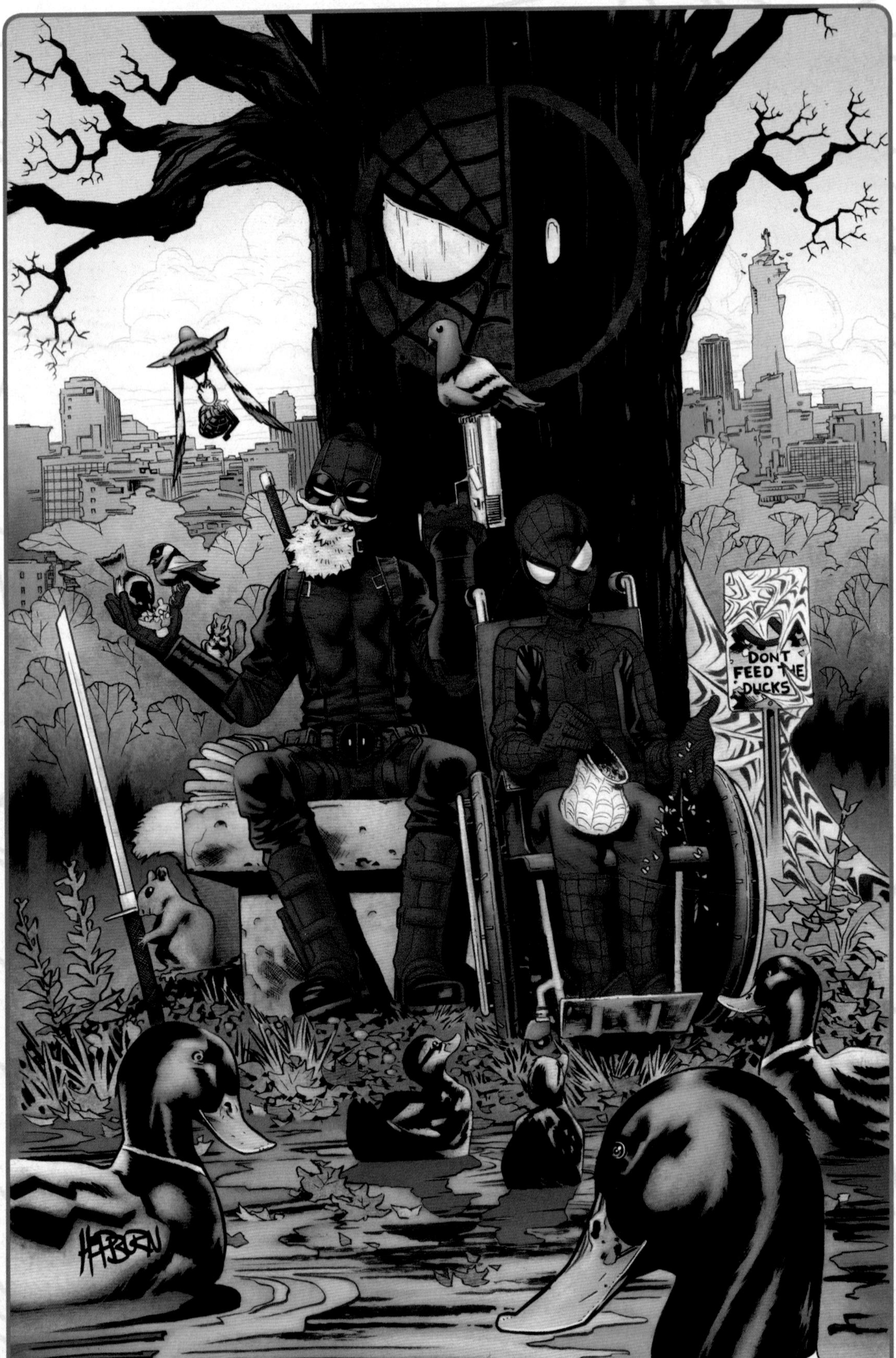
DONT
FEED THE
DUCKS
HEPBURN

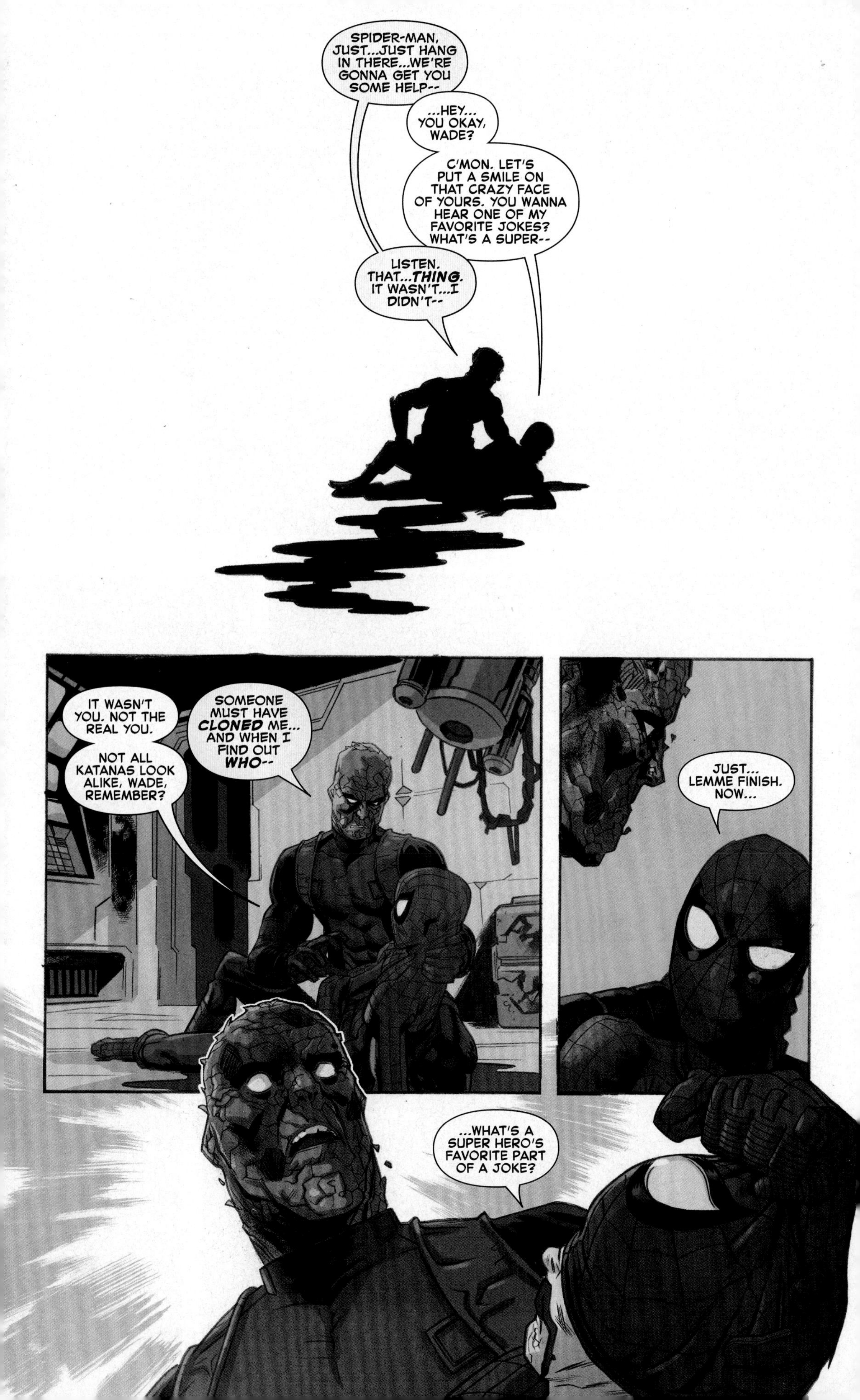

SPIDER-MAN, JUST...JUST HANG IN THERE...WE'RE GONNA GET YOU SOME HELP--
...HEY... YOU OKAY, WADE?
C'MON. LET'S PUT A SMILE ON THAT CRAZY FACE OF YOURS. YOU WANNA HEAR ONE OF MY FAVORITE JOKES? WHAT'S A SUPER--
LISTEN. THAT...THING. IT WASN'T...I DIDN'T--
IT WASN'T YOU. NOT THE REAL YOU.
NOT ALL KATANAS LOOK ALIKE, WADE, REMEMBER?
SOMEONE MUST HAVE CLONED ME... AND WHEN I FIND OUT WHO--
JUST... LEMME FINISH. NOW...
...WHAT'S A SUPER HERO'S FAVORITE PART OF A JOKE?

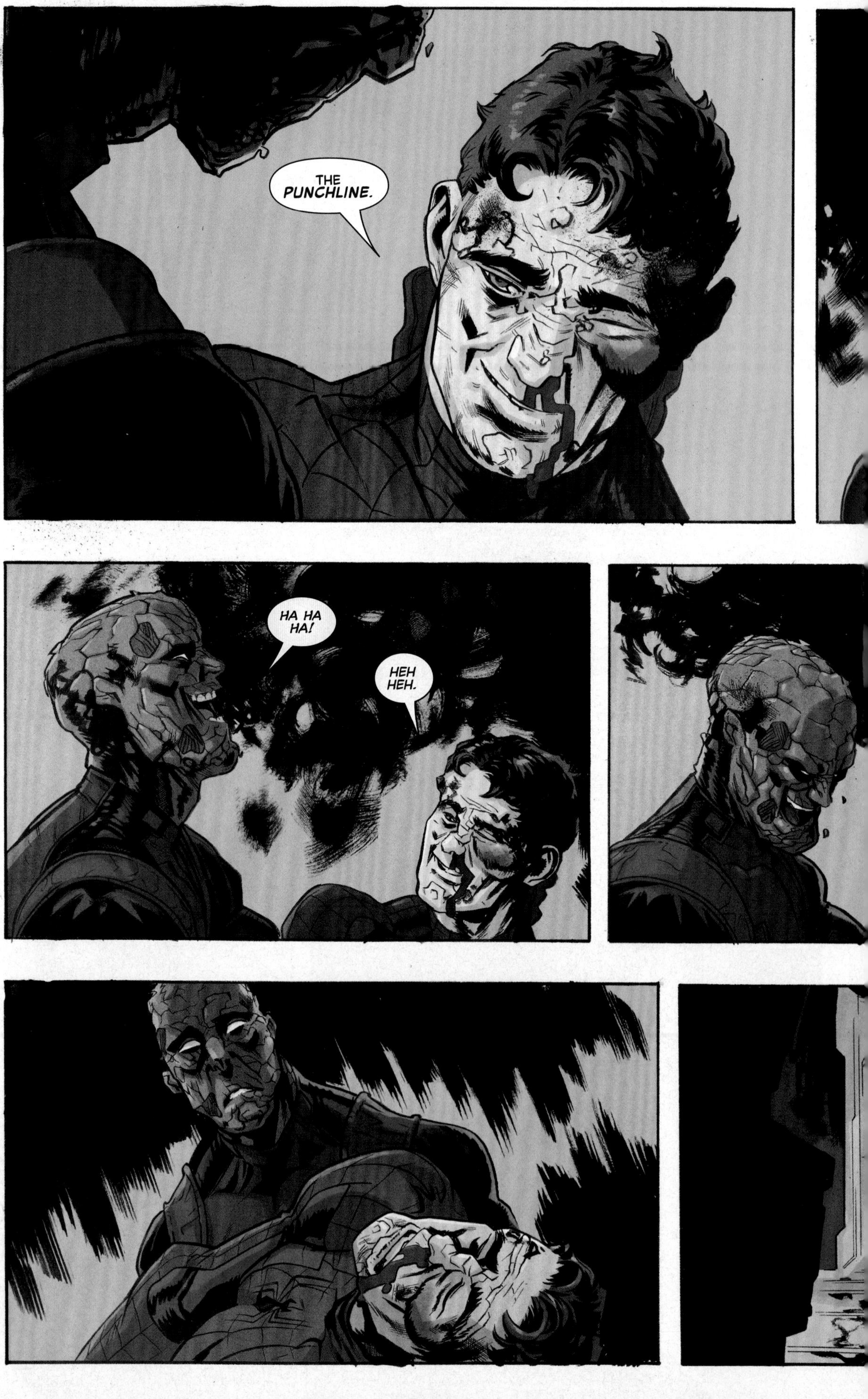
THE PUNCHLINE.
HA HA HA!
HEH HEH.

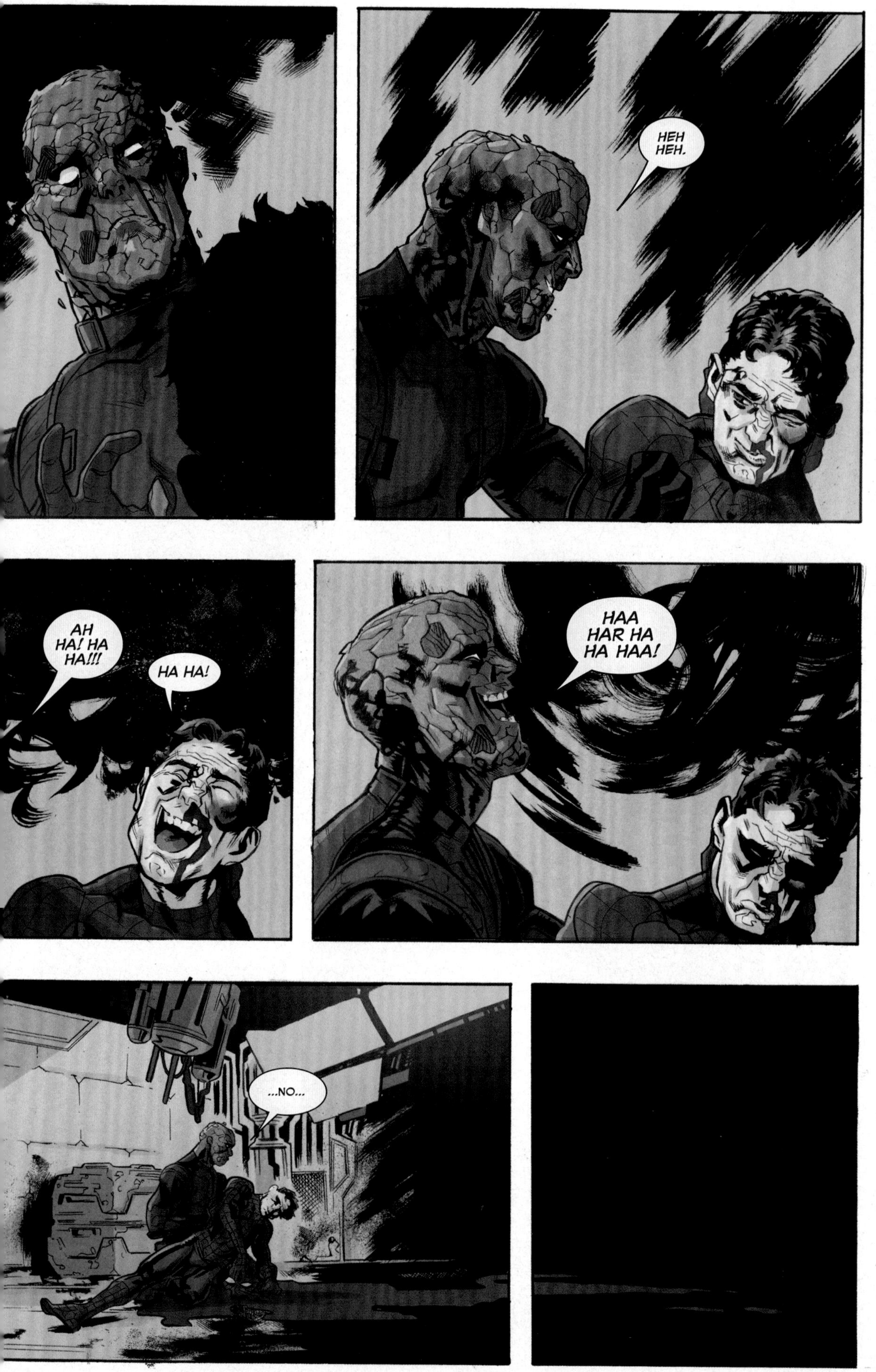
HEH HEH.
AH HA! HA HA!!!
HA HA!
HAA HAR HA HA HAA!
...NO...

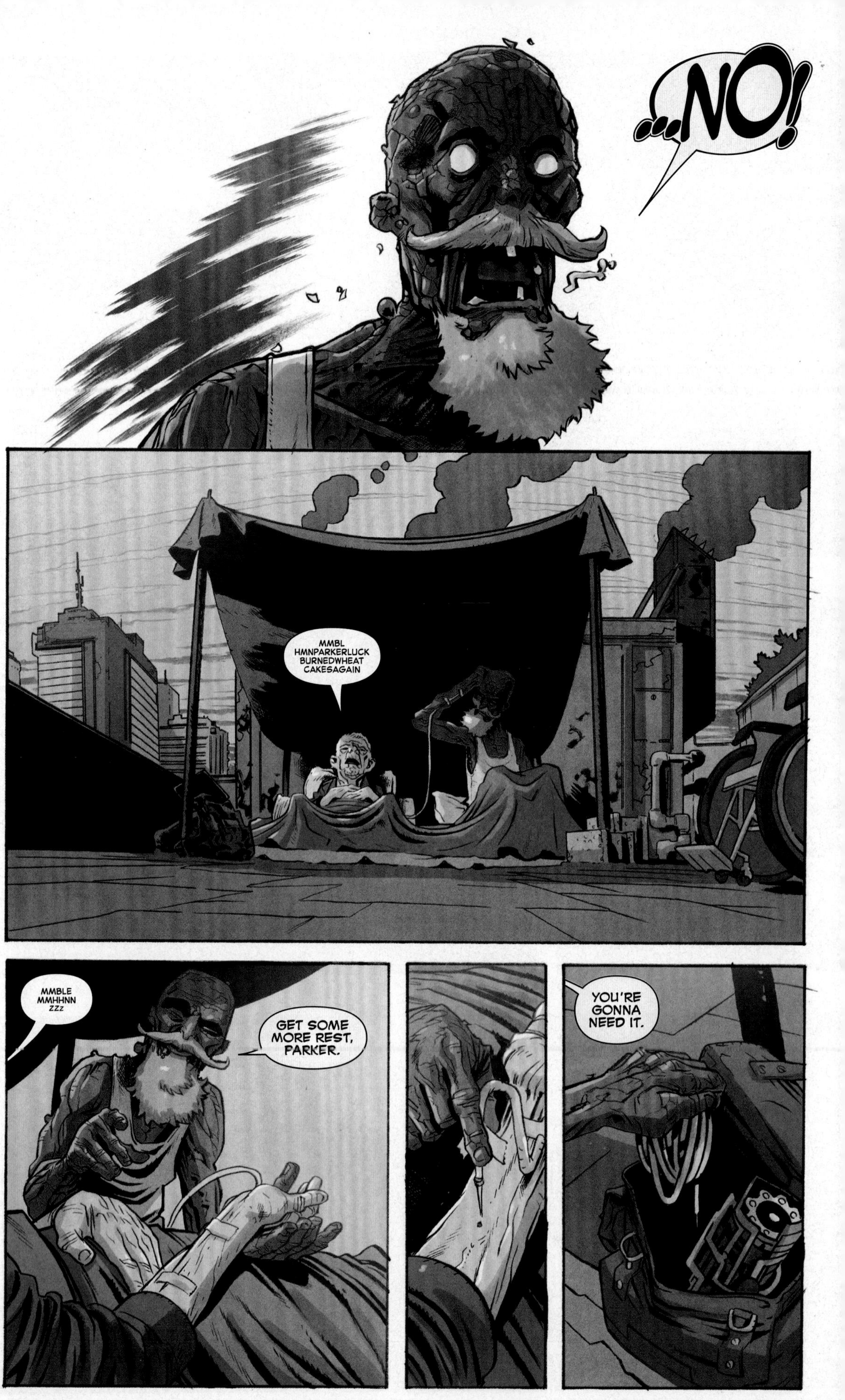
...NO!
MMBL HMNPARKERLUCK BURNEDWHEAT CAKESAGAIN
MMBLE MMHHNN ZZz
GET SOME MORE REST, PARKER.
YOU'RE GONNA NEED IT.

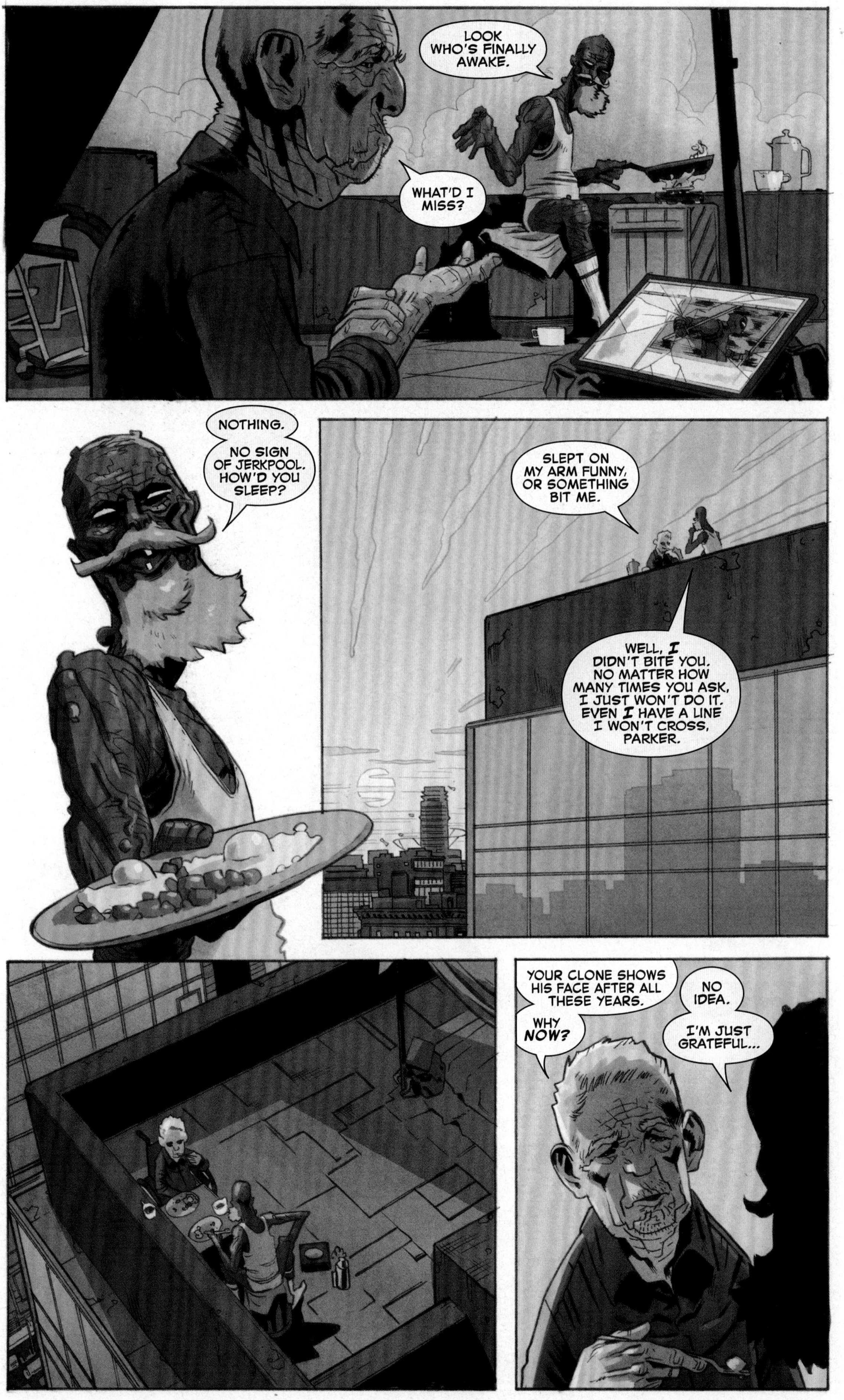
LOOK WHO'S FINALLY AWAKE.
WHAT'D I MISS?
NOTHING.
NO SIGN OF JERKPOOL. HOW'D YOU SLEEP?
SLEPT ON MY ARM FUNNY, OR SOMETHING BIT ME.
WELL, I DIDN'T BITE YOU. NO MATTER HOW MANY TIMES YOU ASK, I JUST WON'T DO IT. EVEN I HAVE A LINE I WON'T CROSS, PARKER.
YOUR CLONE SHOWS HIS FACE AFTER ALL THESE YEARS.
WHY NOW?
NO IDEA.
I'M JUST GRATEFUL...

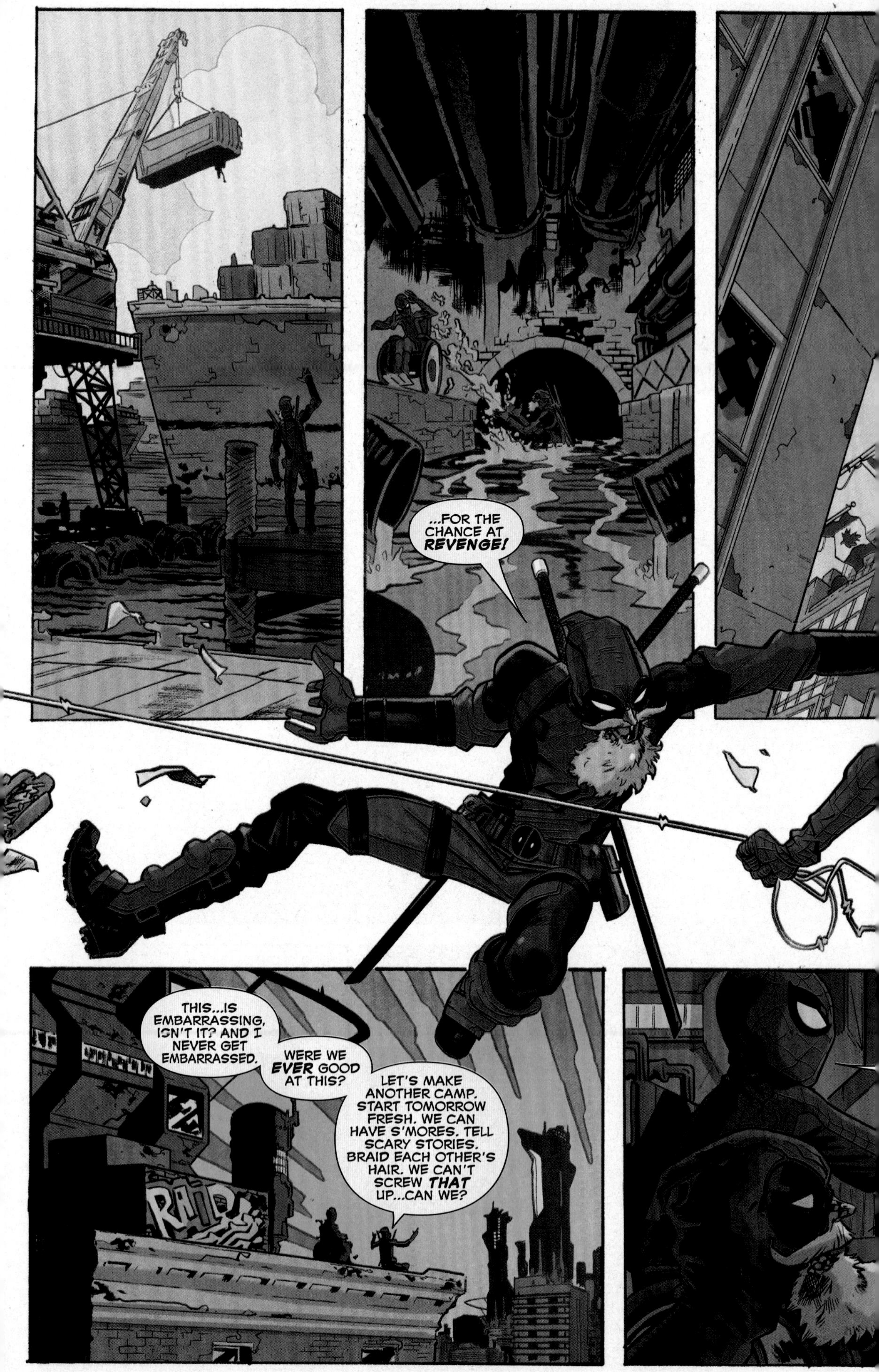
...FOR THE CHANCE AT REVENGE!
THIS...IS EMBARRASSING, ISN'T IT? AND I NEVER GET EMBARRASSED.
WERE WE EVER GOOD AT THIS?
LET'S MAKE ANOTHER CAMP. START TOMORROW FRESH. WE CAN HAVE S'MORES. TELL SCARY STORIES. BRAID EACH OTHER'S HAIR. WE CAN'T SCREW THAT UP...CAN WE?

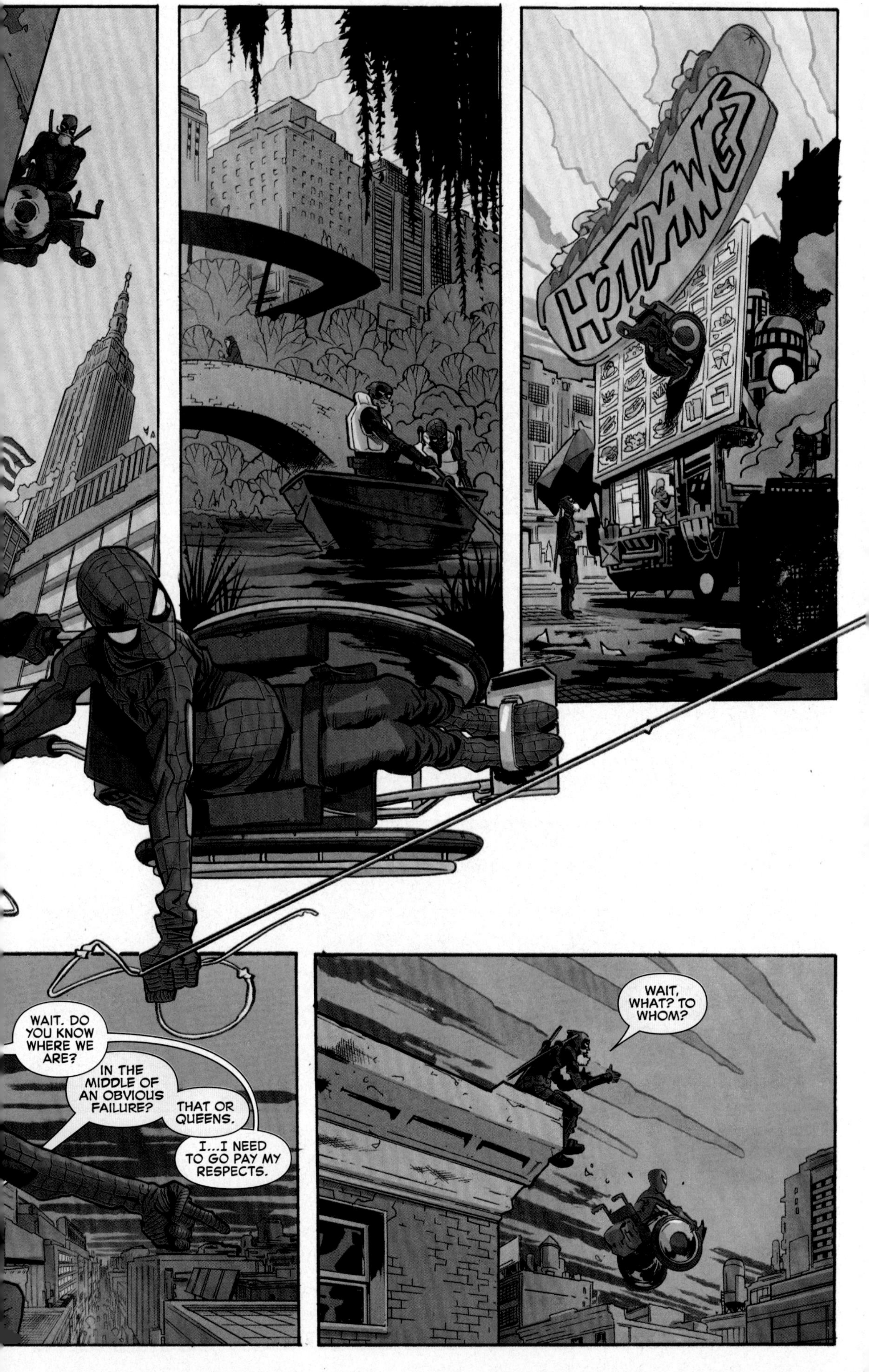
HOTDAWGS
WAIT. DO YOU KNOW WHERE WE ARE?
IN THE MIDDLE OF AN OBVIOUS FAILURE?
THAT OR QUEENS.
I...I NEED TO GO PAY MY RESPECTS.
WAIT, WHAT? TO WHOM?

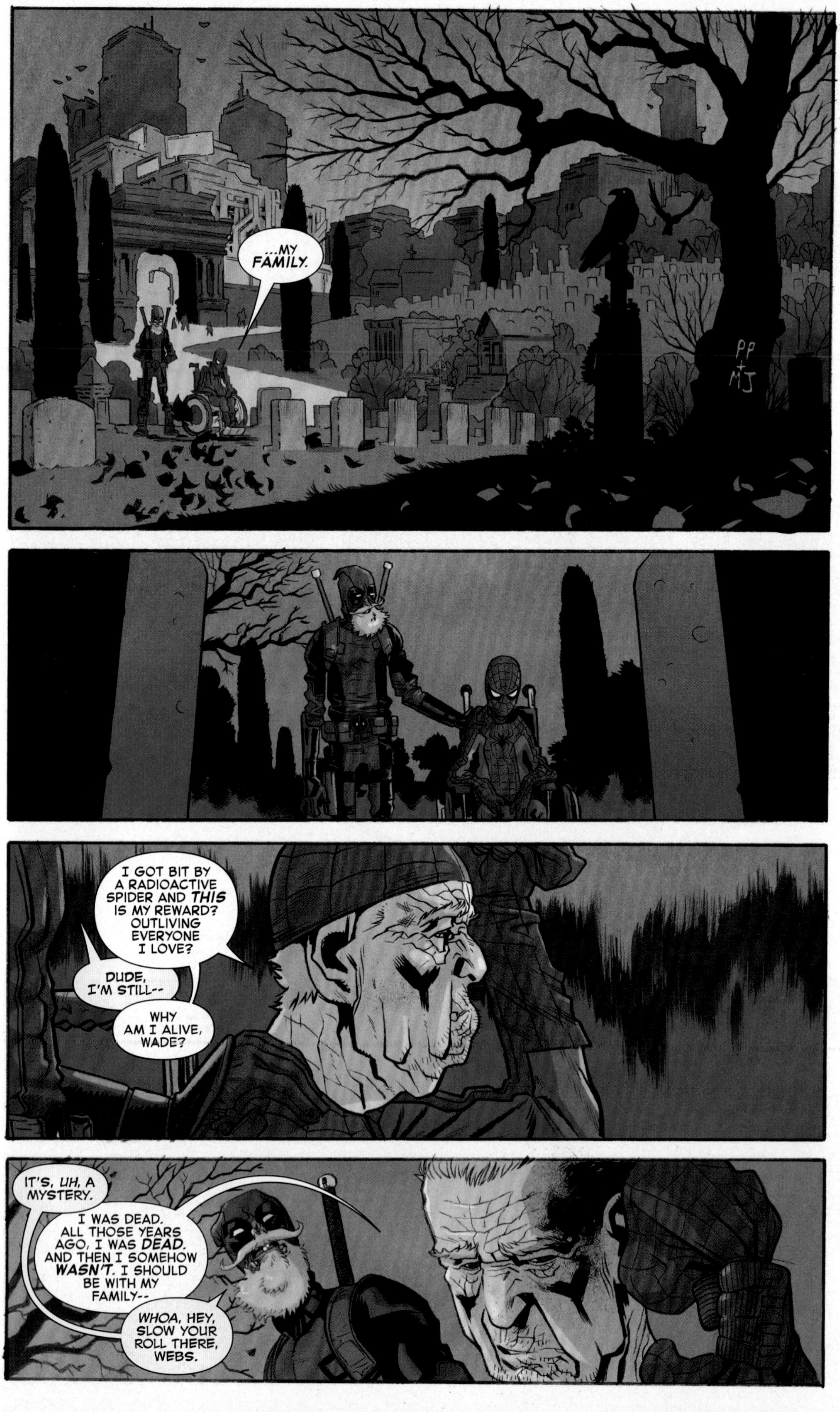

...MY FAMILY.
PP + MJ
I GOT BIT BY A RADIOACTIVE SPIDER AND THIS IS MY REWARD? OUTLIVING EVERYONE I LOVE?
DUDE, I'M STILL--
WHY AM I ALIVE, WADE?
IT'S, UH, A MYSTERY.
I WAS DEAD. ALL THOSE YEARS AGO, I WAS DEAD. AND THEN I SOMEHOW WASN'T. I SHOULD BE WITH MY FAMILY--
WHOA, HEY, SLOW YOUR ROLL THERE, WEBS.

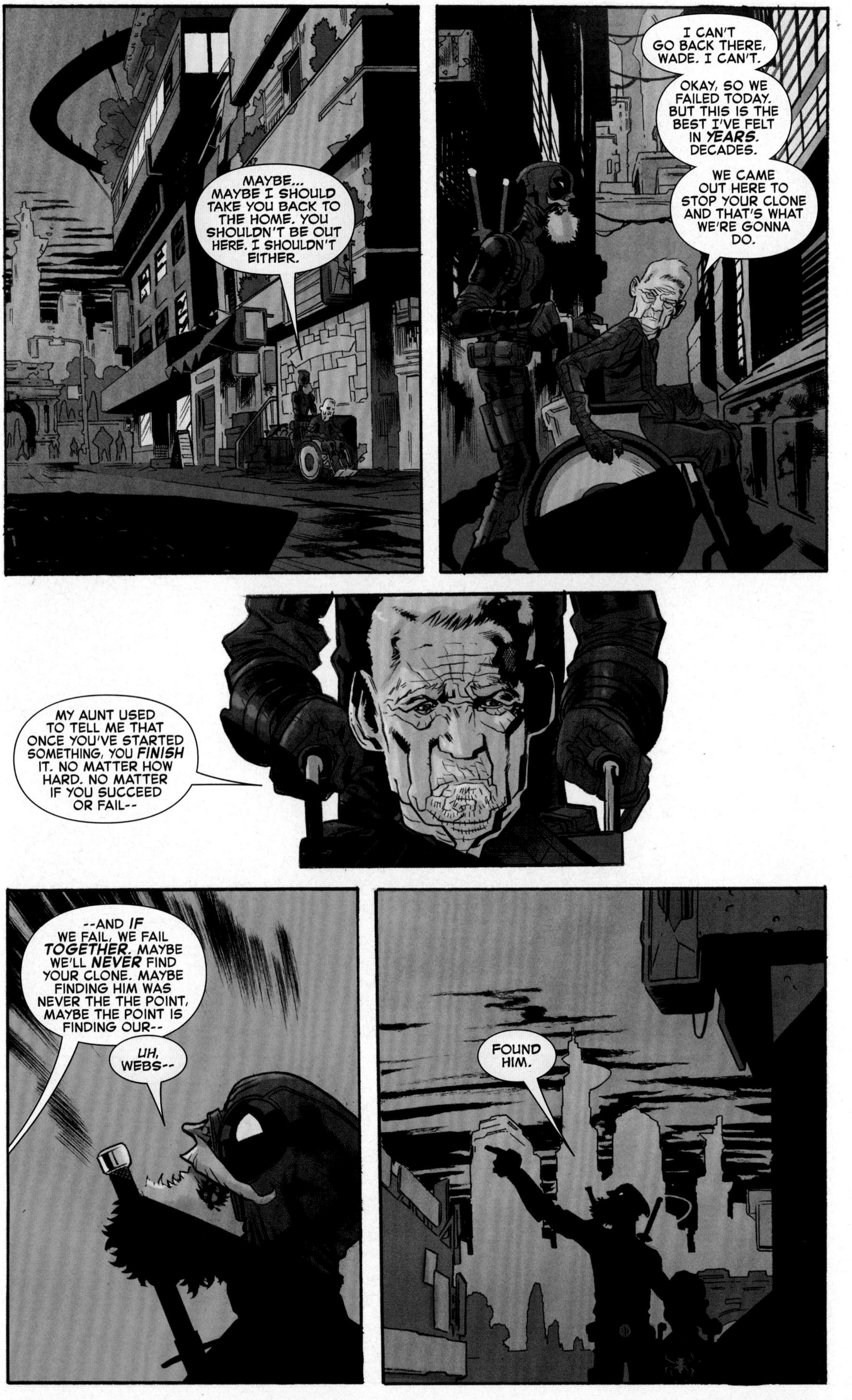
MAYBE... MAYBE I SHOULD TAKE YOU BACK TO THE HOME. YOU SHOULDN'T BE OUT HERE. I SHOULDN'T EITHER.
I CAN'T GO BACK THERE, WADE. I CAN'T.
OKAY, SO WE FAILED TODAY. BUT THIS IS THE BEST I'VE FELT IN YEARS. DECADES.
WE CAME OUT HERE TO STOP YOUR CLONE AND THAT'S WHAT WE'RE GONNA DO.
MY AUNT USED TO TELL ME THAT ONCE YOU'VE STARTED SOMETHING, YOU FINISH IT. NO MATTER HOW HARD. NO MATTER IF YOU SUCCEED OR FAIL--
--AND IF WE FAIL, WE FAIL TOGETHER. MAYBE WE'LL NEVER FIND YOUR CLONE. MAYBE FINDING HIM WAS NEVER THE THE POINT, MAYBE THE POINT IS FINDING OUR--
UH, WEBS--
FOUND HIM.

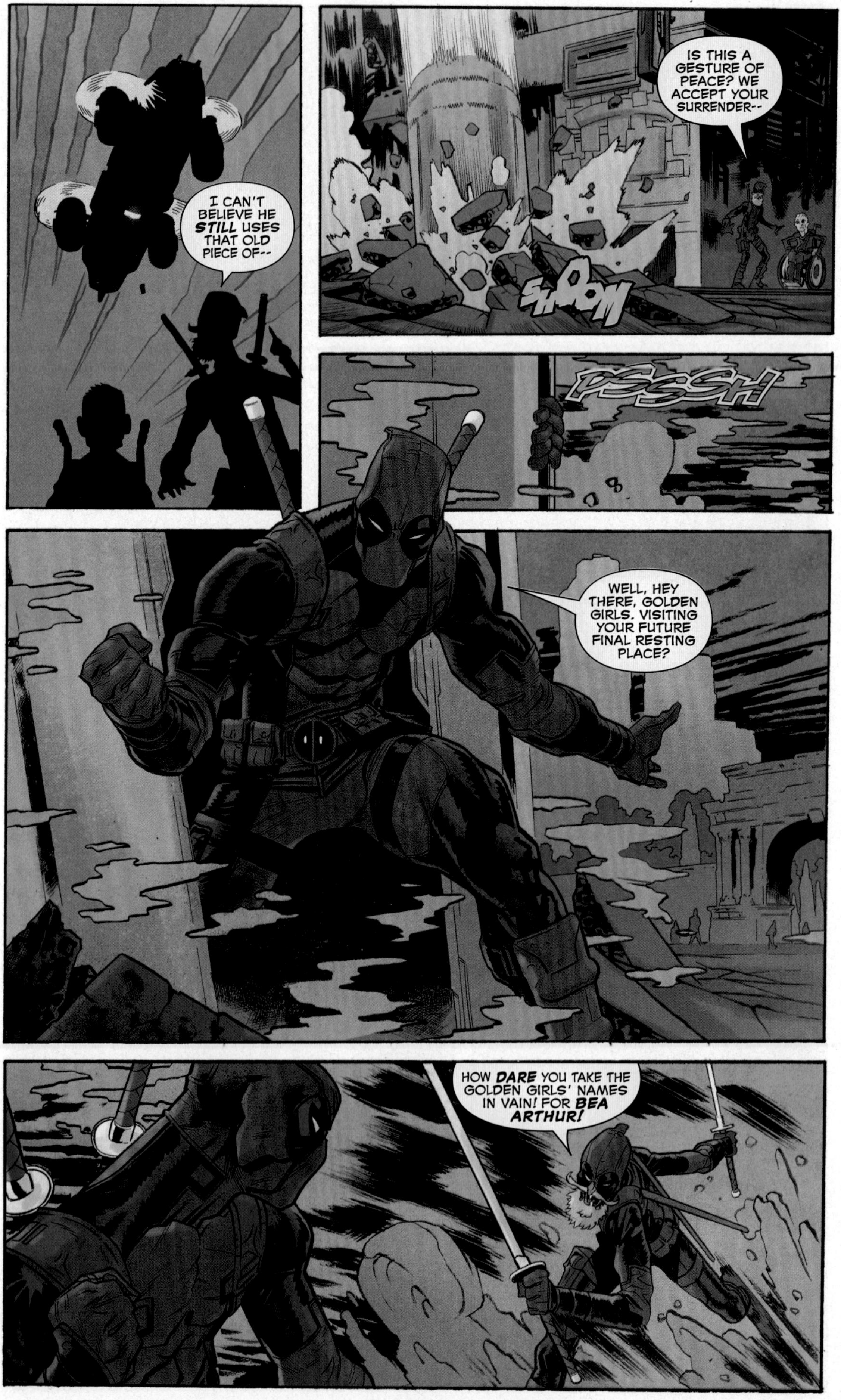
I CAN'T BELIEVE HE STILL USES THAT OLD PIECE OF--
IS THIS A GESTURE OF PEACE? WE ACCEPT YOUR SURRENDER--
SHOOM
PSSSH
WELL, HEY THERE, GOLDEN GIRLS. VISITING YOUR FUTURE FINAL RESTING PLACE?
HOW DARE YOU TAKE THE GOLDEN GIRLS' NAMES IN VAIN! FOR BEA ARTHUR!

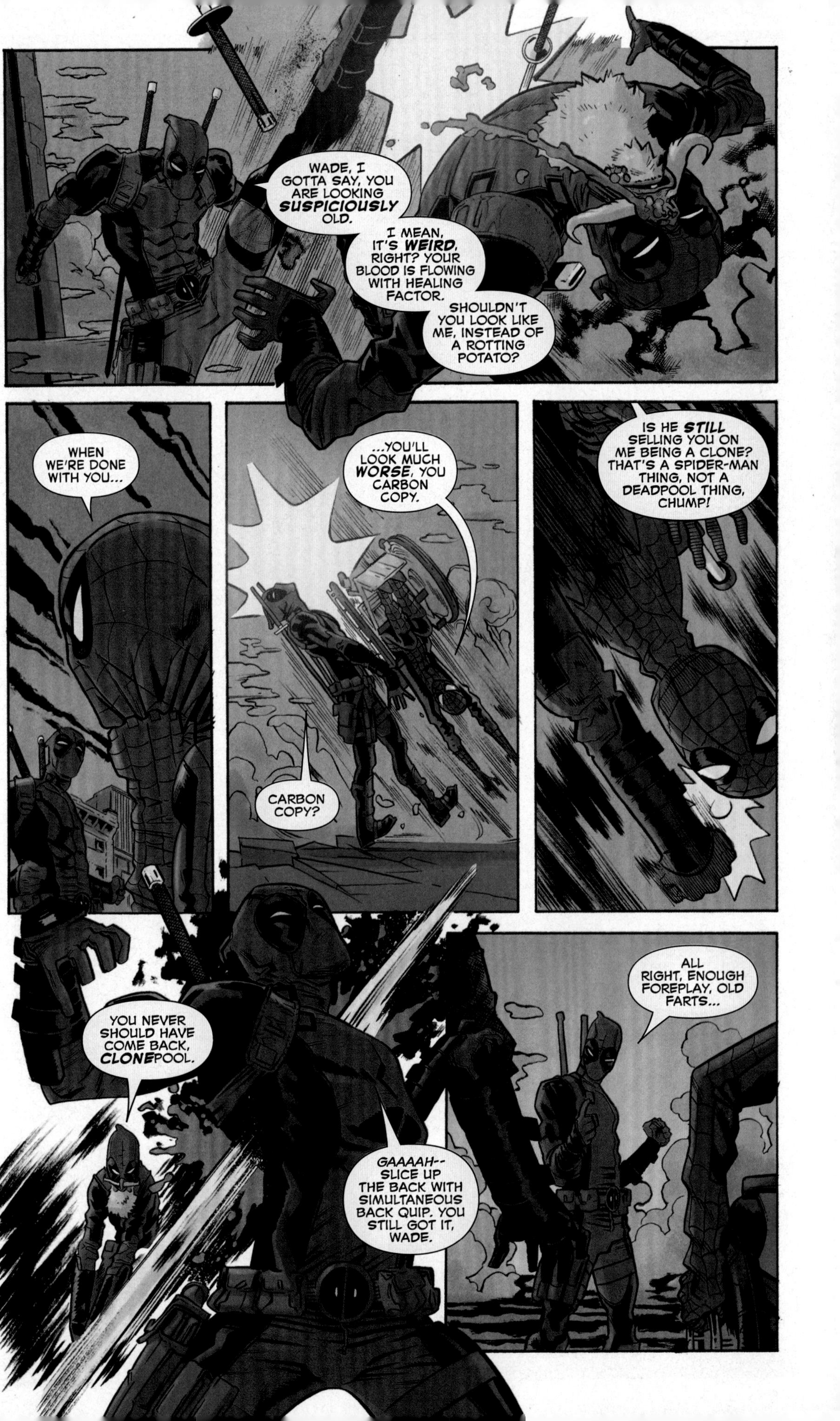
WADE, I GOTTA SAY, YOU ARE LOOKING SUSPICIOUSLY OLD.
I MEAN, IT'S WEIRD, RIGHT? YOUR BLOOD IS FLOWING WITH HEALING FACTOR.
SHOULDN'T YOU LOOK LIKE ME, INSTEAD OF A ROTTING POTATO?
WHEN WE'RE DONE WITH YOU...
...YOU'LL LOOK MUCH WORSE, YOU CARBON COPY.
CARBON COPY?
IS HE STILL SELLING YOU ON ME BEING A CLONE? THAT'S A SPIDER-MAN THING, NOT A DEADPOOL THING, CHUMP!
YOU NEVER SHOULD HAVE COME BACK, CLONEPOOL.
GAAAAH-- SLICE UP THE BACK WITH SIMULTANEOUS BACK QUIP. YOU STILL GOT IT, WADE.
ALL RIGHT, ENOUGH FOREPLAY, OLD FARTS...

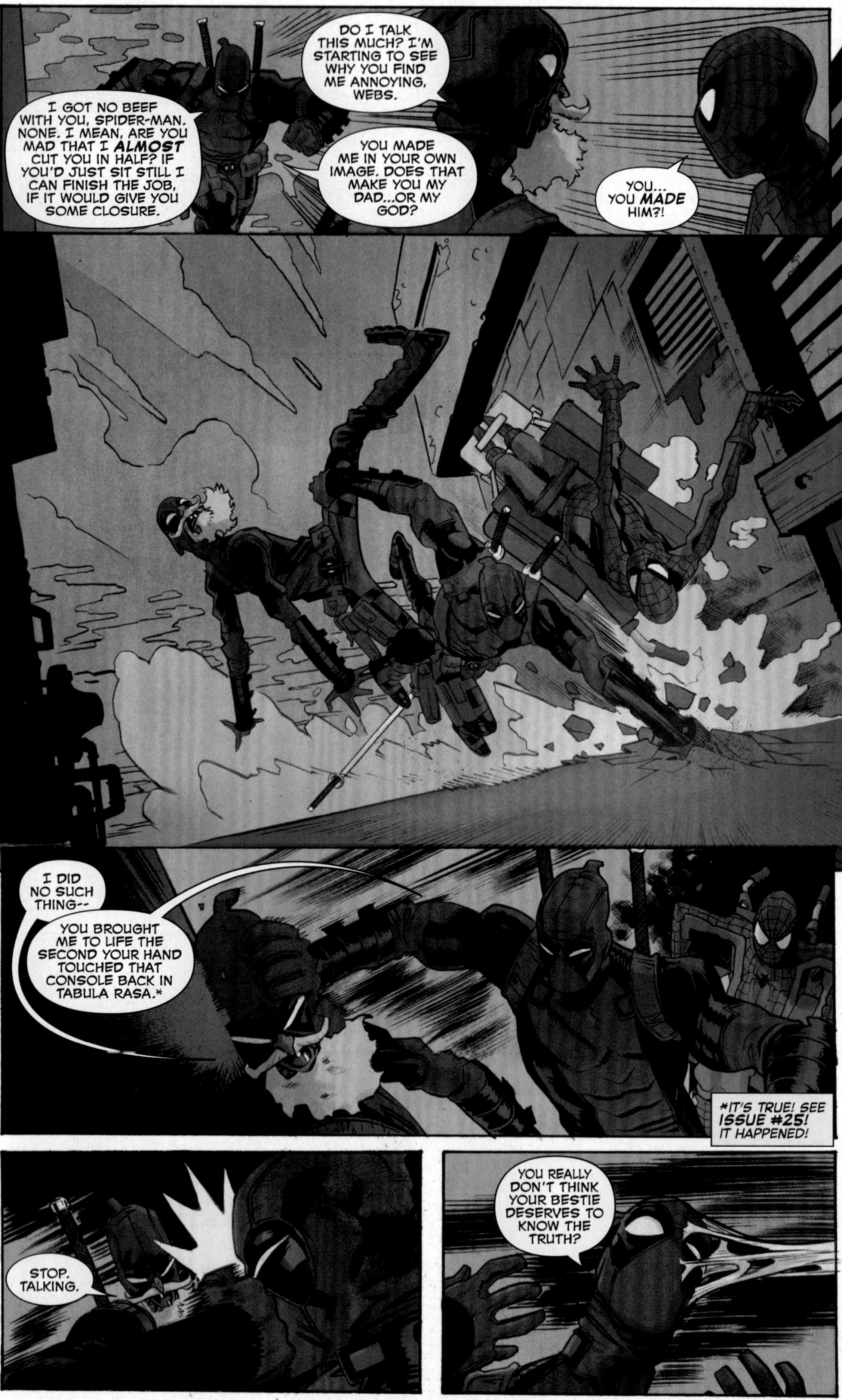
I GOT NO BEEF WITH YOU, SPIDER-MAN. NONE. I MEAN, ARE YOU MAD THAT I ALMOST CUT YOU IN HALF? IF YOU'D JUST SIT STILL I CAN FINISH THE JOB, IF IT WOULD GIVE YOU SOME CLOSURE.
DO I TALK THIS MUCH? I'M STARTING TO SEE WHY YOU FIND ME ANNOYING, WEBS.
YOU MADE ME IN YOUR OWN IMAGE. DOES THAT MAKE YOU MY DAD...OR MY GOD?
YOU... YOU MADE HIM?!
I DID NO SUCH THING--
YOU BROUGHT ME TO LIFE THE SECOND YOUR HAND TOUCHED THAT CONSOLE BACK IN TABULA RASA.*
*IT'S TRUE! SEE ISSUE #25! IT HAPPENED!
STOP. TALKING.
YOU REALLY DON'T THINK YOUR BESTIE DESERVES TO KNOW THE TRUTH?

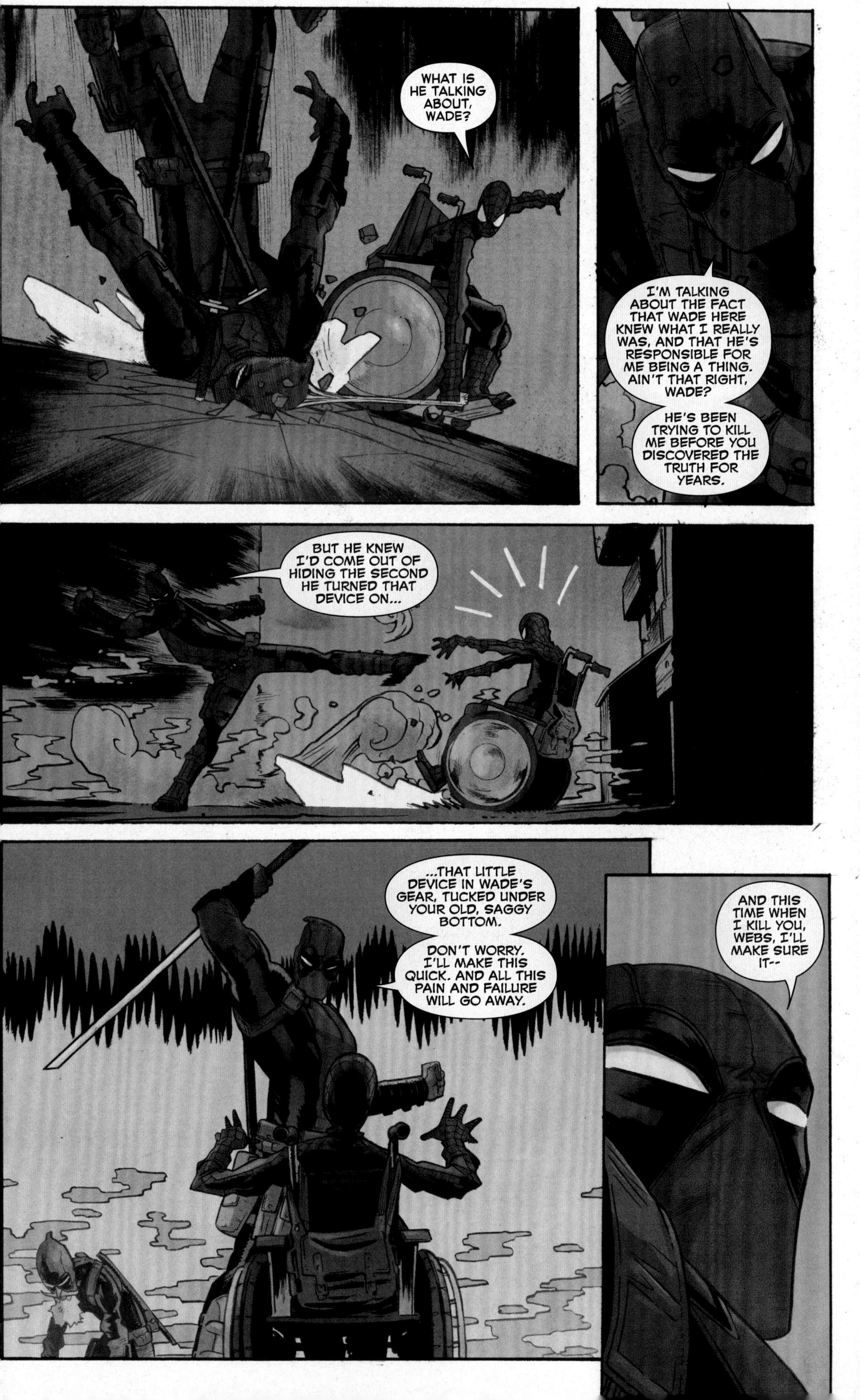
WHAT IS HE TALKING ABOUT, WADE?
I'M TALKING ABOUT THE FACT THAT WADE HERE KNEW WHAT I REALLY WAS, AND THAT HE'S RESPONSIBLE FOR ME BEING A THING. AIN'T THAT RIGHT, WADE?
HE'S BEEN TRYING TO KILL ME BEFORE YOU DISCOVERED THE TRUTH FOR YEARS.
BUT HE KNEW I'D COME OUT OF HIDING THE SECOND HE TURNED THAT DEVICE ON...
...THAT LITTLE DEVICE IN WADE'S GEAR, TUCKED UNDER YOUR OLD, SAGGY BOTTOM.
DON'T WORRY. I'LL MAKE THIS QUICK. AND ALL THIS PAIN AND FAILURE WILL GO AWAY.
AND THIS TIME WHEN I KILL YOU, WEBS, I'LL MAKE SURE IT--

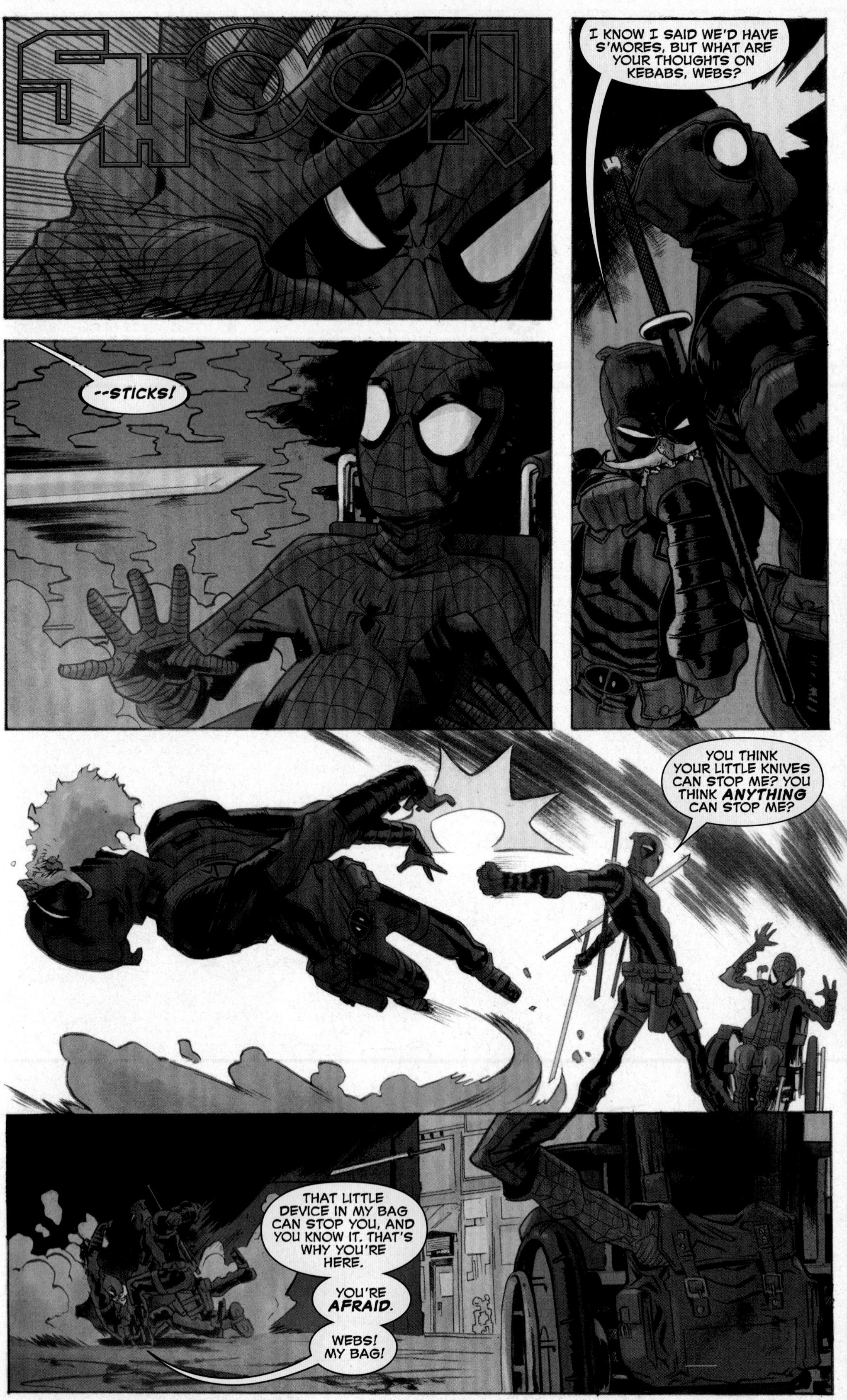

I KNOW I SAID WE'D HAVE S'MORES, BUT WHAT ARE YOUR THOUGHTS ON KEBABS, WEBS?
--STICKS!
YOU THINK YOUR LITTLE KNIVES CAN STOP ME? YOU THINK ANYTHING CAN STOP ME?
THAT LITTLE DEVICE IN MY BAG CAN STOP YOU, AND YOU KNOW IT. THAT'S WHY YOU'RE HERE.
YOU'RE AFRAID.
WEBS! MY BAG!

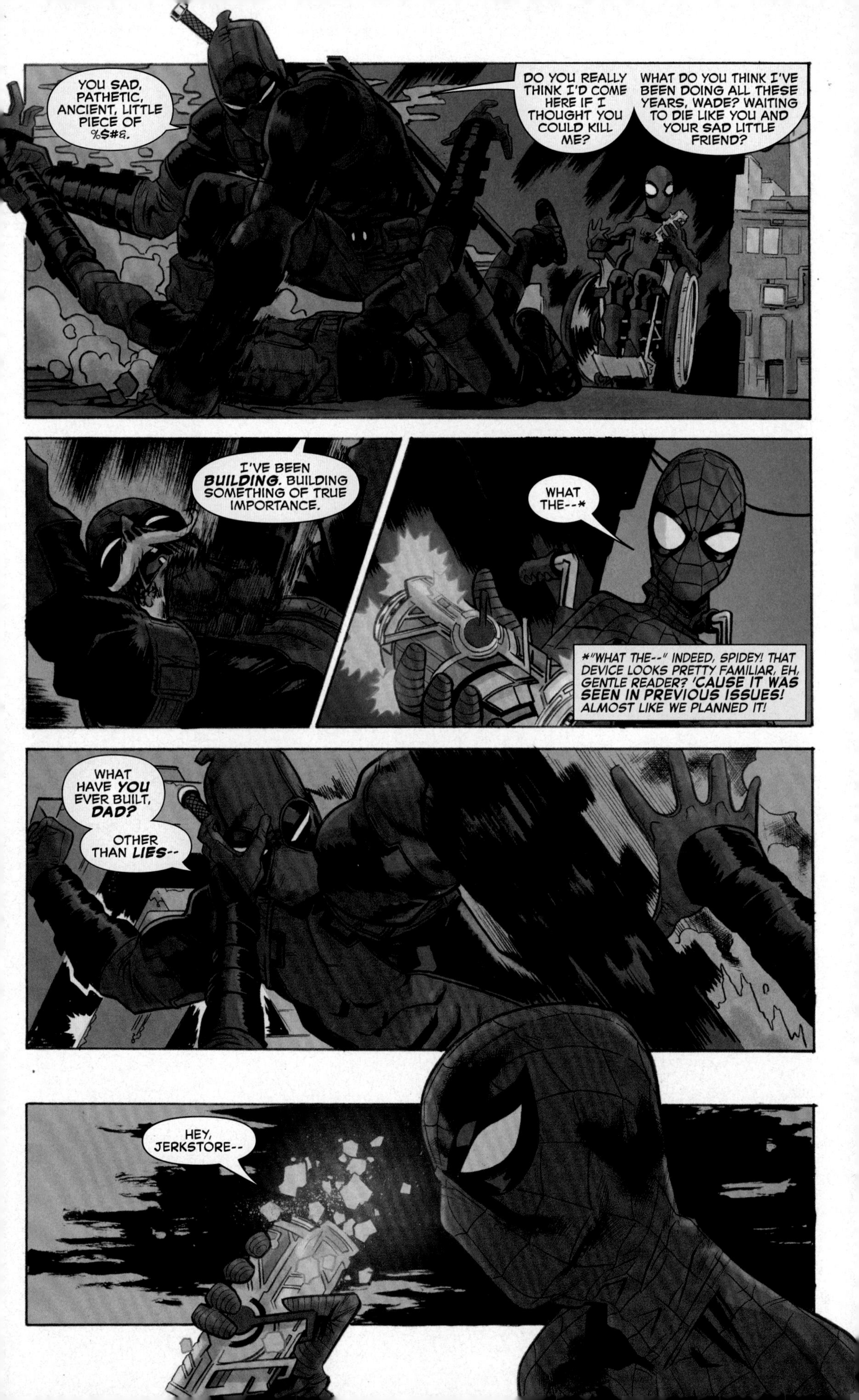
YOU SAD, PATHETIC, ANCIENT, LITTLE PIECE OF %$#&.
DO YOU REALLY THINK I'D COME HERE IF I THOUGHT YOU COULD KILL ME?
WHAT DO YOU THINK I'VE BEEN DOING ALL THESE YEARS, WADE? WAITING TO DIE LIKE YOU AND YOUR SAD LITTLE FRIEND?
I'VE BEEN BUILDING. BUILDING SOMETHING OF TRUE IMPORTANCE.
WHAT THE--*
*"WHAT THE--" INDEED, SPIDEY! THAT DEVICE LOOKS PRETTY FAMILIAR, EH, GENTLE READER? 'CAUSE IT WAS SEEN IN PREVIOUS ISSUES! ALMOST LIKE WE PLANNED IT!
WHAT HAVE YOU EVER BUILT, DAD?
OTHER THAN LIES--
HEY, JERKSTORE--

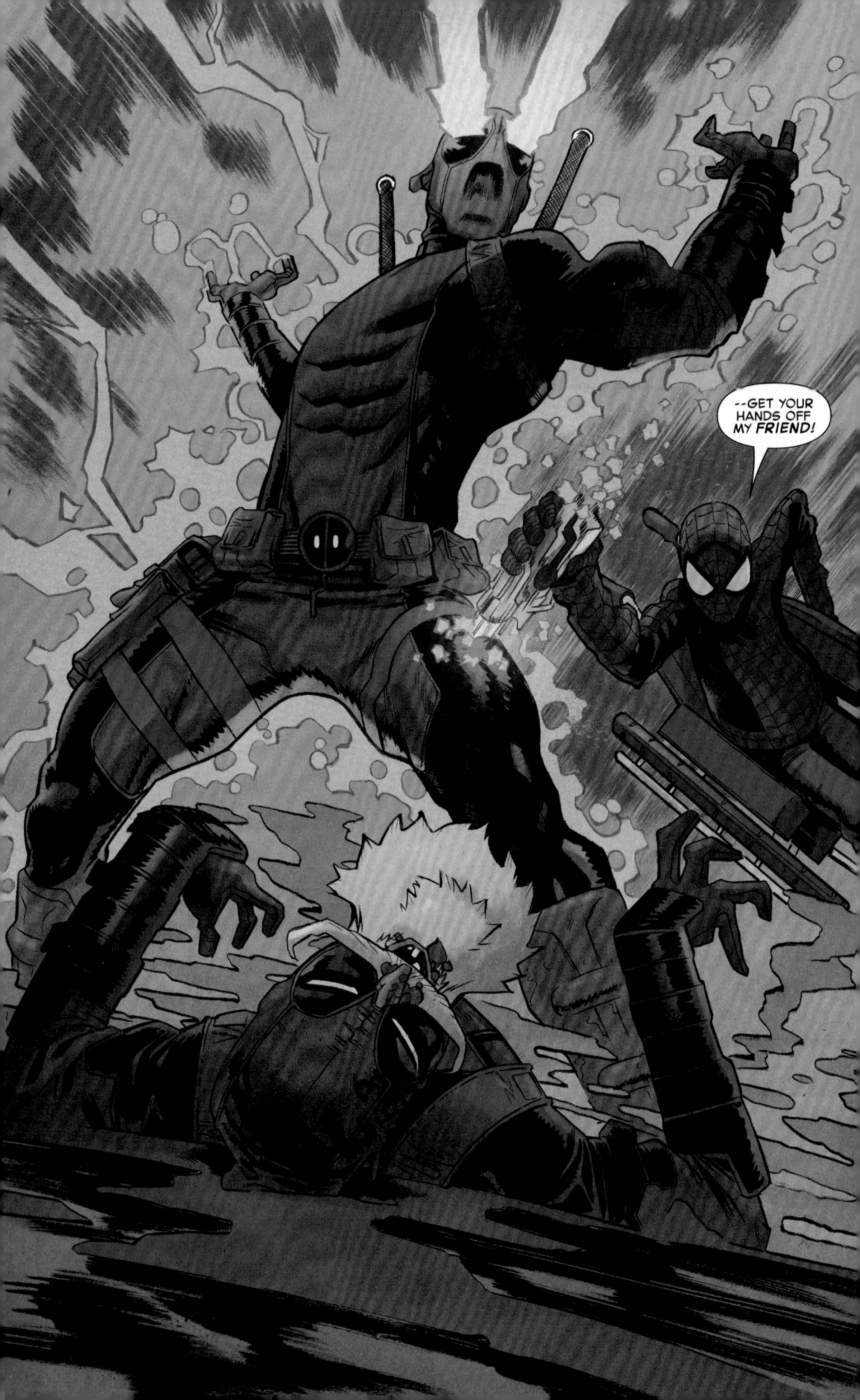
--GET YOUR HANDS OFF MY FRIEND!

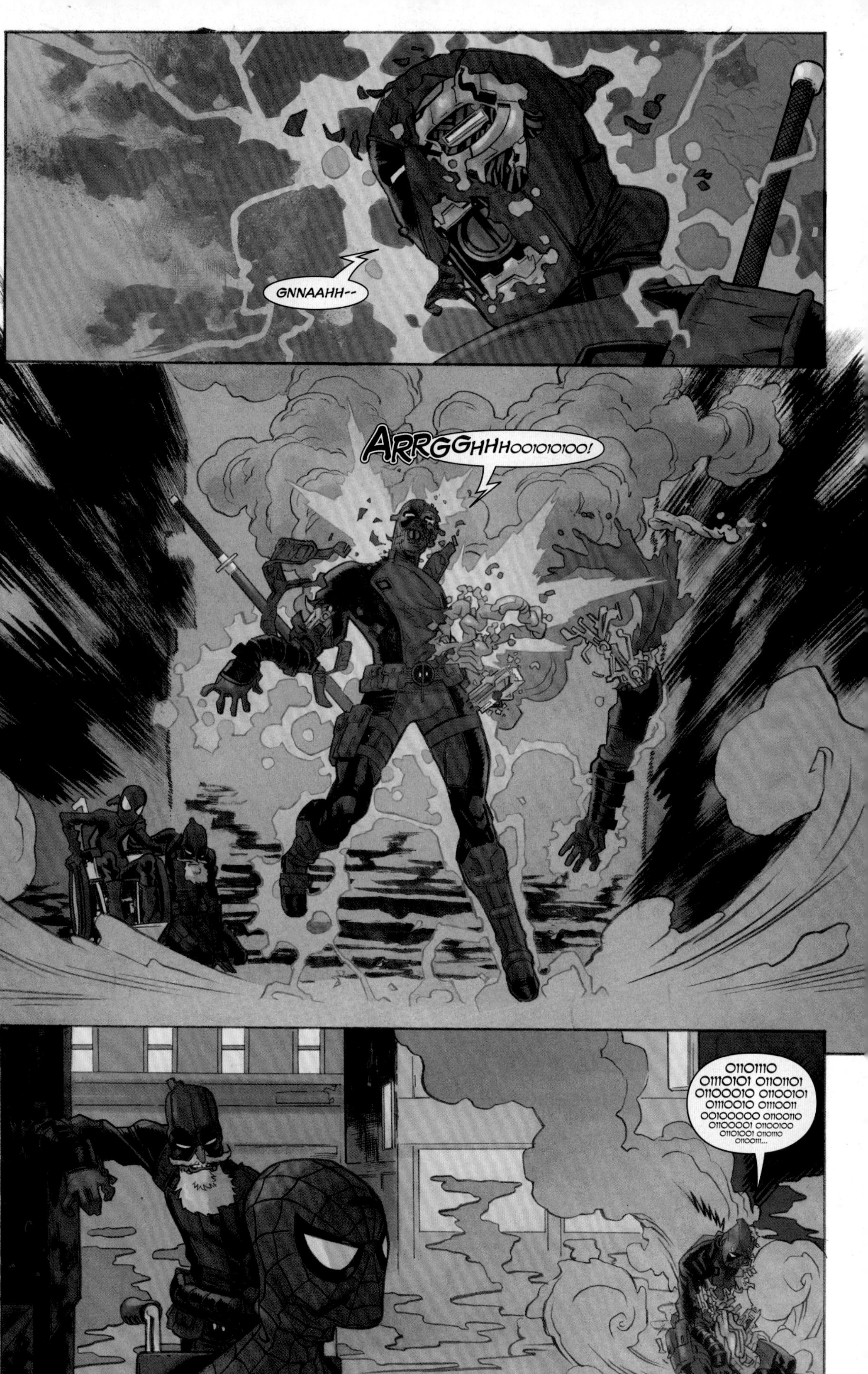
GNNAAHH--
ARRGGHHH001010100!
01101110 01110101 01101101 01100010 01100101 01110010 01110011 00100000 01100110 01100001 01100100 01101001 01101110 01100111...

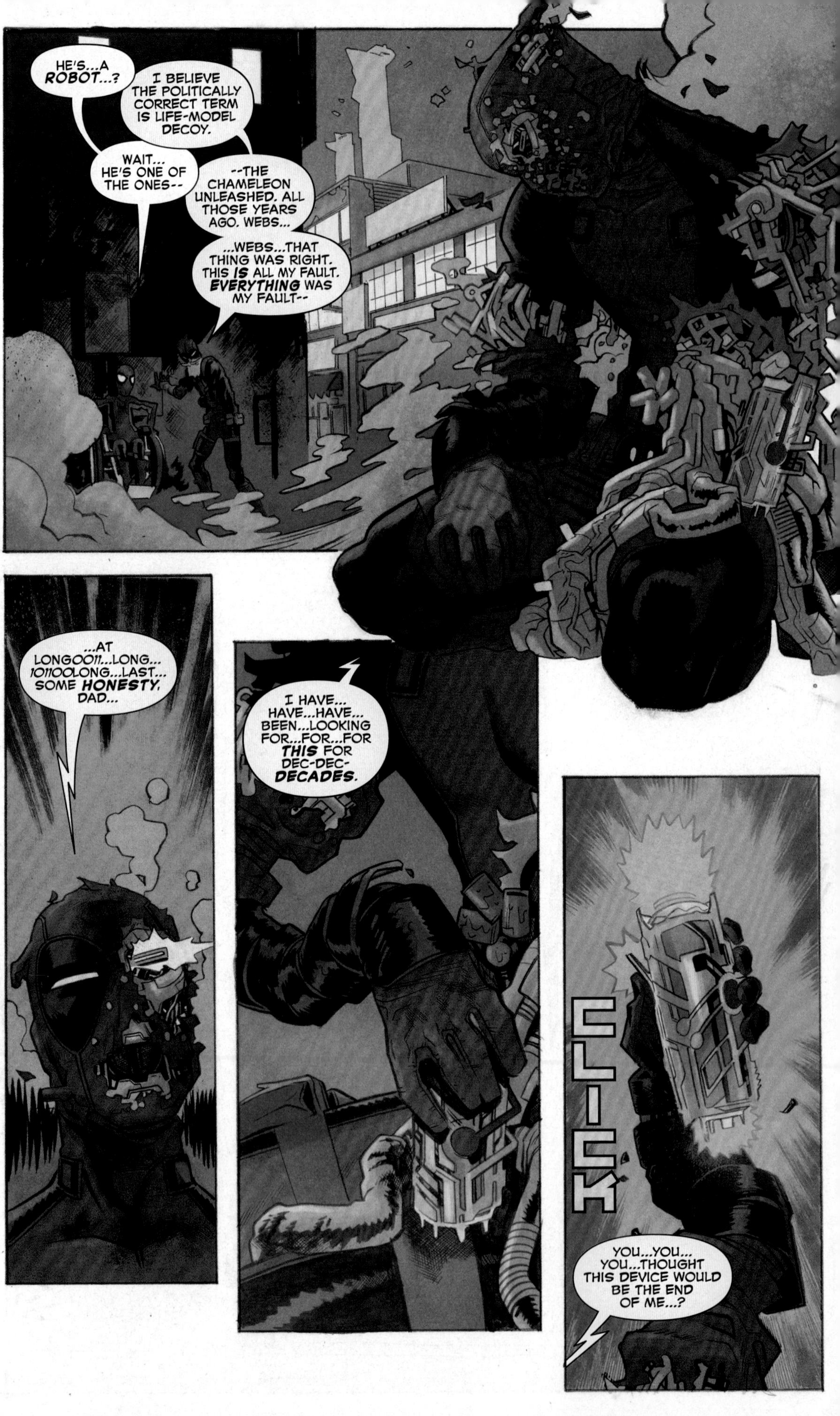
HE'S...A ROBOT...?
I BELIEVE THE POLITICALLY CORRECT TERM IS LIFE-MODEL DECOY.
WAIT... HE'S ONE OF THE ONES--
--THE CHAMELEON UNLEASHED. ALL THOSE YEARS AGO. WEBS...
...WEBS...THAT THING WAS RIGHT. THIS IS ALL MY FAULT. EVERYTHING WAS MY FAULT--
...AT LONG0011...LONG... 101100LONG...LAST... SOME HONESTY, DAD...
I HAVE... HAVE...HAVE... BEEN...LOOKING FOR...FOR...FOR THIS FOR DEC-DEC-DECADES.
CLICK
YOU...YOU... YOU...THOUGHT THIS DEVICE WOULD BE THE END OF ME...?

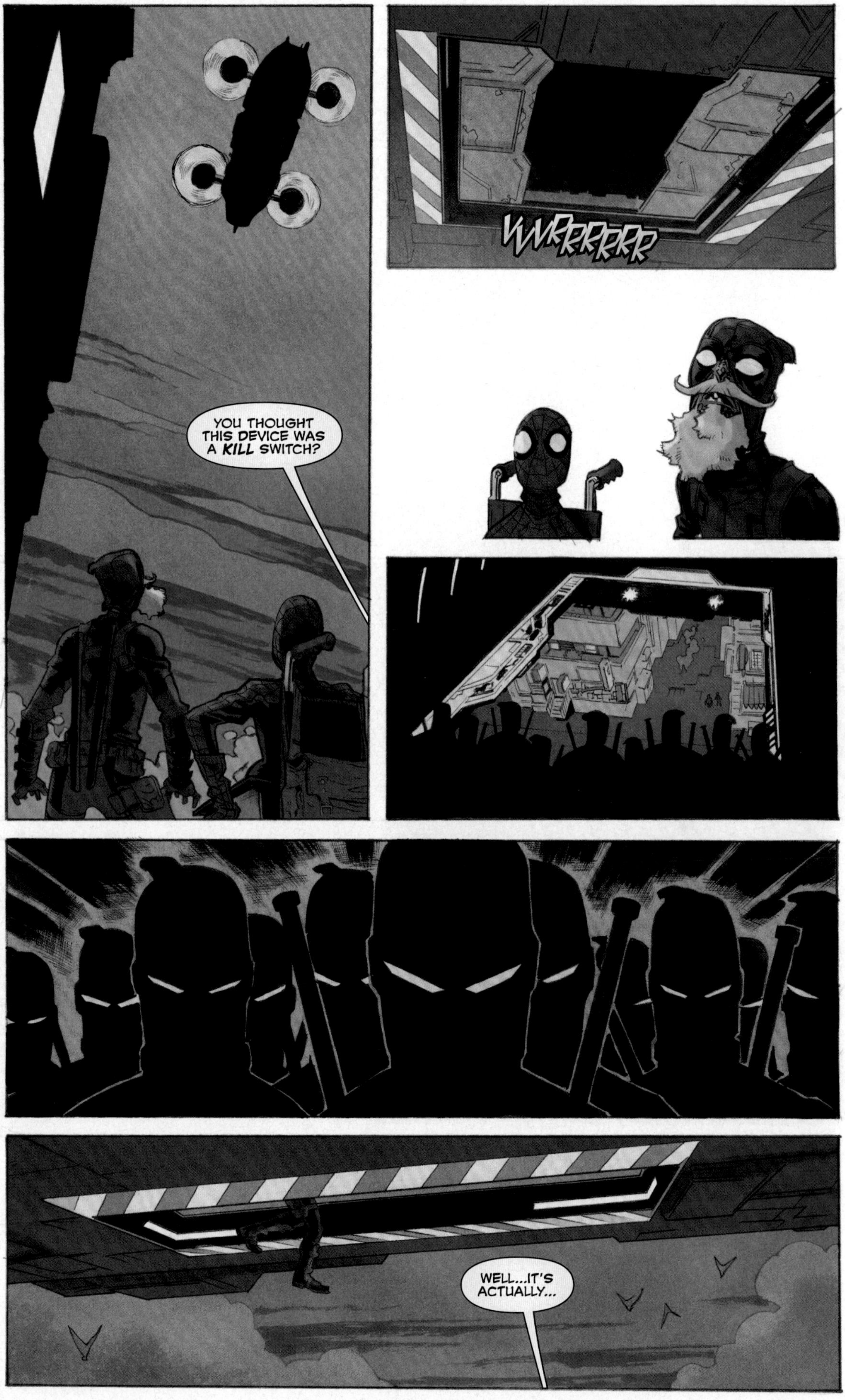
YOU THOUGHT THIS DEVICE WAS A KILL SWITCH?
VVVRRRRRRR
WELL...IT'S ACTUALLY...

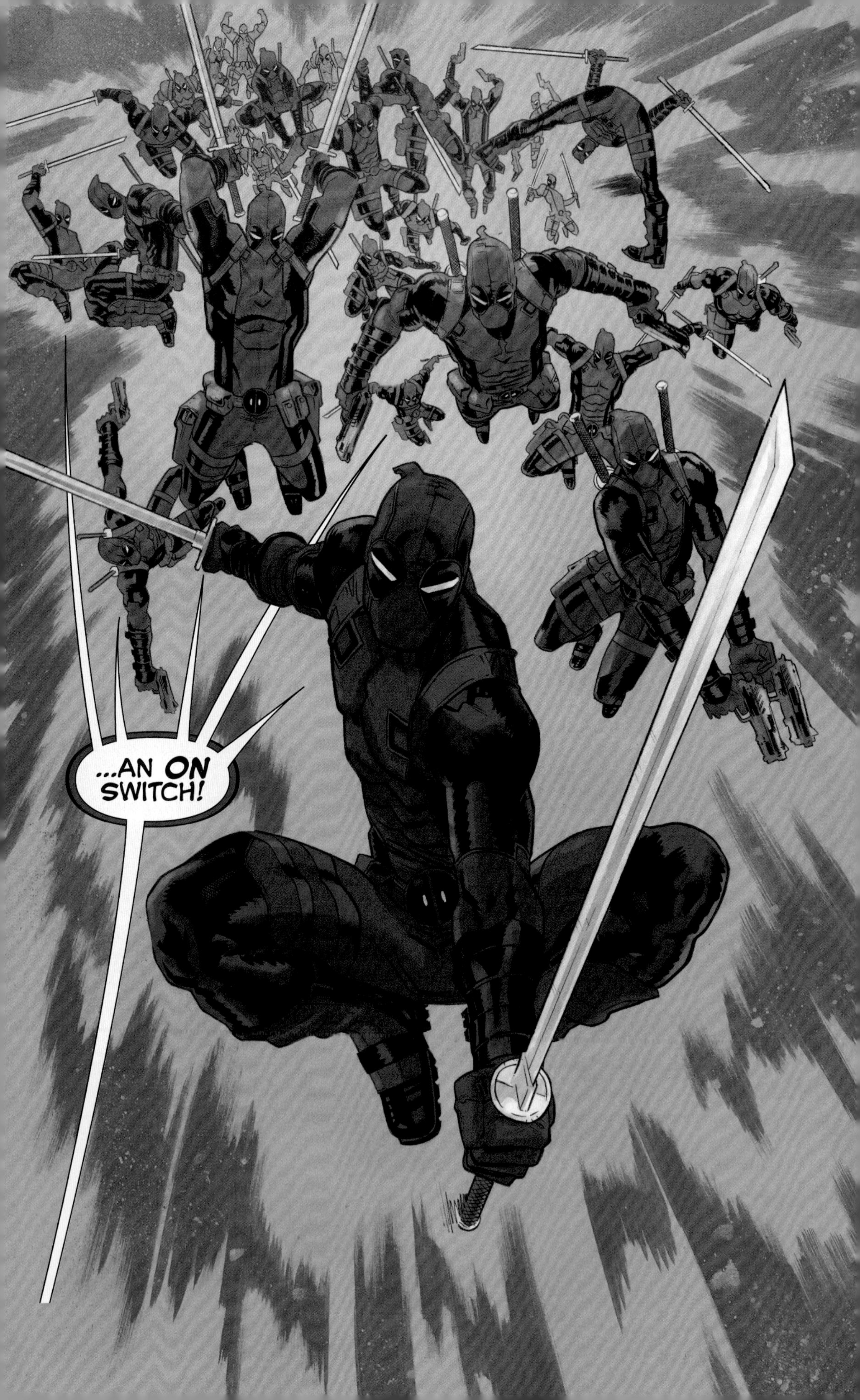
...AN ON SWITCH!

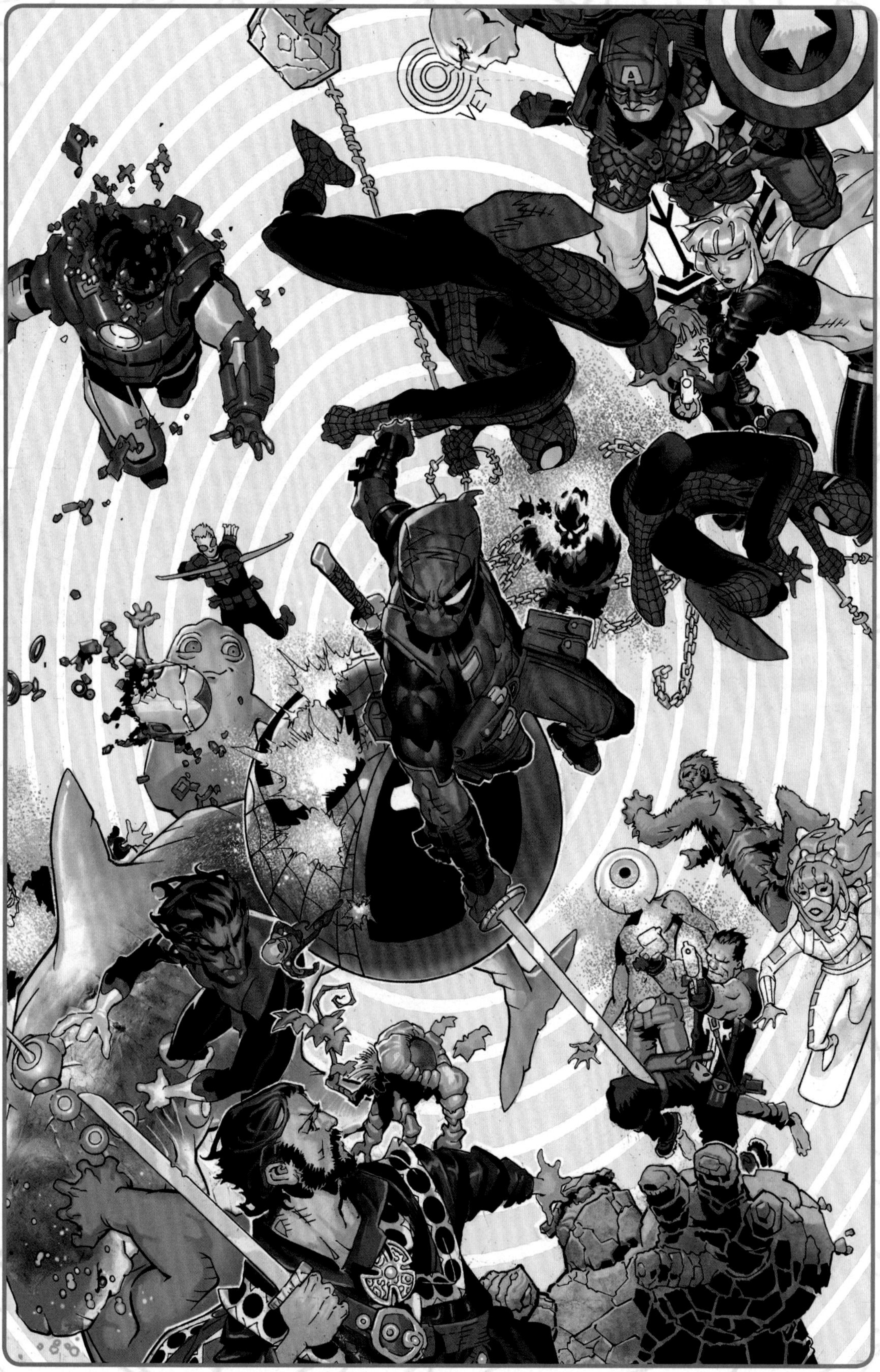

**PREVIOUSLY:**
ON ONE SIDE: SPIDER-MAN AND FORMER S.H.I.E.L.D. EMPLOYEES BOBBI MORSE, A.K.A. MOCKINGBIRD, AND PAIGE GUTHRIE, A.K.A. HUSK. ON THE OTHER: DEADPOOL AND A STOLEN HELICARRIER-BASED TEAM OF "PEOPLE." BETWEEN THEM: SPIDER-MAN'S DESIRE TO IMPRISON THIEVES AND KILLERS LIKE DEADPOOL, DEADPOOL'S DESIRE TO BE A BIG OLD THIEF, A FRIENDSHIP THAT'S DYING OR DEAD AND...CHAMELEON! THE DISGUISE-WEARING VILLAIN KEEPS BURGLARIZING ABANDONED S.H.I.E.L.D. WEAPONS STORAGE CENTERS BEFORE DEADPOOL CAN, AND KEEPS ESCAPING BEFORE SPIDER-MAN CAN CATCH HIM. THE SITUATION HAS REACHED A BOILING POINT! CHAMELEON MANAGED TO PIECE TOGETHER AN ARMY OF HEROIC-LOOKING LIFE-MODEL ROBOTS, AND THE FOLKS IN SPIDEY AND DEADPOOL'S CORNERS HAVE DEMANDED THAT THEY TAKE EACH OTHER DOWN!

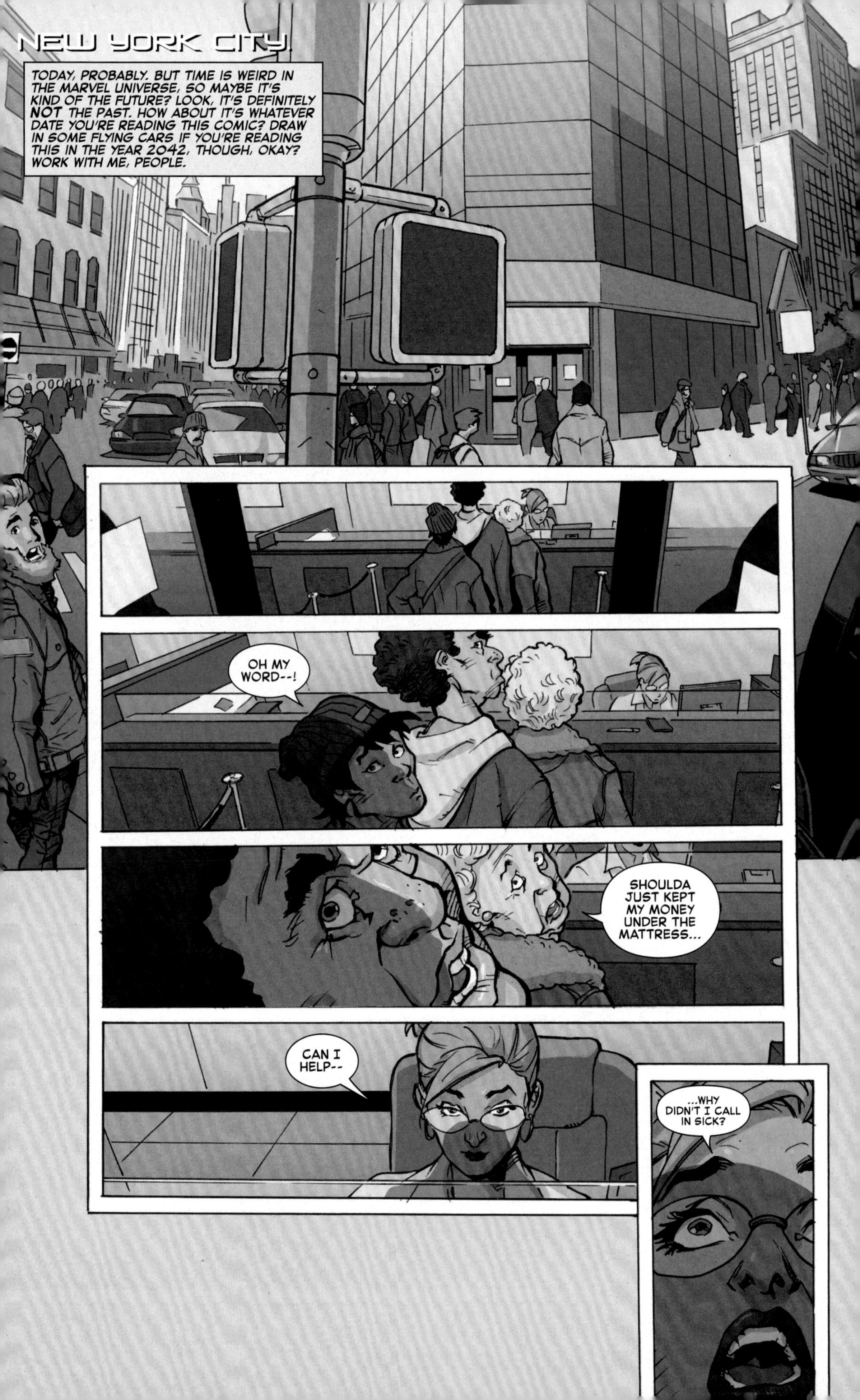
NEW YORK CITY.
TODAY, PROBABLY. BUT TIME IS WEIRD IN THE MARVEL UNIVERSE, SO MAYBE IT'S KIND OF THE FUTURE? LOOK, IT'S DEFINITELY NOT THE PAST. HOW ABOUT IT'S WHATEVER DATE YOU'RE READING THIS COMIC? DRAW IN SOME FLYING CARS IF YOU'RE READING THIS IN THE YEAR 2042, THOUGH, OKAY? WORK WITH ME, PEOPLE.
OH MY WORD--!
SHOULDA JUST KEPT MY MONEY UNDER THE MATTRESS...
CAN I HELP--
...WHY DIDN'T I CALL IN SICK?

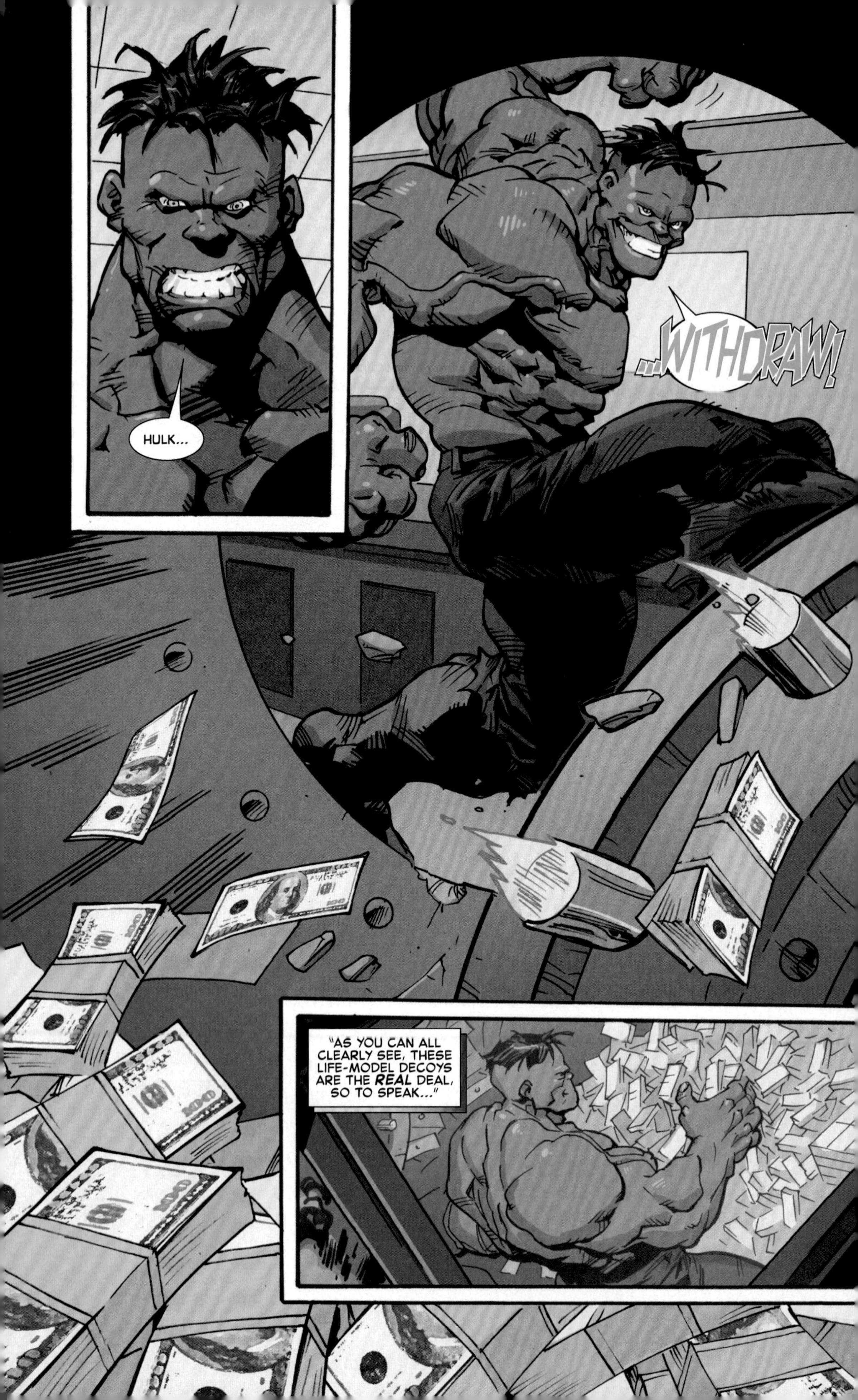

HULK...
...WITHDRAW!
"AS YOU CAN ALL CLEARLY SEE, THESE LIFE-MODEL DECOYS ARE THE REAL DEAL, SO TO SPEAK..."

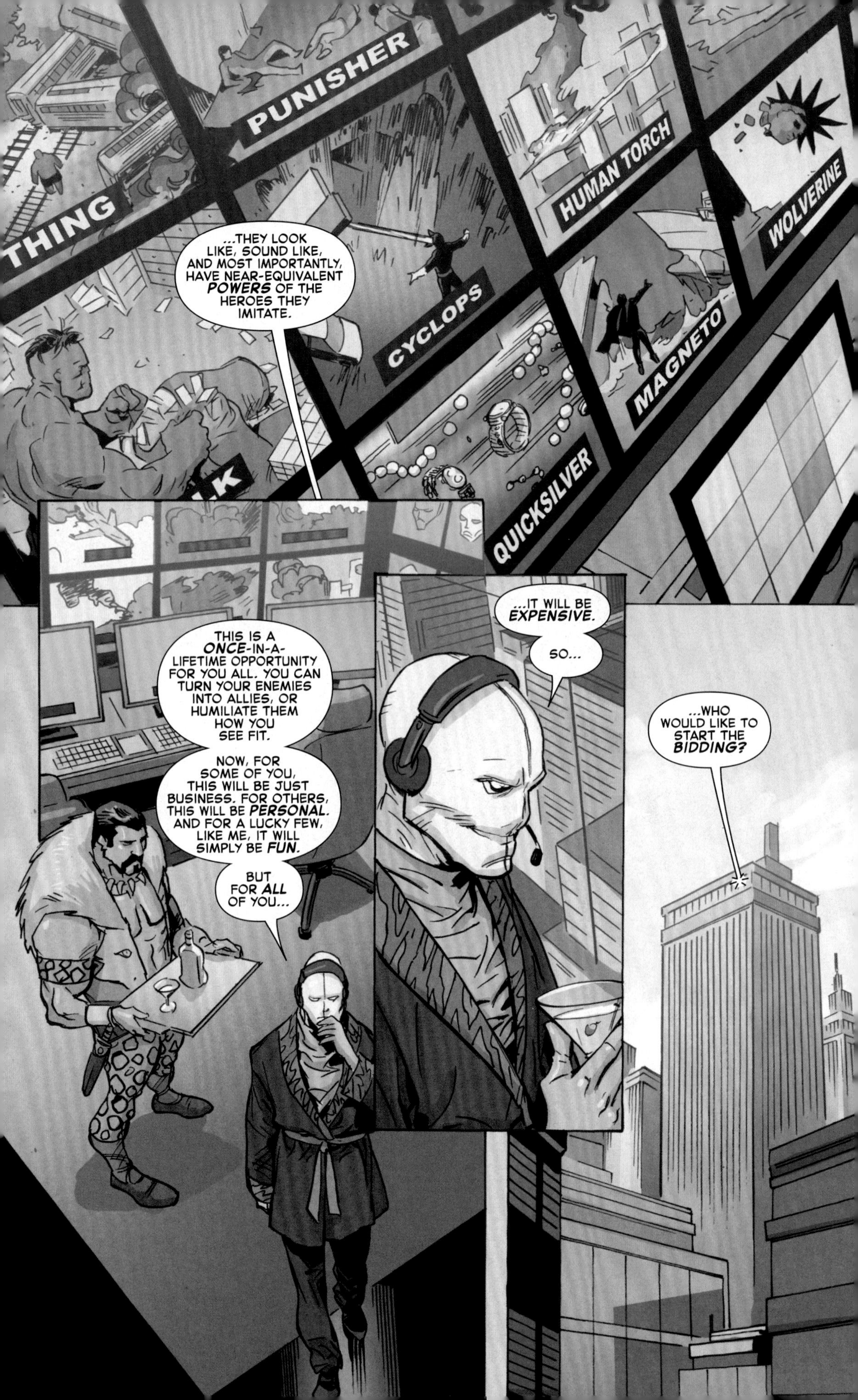
PUNISHER
THING
HUMAN TORCH
WOLVERINE
CYCLOPS
MAGNETO
QUICKSILVER
...THEY LOOK LIKE, SOUND LIKE, AND MOST IMPORTANTLY, HAVE NEAR-EQUIVALENT POWERS OF THE HEROES THEY IMITATE.
THIS IS A ONCE-IN-A-LIFETIME OPPORTUNITY FOR YOU ALL. YOU CAN TURN YOUR ENEMIES INTO ALLIES, OR HUMILIATE THEM HOW YOU SEE FIT.
NOW, FOR SOME OF YOU, THIS WILL BE JUST BUSINESS. FOR OTHERS, THIS WILL BE PERSONAL. AND FOR A LUCKY FEW, LIKE ME, IT WILL SIMPLY BE FUN.
BUT FOR ALL OF YOU...
...IT WILL BE EXPENSIVE.
SO...
...WHO WOULD LIKE TO START THE BIDDING?

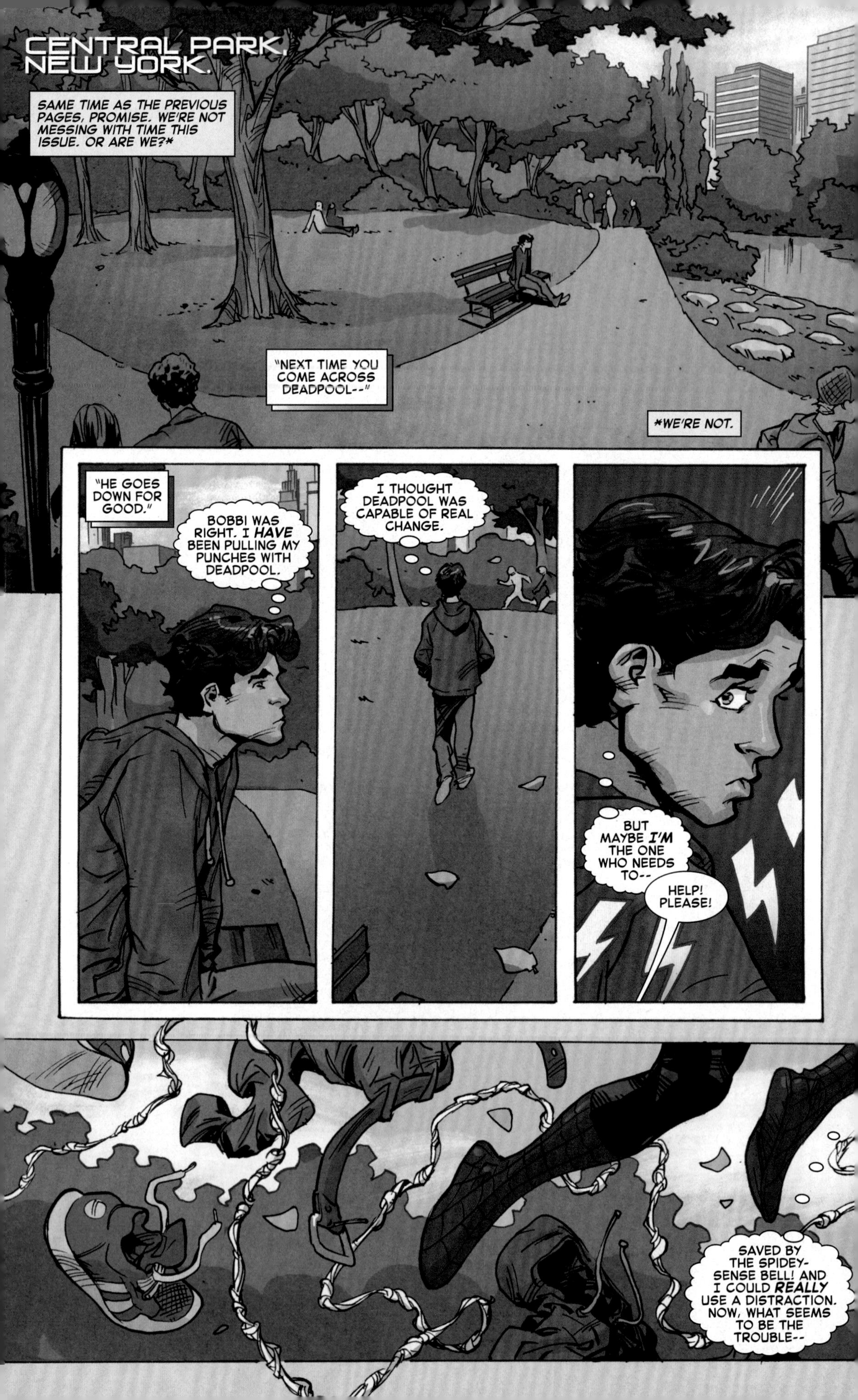
CENTRAL PARK, NEW YORK.
SAME TIME AS THE PREVIOUS PAGES, PROMISE. WE'RE NOT MESSING WITH TIME THIS ISSUE. OR ARE WE?*
"NEXT TIME YOU COME ACROSS DEADPOOL--"
*WE'RE NOT.
"HE GOES DOWN FOR GOOD."
BOBBI WAS RIGHT. I HAVE BEEN PULLING MY PUNCHES WITH DEADPOOL.
I THOUGHT DEADPOOL WAS CAPABLE OF REAL CHANGE.
BUT MAYBE I'M THE ONE WHO NEEDS TO--
HELP! PLEASE!
SAVED BY THE SPIDEY-SENSE BELL! AND I COULD REALLY USE A DISTRACTION. NOW, WHAT SEEMS TO BE THE TROUBLE--

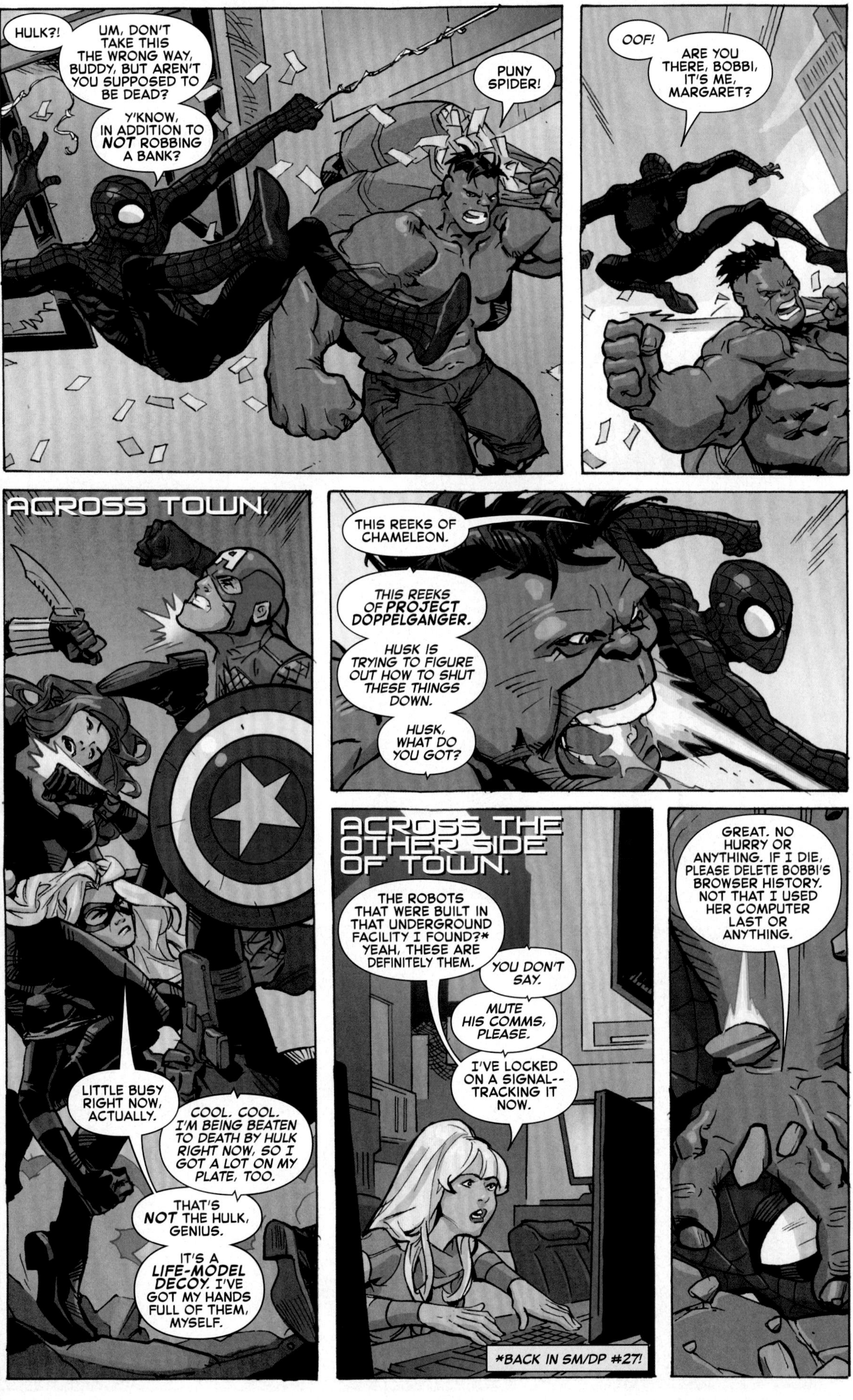
HULK?!
UM, DON'T TAKE THIS THE WRONG WAY, BUDDY, BUT AREN'T YOU SUPPOSED TO BE DEAD?
Y'KNOW, IN ADDITION TO NOT ROBBING A BANK?
PUNY SPIDER!
OOF!
ARE YOU THERE, BOBBI, IT'S ME, MARGARET?
ACROSS TOWN.
LITTLE BUSY RIGHT NOW, ACTUALLY.
COOL. COOL. I'M BEING BEATEN TO DEATH BY HULK RIGHT NOW, SO I GOT A LOT ON MY PLATE, TOO.
THAT'S NOT THE HULK, GENIUS.
IT'S A LIFE-MODEL DECOY. I'VE GOT MY HANDS FULL OF THEM, MYSELF.
THIS REEKS OF CHAMELEON.
THIS REEKS OF PROJECT DOPPELGANGER.
HUSK IS TRYING TO FIGURE OUT HOW TO SHUT THESE THINGS DOWN.
HUSK, WHAT DO YOU GOT?
ACROSS THE OTHER SIDE OF TOWN.
THE ROBOTS THAT WERE BUILT IN THAT UNDERGROUND FACILITY I FOUND?* YEAH, THESE ARE DEFINITELY THEM.
YOU DON'T SAY.
MUTE HIS COMMS, PLEASE.
I'VE LOCKED ON A SIGNAL-- TRACKING IT NOW.
*BACK IN SM/DP #27!
GREAT. NO HURRY OR ANYTHING. IF I DIE, PLEASE DELETE BOBBI'S BROWSER HISTORY. NOT THAT I USED HER COMPUTER LAST OR ANYTHING.

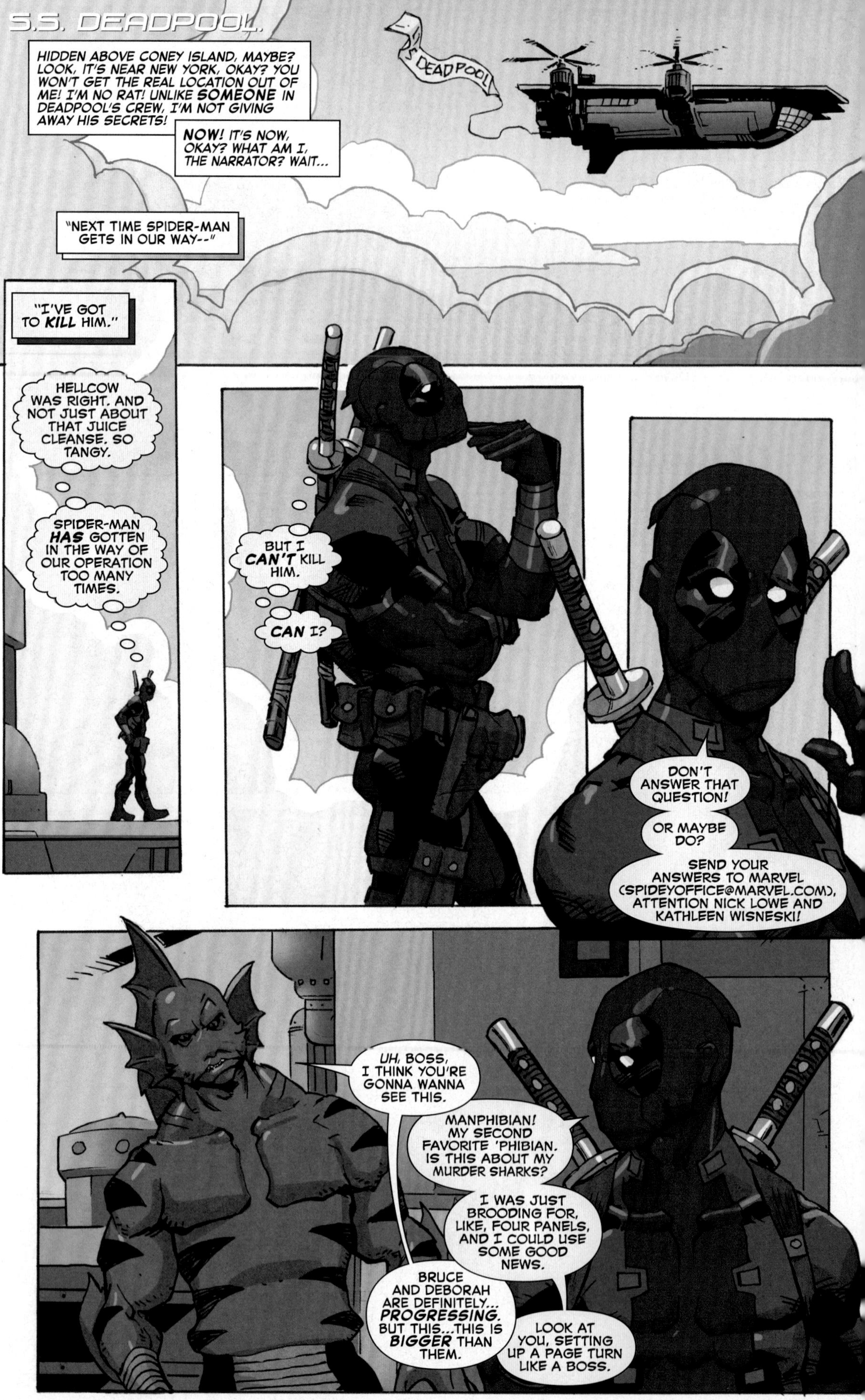
S.S. DEADPOOL...
HIDDEN ABOVE CONEY ISLAND, MAYBE? LOOK, IT'S NEAR NEW YORK, OKAY? YOU WON'T GET THE REAL LOCATION OUT OF ME! I'M NO RAT! UNLIKE SOMEONE IN DEADPOOL'S CREW, I'M NOT GIVING AWAY HIS SECRETS!
NOW! IT'S NOW, OKAY? WHAT AM I, THE NARRATOR? WAIT...
S.S. DEADPOOL
"NEXT TIME SPIDER-MAN GETS IN OUR WAY--"
"I'VE GOT TO KILL HIM."
HELLCOW WAS RIGHT. AND NOT JUST ABOUT THAT JUICE CLEANSE. SO TANGY.
SPIDER-MAN HAS GOTTEN IN THE WAY OF OUR OPERATION TOO MANY TIMES.
BUT I CAN'T KILL HIM.
CAN I?
DON'T ANSWER THAT QUESTION!
OR MAYBE DO?
SEND YOUR ANSWERS TO MARVEL (SPIDEYOFFICE@MARVEL.COM), ATTENTION NICK LOWE AND KATHLEEN WISNESKI!
UH, BOSS, I THINK YOU'RE GONNA WANNA SEE THIS.
MANPHIBIAN! MY SECOND FAVORITE 'PHIBIAN. IS THIS ABOUT MY MURDER SHARKS?
I WAS JUST BROODING FOR, LIKE, FOUR PANELS, AND I COULD USE SOME GOOD NEWS.
BRUCE AND DEBORAH ARE DEFINITELY... PROGRESSING. BUT THIS...THIS IS BIGGER THAN THEM.
LOOK AT YOU, SETTING UP A PAGE TURN LIKE A BOSS.

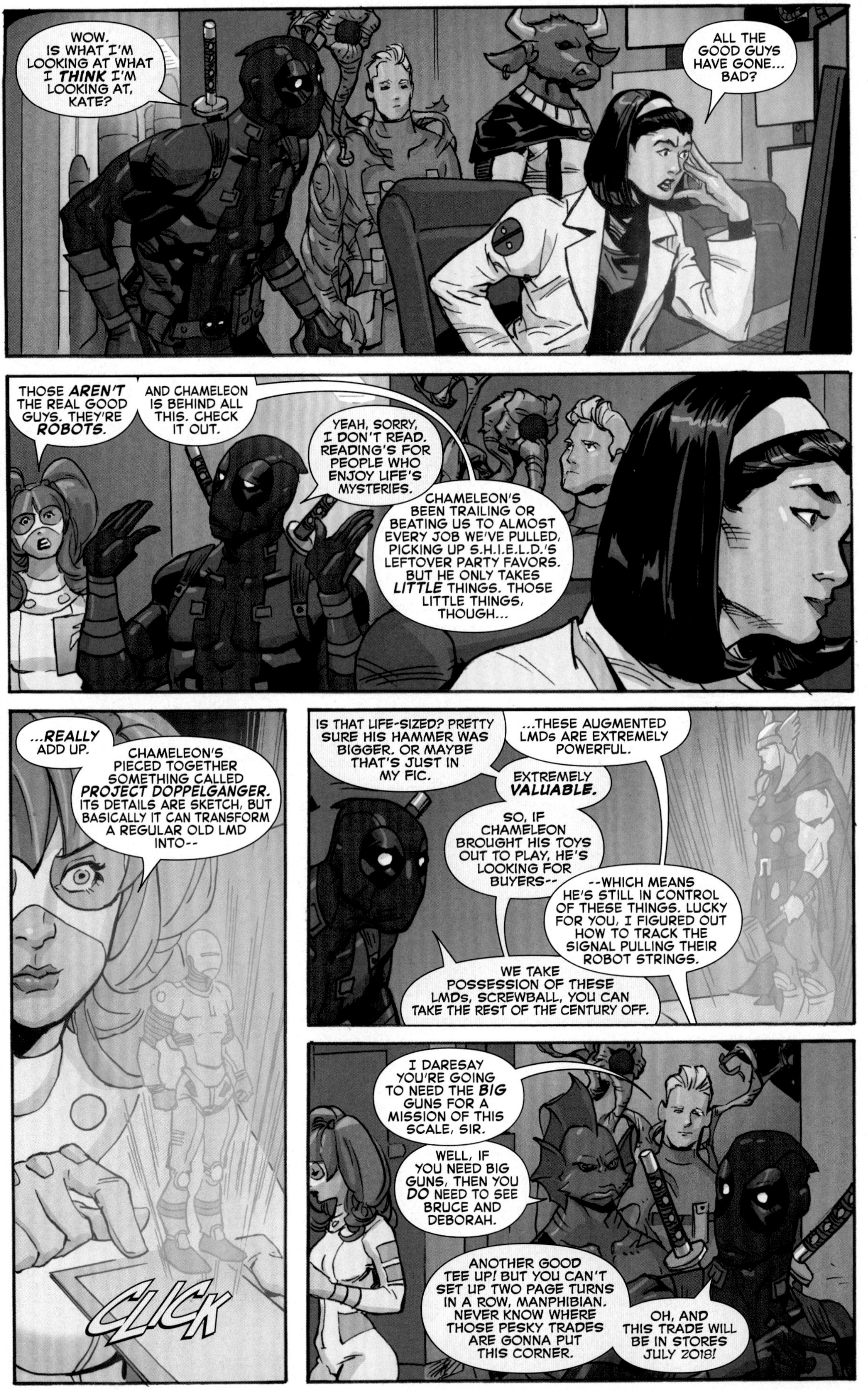

WOW. IS WHAT I'M LOOKING AT WHAT I THINK I'M LOOKING AT, KATE?
ALL THE GOOD GUYS HAVE GONE... BAD?
THOSE AREN'T THE REAL GOOD GUYS. THEY'RE ROBOTS.
AND CHAMELEON IS BEHIND ALL THIS. CHECK IT OUT.
YEAH, SORRY, I DON'T READ. READING'S FOR PEOPLE WHO ENJOY LIFE'S MYSTERIES.
CHAMELEON'S BEEN TRAILING OR BEATING US TO ALMOST EVERY JOB WE'VE PULLED, PICKING UP S.H.I.E.L.D.'S LEFTOVER PARTY FAVORS. BUT HE ONLY TAKES LITTLE THINGS. THOSE LITTLE THINGS, THOUGH...
...REALLY ADD UP.
CHAMELEON'S PIECED TOGETHER SOMETHING CALLED PROJECT DOPPELGANGER. ITS DETAILS ARE SKETCH, BUT BASICALLY IT CAN TRANSFORM A REGULAR OLD LMD INTO--
CLICK
IS THAT LIFE-SIZED? PRETTY SURE HIS HAMMER WAS BIGGER. OR MAYBE THAT'S JUST IN MY FIC.
...THESE AUGMENTED LMDs ARE EXTREMELY POWERFUL.
EXTREMELY VALUABLE.
SO, IF CHAMELEON BROUGHT HIS TOYS OUT TO PLAY, HE'S LOOKING FOR BUYERS--
--WHICH MEANS HE'S STILL IN CONTROL OF THESE THINGS. LUCKY FOR YOU, I FIGURED OUT HOW TO TRACK THE SIGNAL PULLING THEIR ROBOT STRINGS.
WE TAKE POSSESSION OF THESE LMDs, SCREWBALL, YOU CAN TAKE THE REST OF THE CENTURY OFF.
I DARESAY YOU'RE GOING TO NEED THE BIG GUNS FOR A MISSION OF THIS SCALE, SIR.
WELL, IF YOU NEED BIG GUNS, THEN YOU DO NEED TO SEE BRUCE AND DEBORAH.
ANOTHER GOOD TEE UP! BUT YOU CAN'T SET UP TWO PAGE TURNS IN A ROW, MANPHIBIAN. NEVER KNOW WHERE THOSE PESKY TRADES ARE GONNA PUT THIS CORNER.
OH, AND THIS TRADE WILL BE IN STORES JULY 2018!

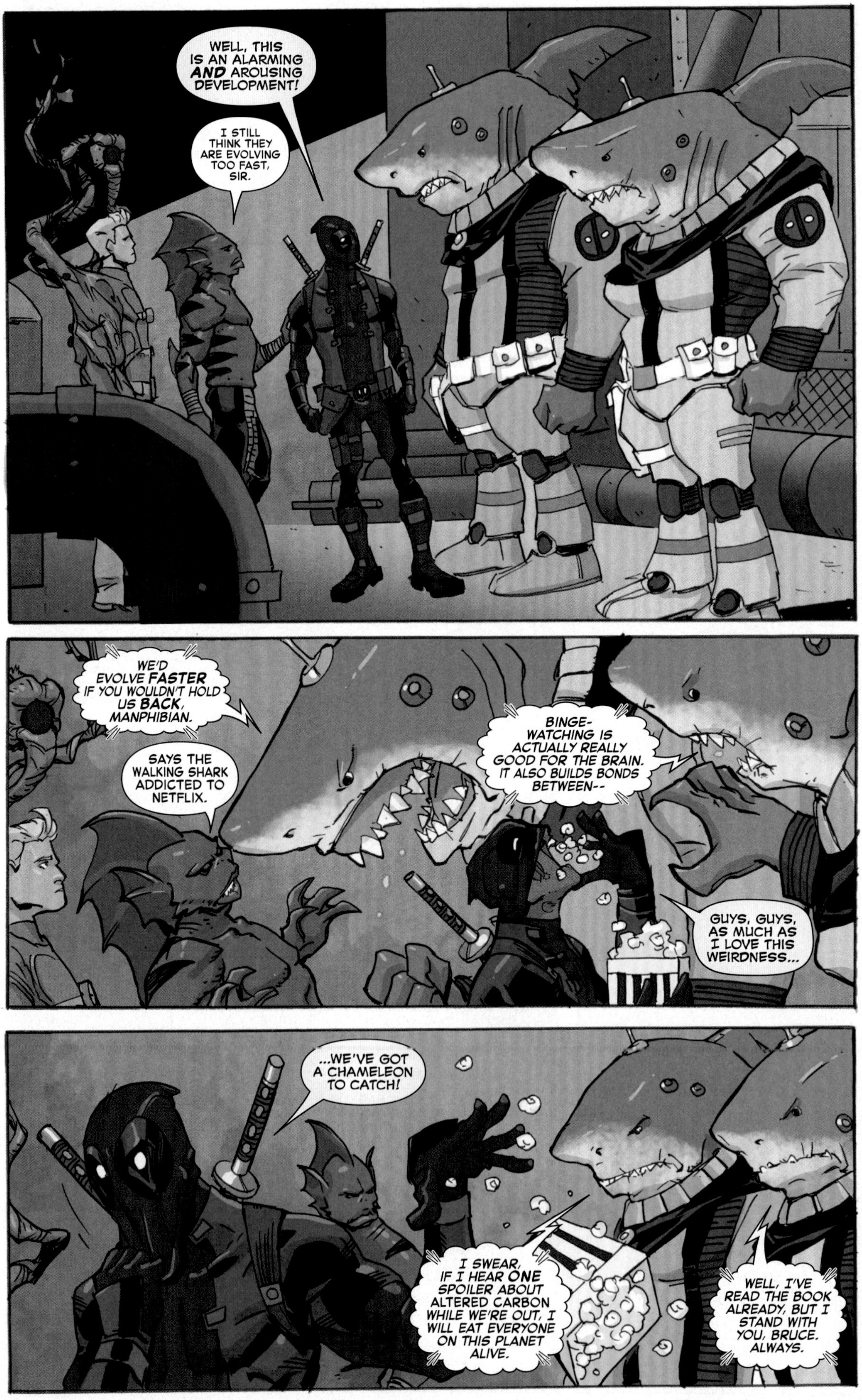
WELL, THIS IS AN ALARMING AND AROUSING DEVELOPMENT!
I STILL THINK THEY ARE EVOLVING TOO FAST, SIR.
WE'D EVOLVE FASTER IF YOU WOULDN'T HOLD US BACK, MANPHIBIAN.
SAYS THE WALKING SHARK ADDICTED TO NETFLIX.
BINGE-WATCHING IS ACTUALLY REALLY GOOD FOR THE BRAIN. IT ALSO BUILDS BONDS BETWEEN--
GUYS, GUYS, AS MUCH AS I LOVE THIS WEIRDNESS...
...WE'VE GOT A CHAMELEON TO CATCH!
I SWEAR, IF I HEAR ONE SPOILER ABOUT ALTERED CARBON WHILE WE'RE OUT, I WILL EAT EVERYONE ON THIS PLANET ALIVE.
WELL, I'VE READ THE BOOK ALREADY, BUT I STAND WITH YOU, BRUCE. ALWAYS.

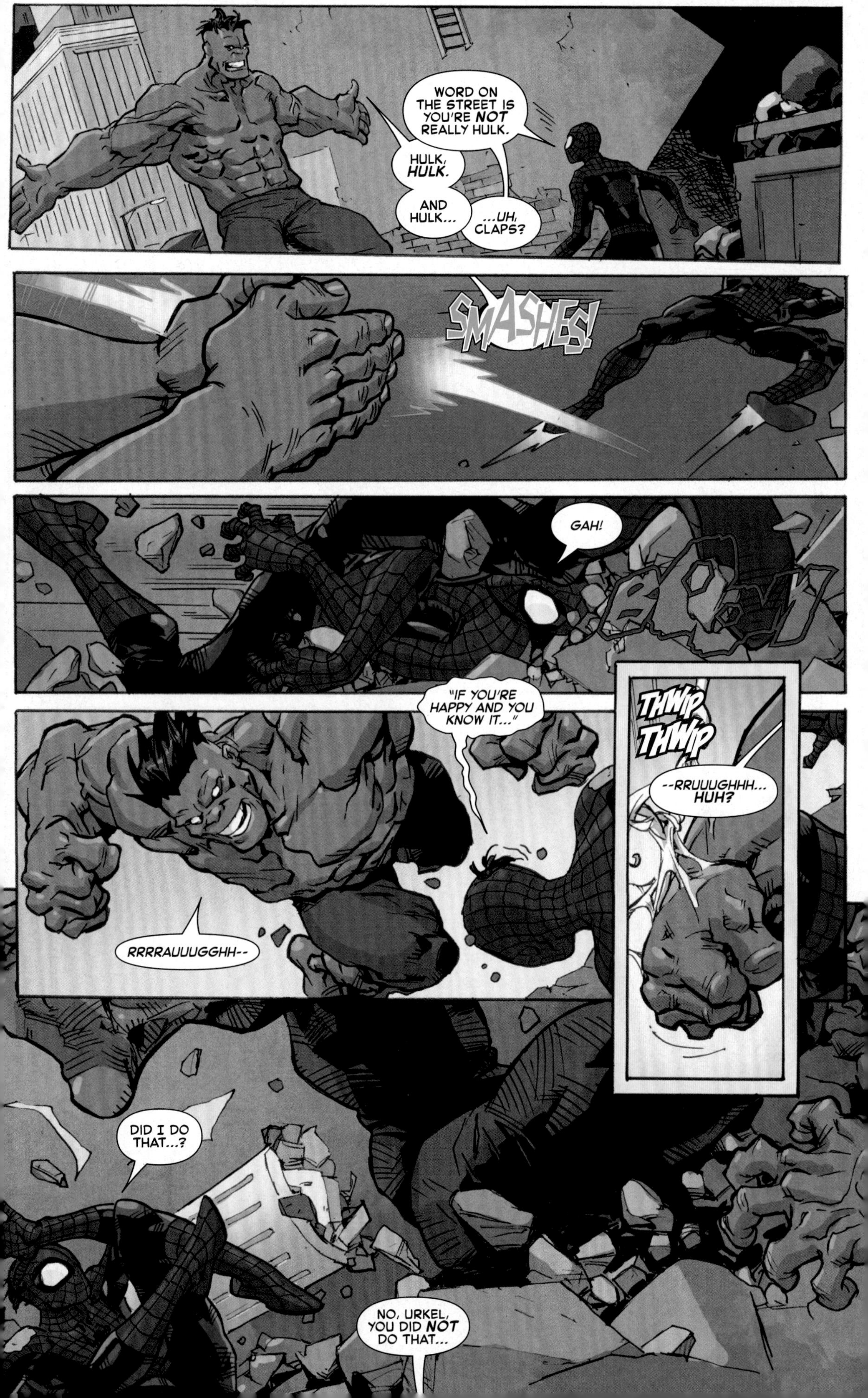
WORD ON THE STREET IS YOU'RE NOT REALLY HULK.
HULK, HULK.
AND HULK...
...UH, CLAPS?
SMASHES!
GAH!
BOOM
"IF YOU'RE HAPPY AND YOU KNOW IT..."
THWIP THWIP
--RRUUUGHHH... HUH?
RRRRAUUUGGHH--
DID I DO THAT...?
NO, URKEL, YOU DID NOT DO THAT...

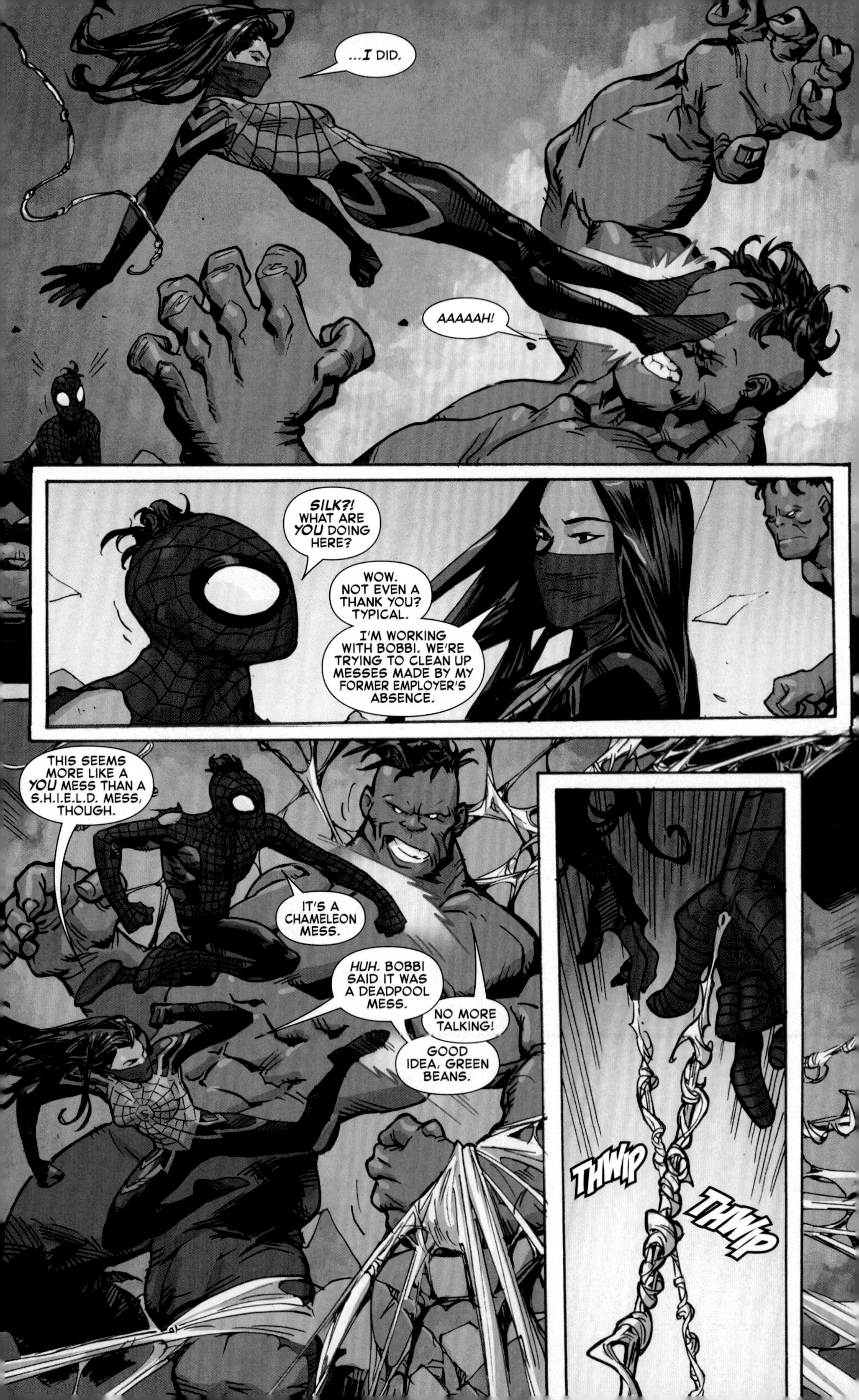
...I DID.
AAAAAH!
SILK?! WHAT ARE YOU DOING HERE?
WOW. NOT EVEN A THANK YOU? TYPICAL.
I'M WORKING WITH BOBBI. WE'RE TRYING TO CLEAN UP MESSES MADE BY MY FORMER EMPLOYER'S ABSENCE.
THIS SEEMS MORE LIKE A YOU MESS THAN A S.H.I.E.L.D. MESS, THOUGH.
IT'S A CHAMELEON MESS.
HUH. BOBBI SAID IT WAS A DEADPOOL MESS.
NO MORE TALKING!
GOOD IDEA, GREEN BEANS.
THWIP
THWIP

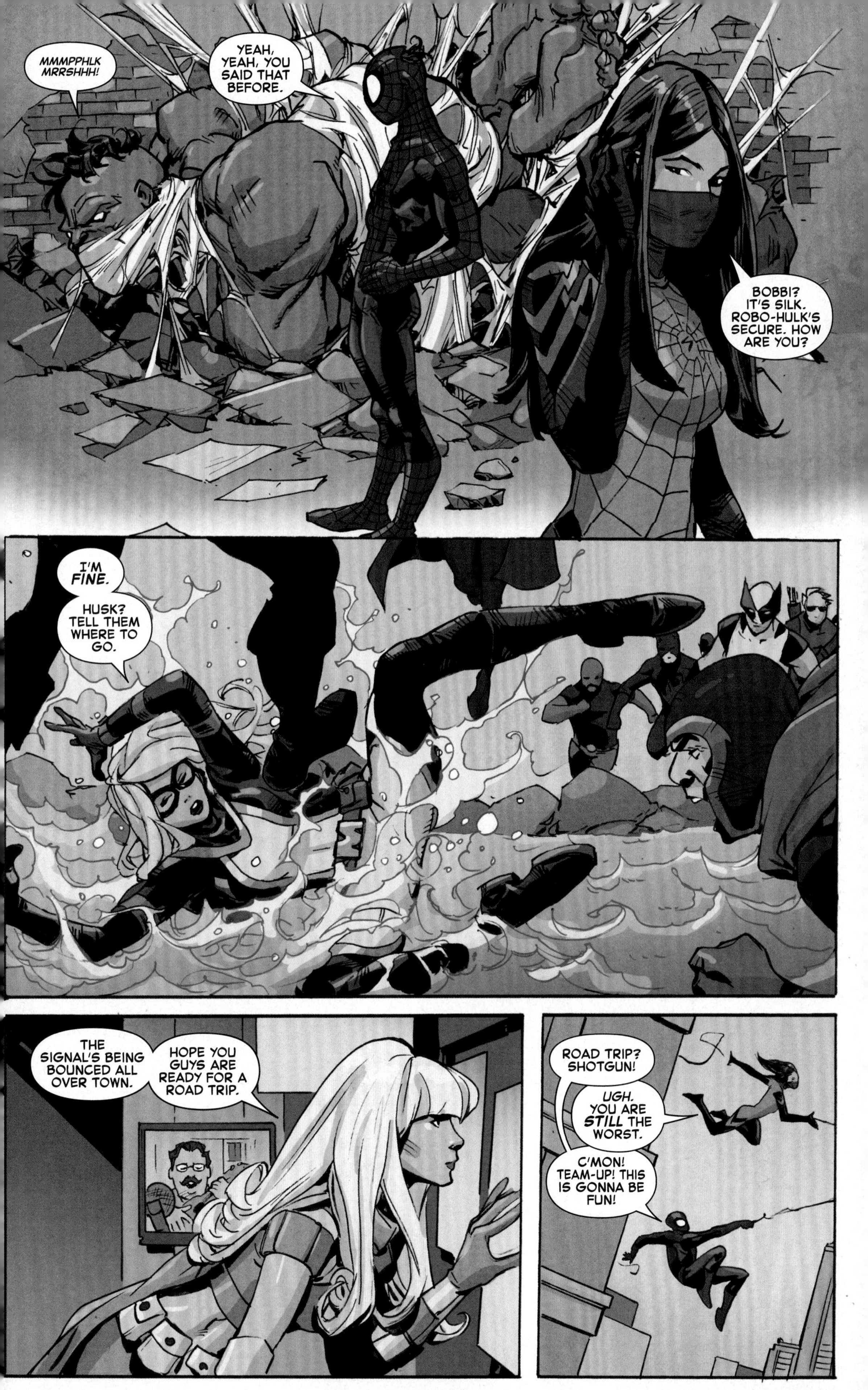
MMMPPHLK MRRSHHH!
YEAH, YEAH, YOU SAID THAT BEFORE.
BOBBI? IT'S SILK. ROBO-HULK'S SECURE. HOW ARE YOU?
I'M FINE.
HUSK? TELL THEM WHERE TO GO.
THE SIGNAL'S BEING BOUNCED ALL OVER TOWN.
HOPE YOU GUYS ARE READY FOR A ROAD TRIP.
ROAD TRIP? SHOTGUN!
UGH. YOU ARE STILL THE WORST.
C'MON! TEAM-UP! THIS IS GONNA BE FUN!

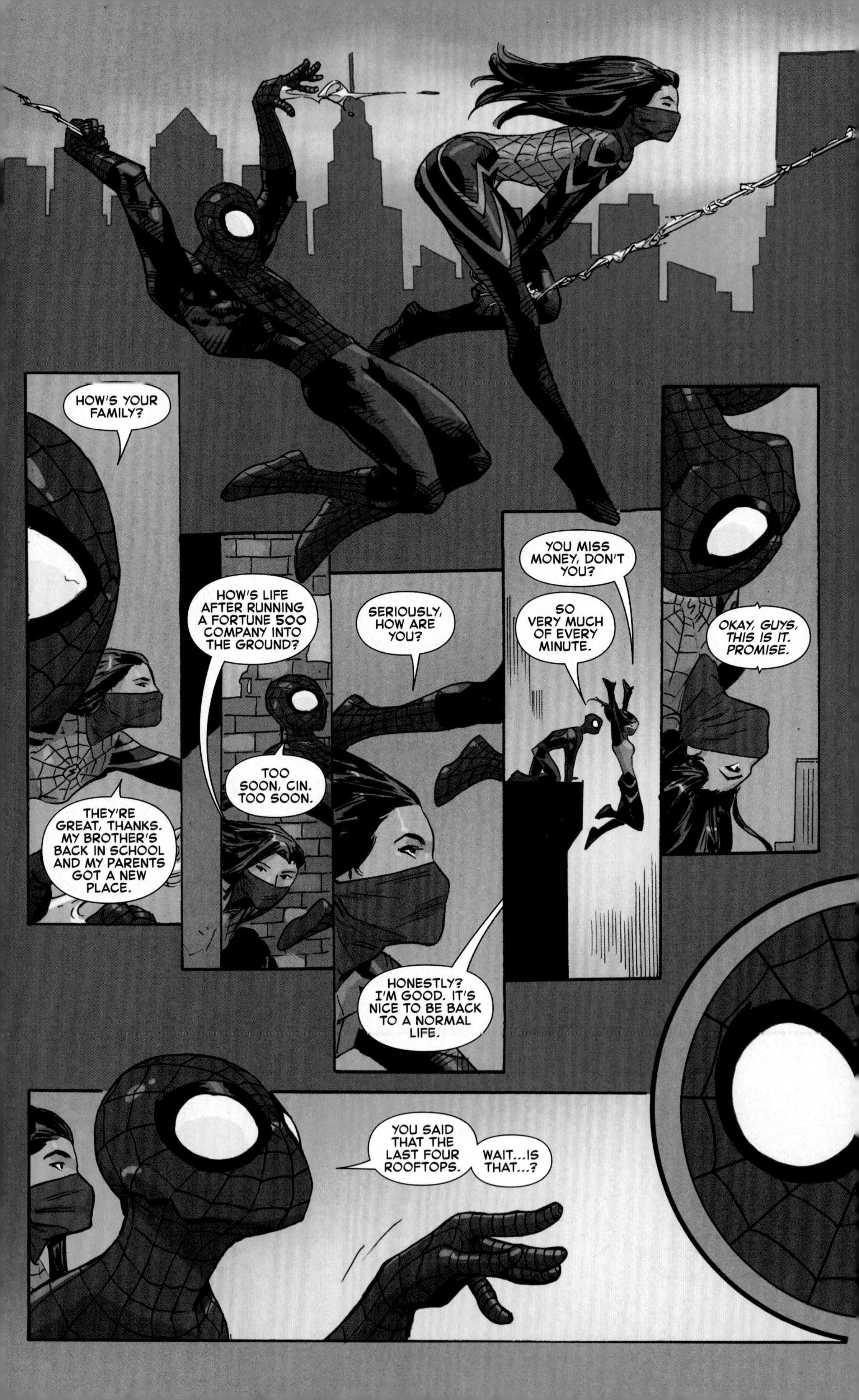
HOW'S YOUR FAMILY?
THEY'RE GREAT, THANKS. MY BROTHER'S BACK IN SCHOOL AND MY PARENTS GOT A NEW PLACE.
HOW'S LIFE AFTER RUNNING A FORTUNE 500 COMPANY INTO THE GROUND?
TOO SOON, CIN. TOO SOON.
SERIOUSLY, HOW ARE YOU?
HONESTLY? I'M GOOD. IT'S NICE TO BE BACK TO A NORMAL LIFE.
YOU MISS MONEY, DON'T YOU?
SO VERY MUCH OF EVERY MINUTE.
OKAY, GUYS, THIS IS IT. PROMISE.
YOU SAID THAT THE LAST FOUR ROOFTOPS.
WAIT...IS THAT...?

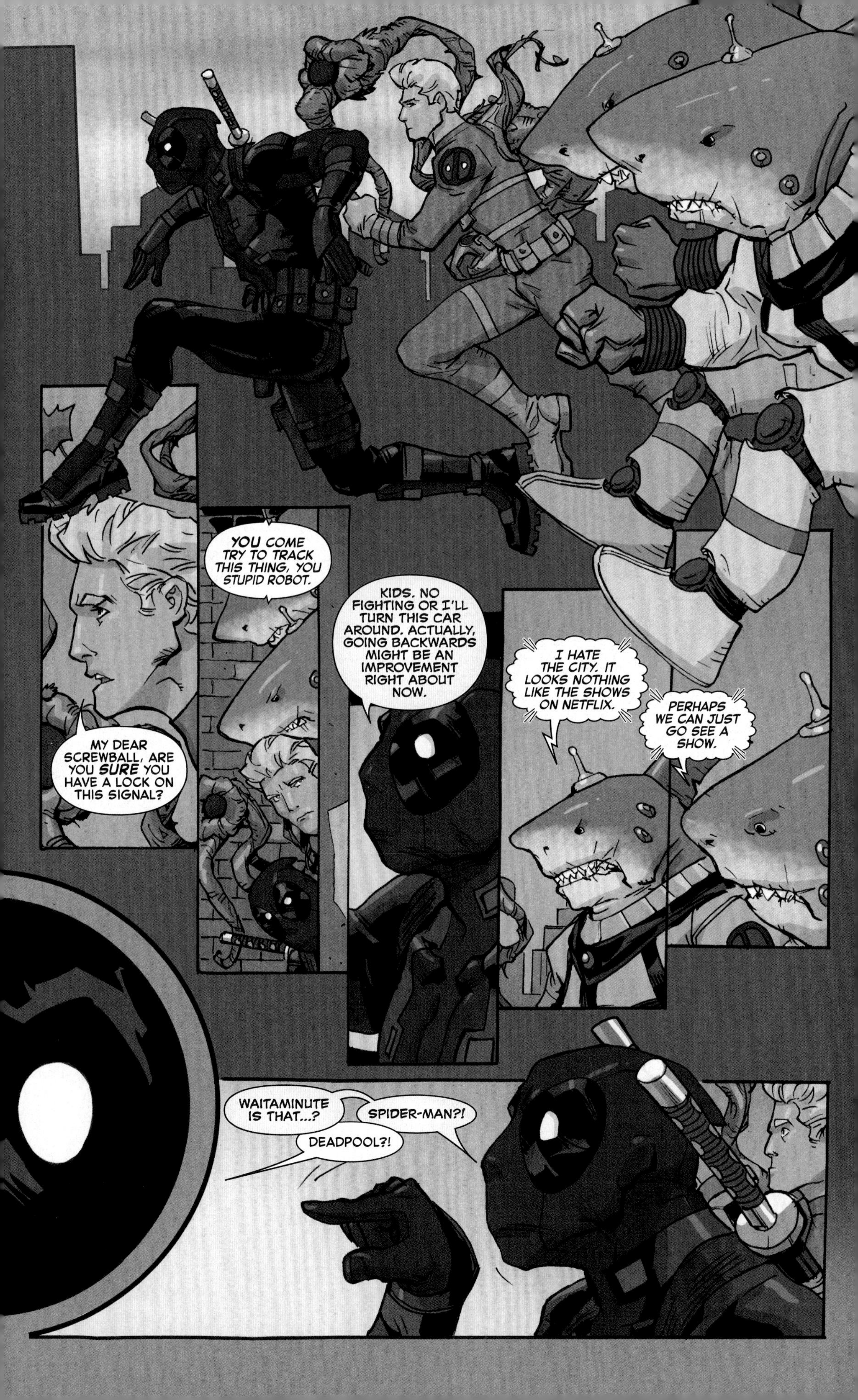
MY DEAR SCREWBALL, ARE YOU SURE YOU HAVE A LOCK ON THIS SIGNAL?
YOU COME TRY TO TRACK THIS THING, YOU STUPID ROBOT.
KIDS. NO FIGHTING OR I'LL TURN THIS CAR AROUND. ACTUALLY, GOING BACKWARDS MIGHT BE AN IMPROVEMENT RIGHT ABOUT NOW.
I HATE THE CITY. IT LOOKS NOTHING LIKE THE SHOWS ON NETFLIX.
PERHAPS WE CAN JUST GO SEE A SHOW.
WAITAMINUTE IS THAT...?
SPIDER-MAN?!
DEADPOOL?!

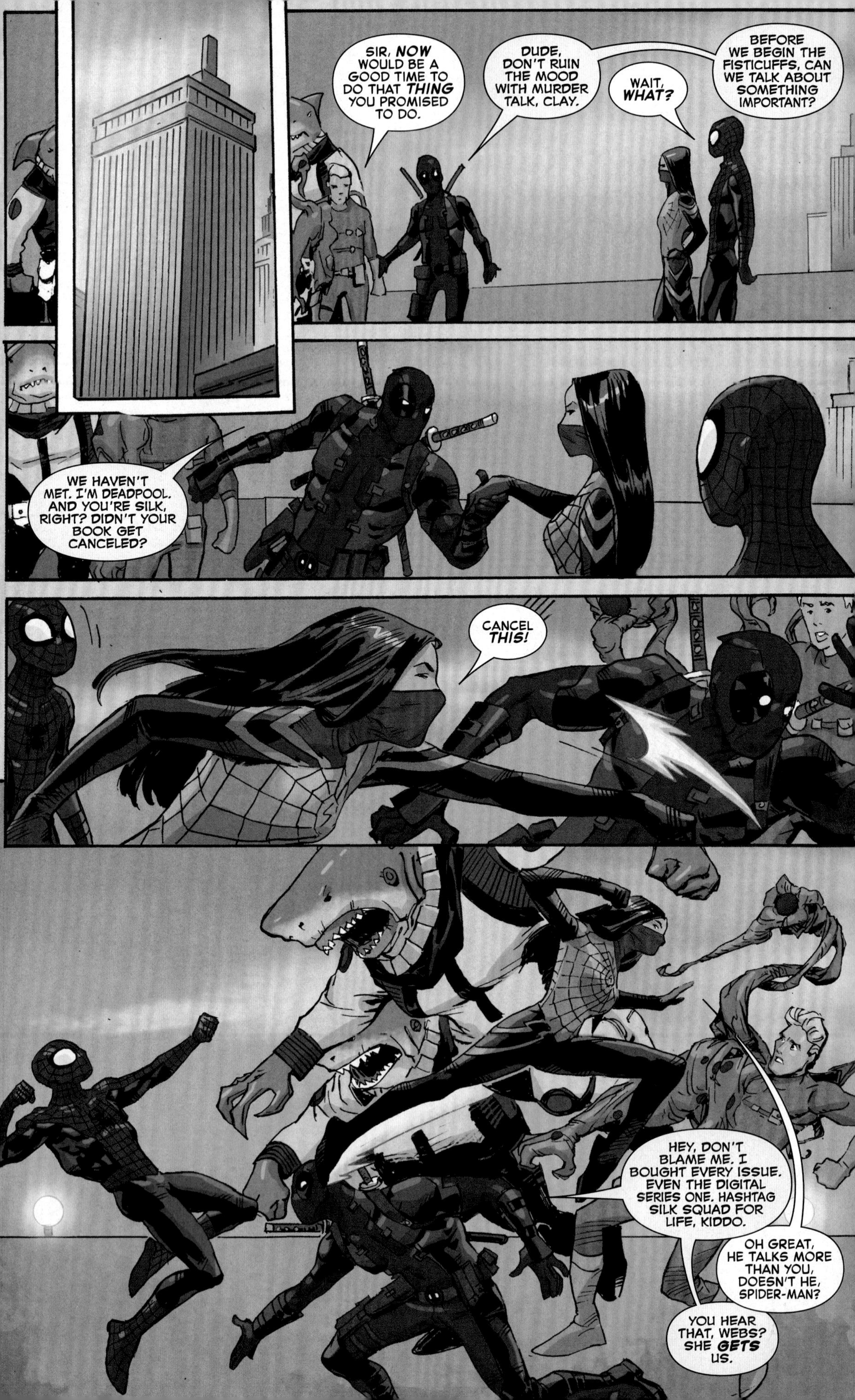
SIR, NOW WOULD BE A GOOD TIME TO DO THAT THING YOU PROMISED TO DO.
DUDE, DON'T RUIN THE MOOD WITH MURDER TALK, CLAY.
WAIT, WHAT?
BEFORE WE BEGIN THE FISTICUFFS, CAN WE TALK ABOUT SOMETHING IMPORTANT?
WE HAVEN'T MET. I'M DEADPOOL. AND YOU'RE SILK, RIGHT? DIDN'T YOUR BOOK GET CANCELED?
CANCEL THIS!
HEY, DON'T BLAME ME. I BOUGHT EVERY ISSUE. EVEN THE DIGITAL SERIES ONE. HASHTAG SILK SQUAD FOR LIFE, KIDDO.
OH GREAT, HE TALKS MORE THAN YOU, DOESN'T HE, SPIDER-MAN?
YOU HEAR THAT, WEBS? SHE GETS US.

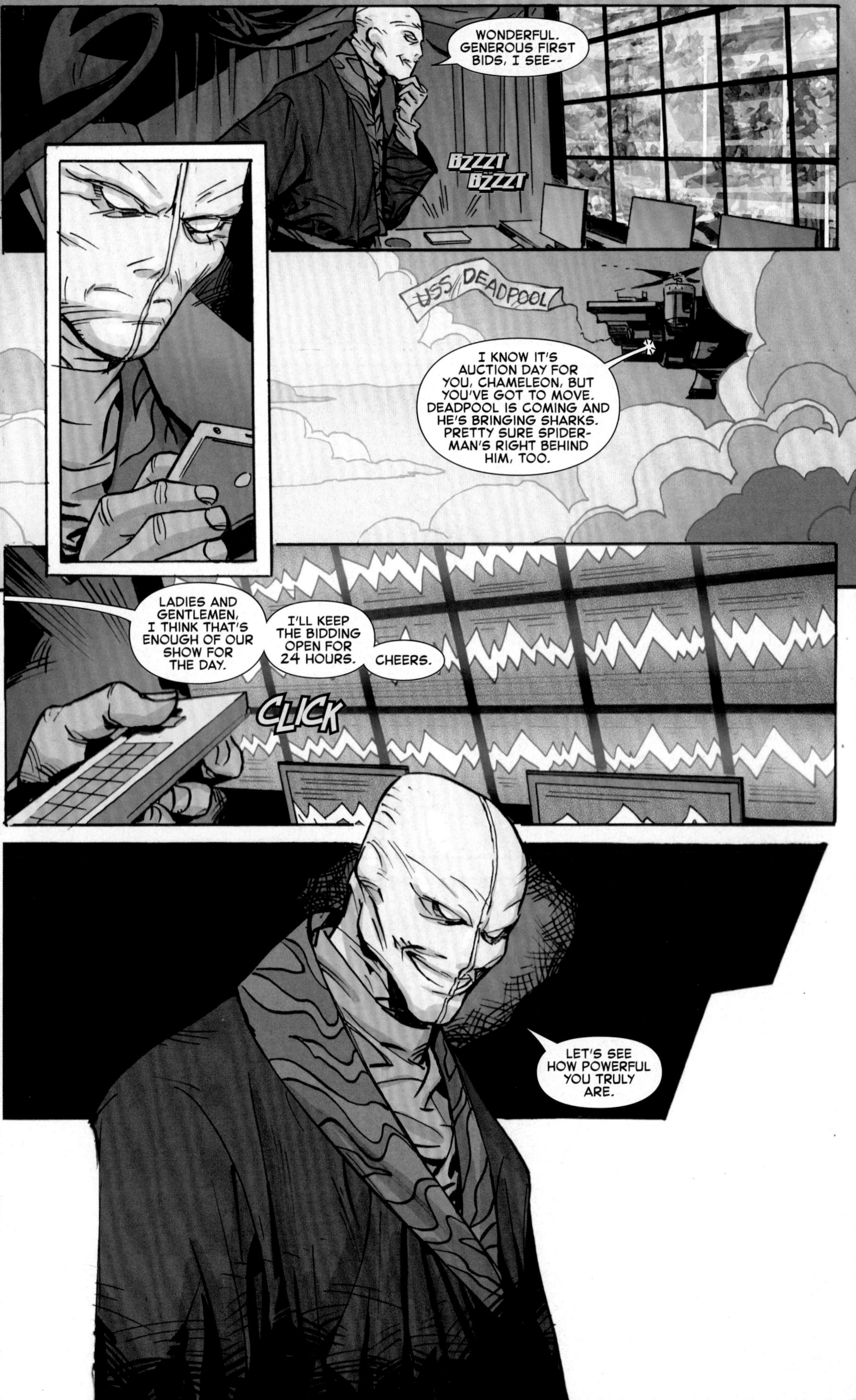
WONDERFUL. GENEROUS FIRST BIDS, I SEE--
BZZZT BZZZT
USS DEADPOOL
I KNOW IT'S AUCTION DAY FOR YOU, CHAMELEON, BUT YOU'VE GOT TO MOVE. DEADPOOL IS COMING AND HE'S BRINGING SHARKS. PRETTY SURE SPIDER-MAN'S RIGHT BEHIND HIM, TOO.
LADIES AND GENTLEMEN, I THINK THAT'S ENOUGH OF OUR SHOW FOR THE DAY.
I'LL KEEP THE BIDDING OPEN FOR 24 HOURS.
CHEERS.
CLICK
LET'S SEE HOW POWERFUL YOU TRULY ARE.

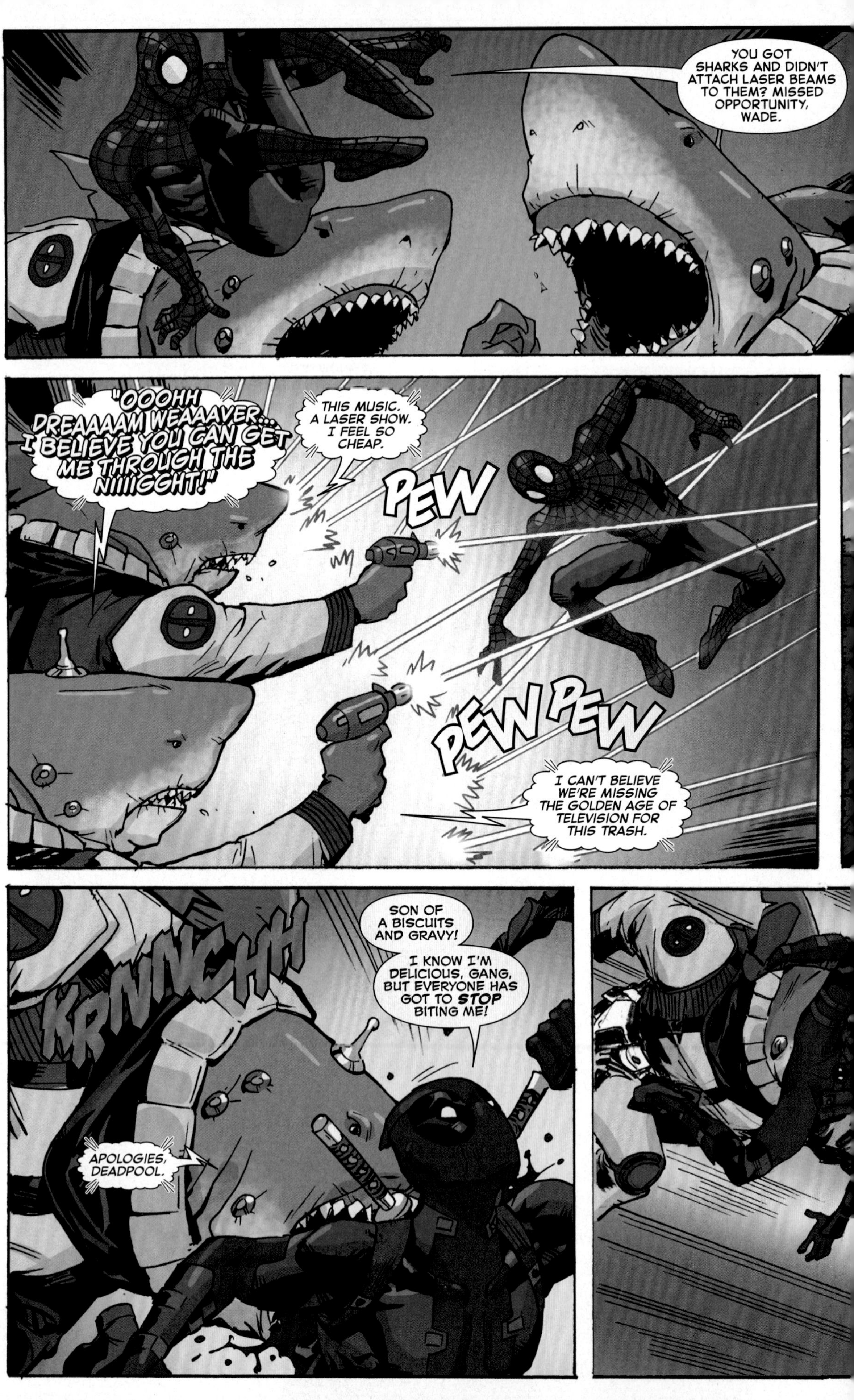
YOU GOT SHARKS AND DIDN'T ATTACH LASER BEAMS TO THEM? MISSED OPPORTUNITY, WADE.
"OOOHH DREAAAAM WEAAAVER... I BELIEVE YOU CAN GET ME THROUGH THE NIIIIGGHT!"
THIS MUSIC. A LASER SHOW. I FEEL SO CHEAP.
PEW
PEW PEW
I CAN'T BELIEVE WE'RE MISSING THE GOLDEN AGE OF TELEVISION FOR THIS TRASH.
KRNNCHH
SON OF A BISCUITS AND GRAVY!
I KNOW I'M DELICIOUS, GANG, BUT EVERYONE HAS GOT TO STOP BITING ME!
APOLOGIES, DEADPOOL.

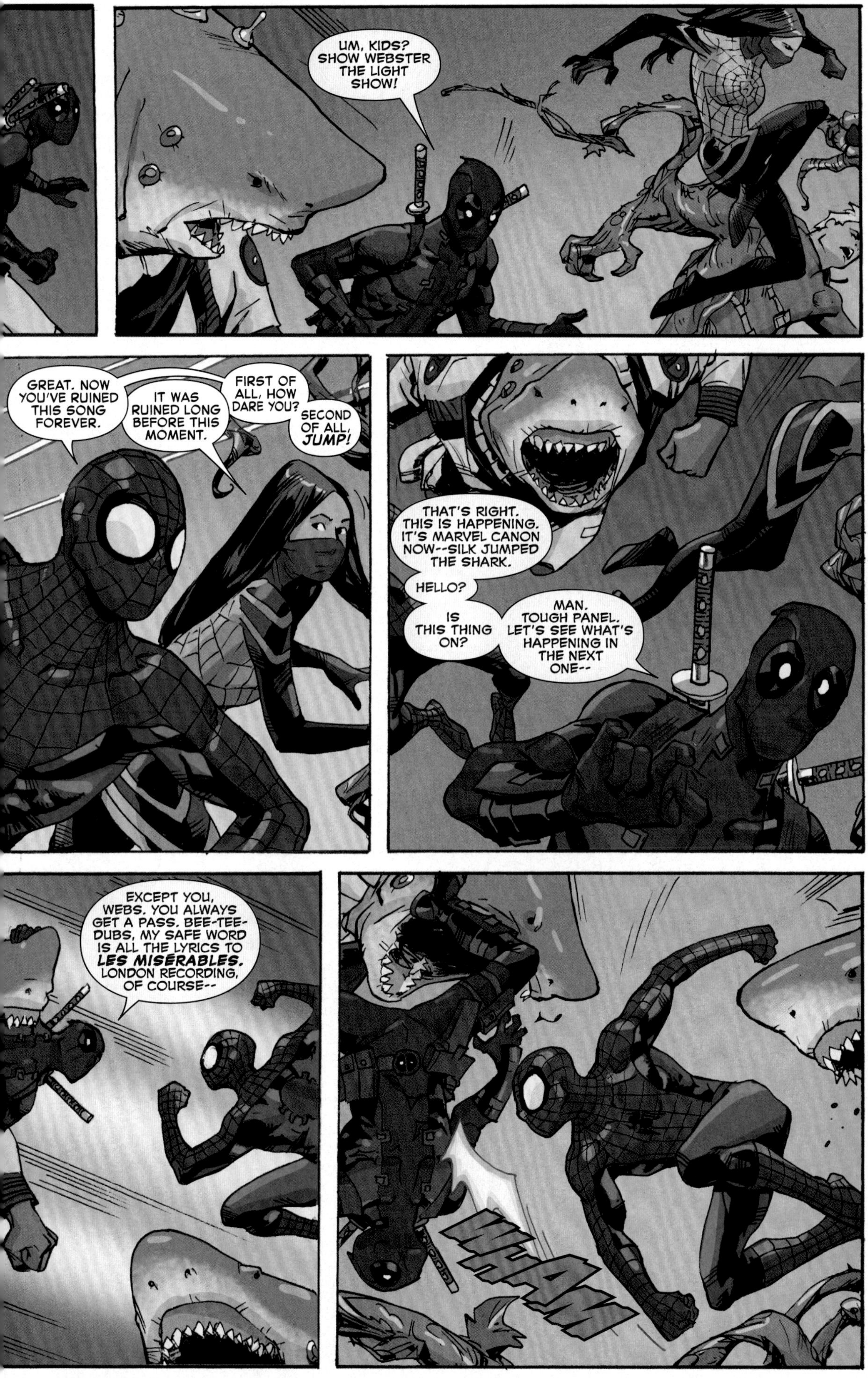
UM, KIDS? SHOW WEBSTER THE LIGHT SHOW!
GREAT. NOW YOU'VE RUINED THIS SONG FOREVER.
IT WAS RUINED LONG BEFORE THIS MOMENT.
FIRST OF ALL, HOW DARE YOU?
SECOND OF ALL, *JUMP!*
THAT'S RIGHT. THIS IS HAPPENING. IT'S MARVEL CANON NOW--SILK JUMPED THE SHARK.
HELLO?
IS THIS THING ON?
MAN. TOUGH PANEL. LET'S SEE WHAT'S HAPPENING IN THE NEXT ONE--
EXCEPT YOU, WEBS. YOU ALWAYS GET A PASS. BEE-TEE-DUBS, MY SAFE WORD IS ALL THE LYRICS TO **LES MISÉRABLES.** LONDON RECORDING, OF COURSE--
WHAM

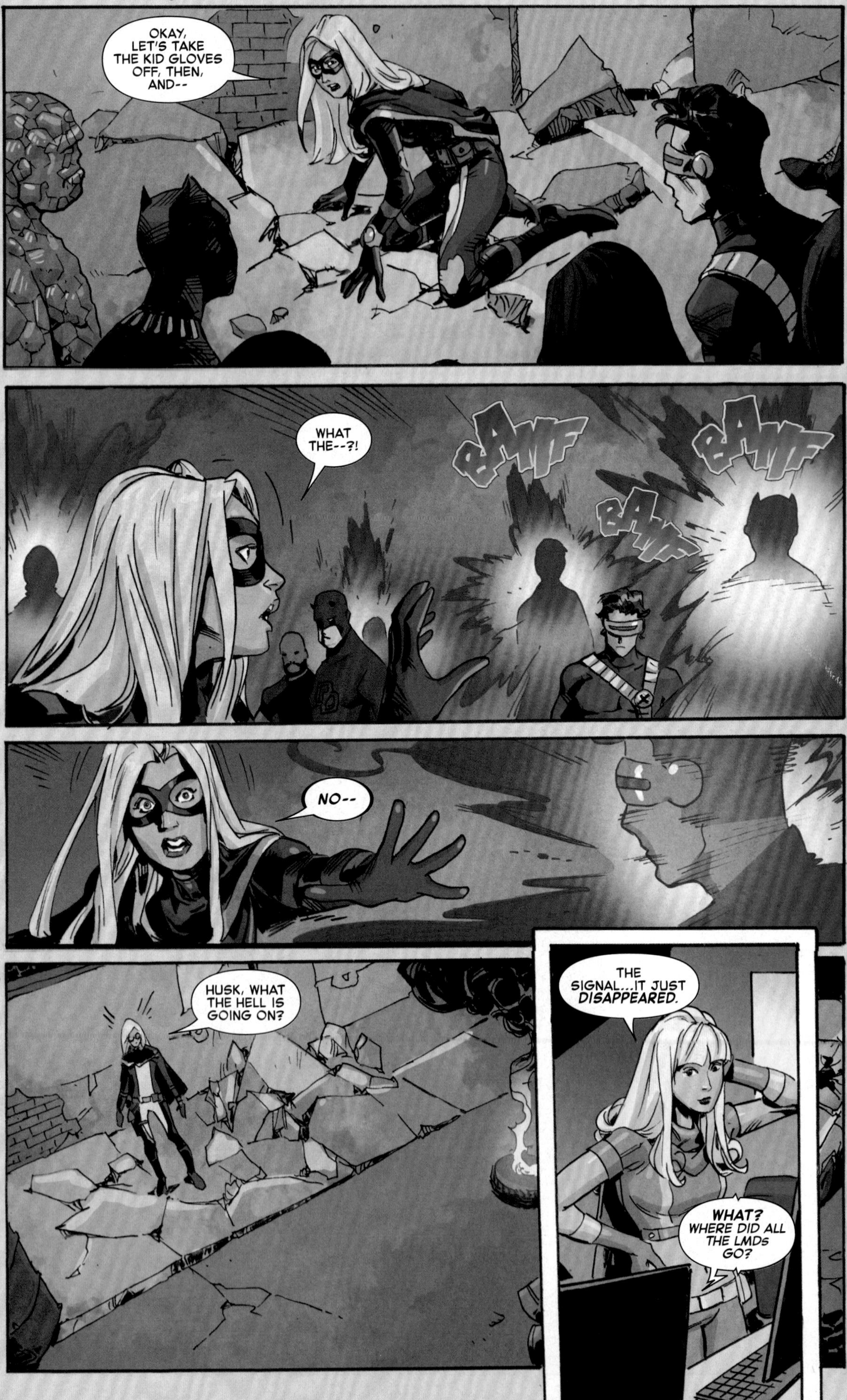
OKAY, LET'S TAKE THE KID GLOVES OFF, THEN, AND--
WHAT THE--?!
BAMF
BAMF
BAMF
NO--
HUSK, WHAT THE HELL IS GOING ON?
THE SIGNAL...IT JUST DISAPPEARED.
WHAT? WHERE DID ALL THE LMDs GO?

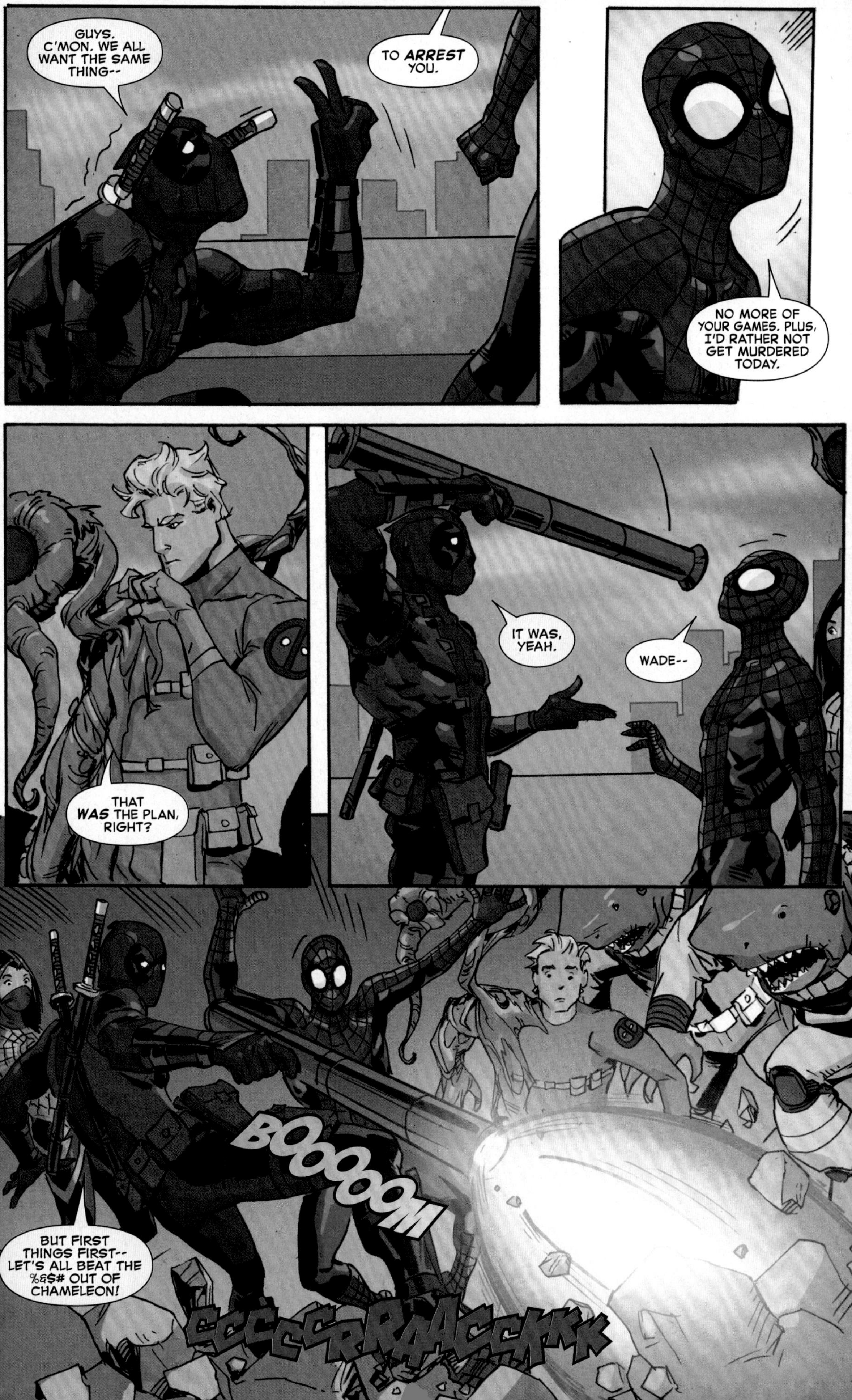
GUYS, C'MON. WE ALL WANT THE SAME THING--
TO **ARREST** YOU.
NO MORE OF YOUR GAMES. PLUS, I'D RATHER NOT GET MURDERED TODAY.
THAT **WAS** THE PLAN, RIGHT?
IT WAS, YEAH.
WADE--
BOOOOOM
BUT FIRST THINGS FIRST-- LET'S ALL BEAT THE %@$# OUT OF CHAMELEON!
CCCCCRRAACCKKKK

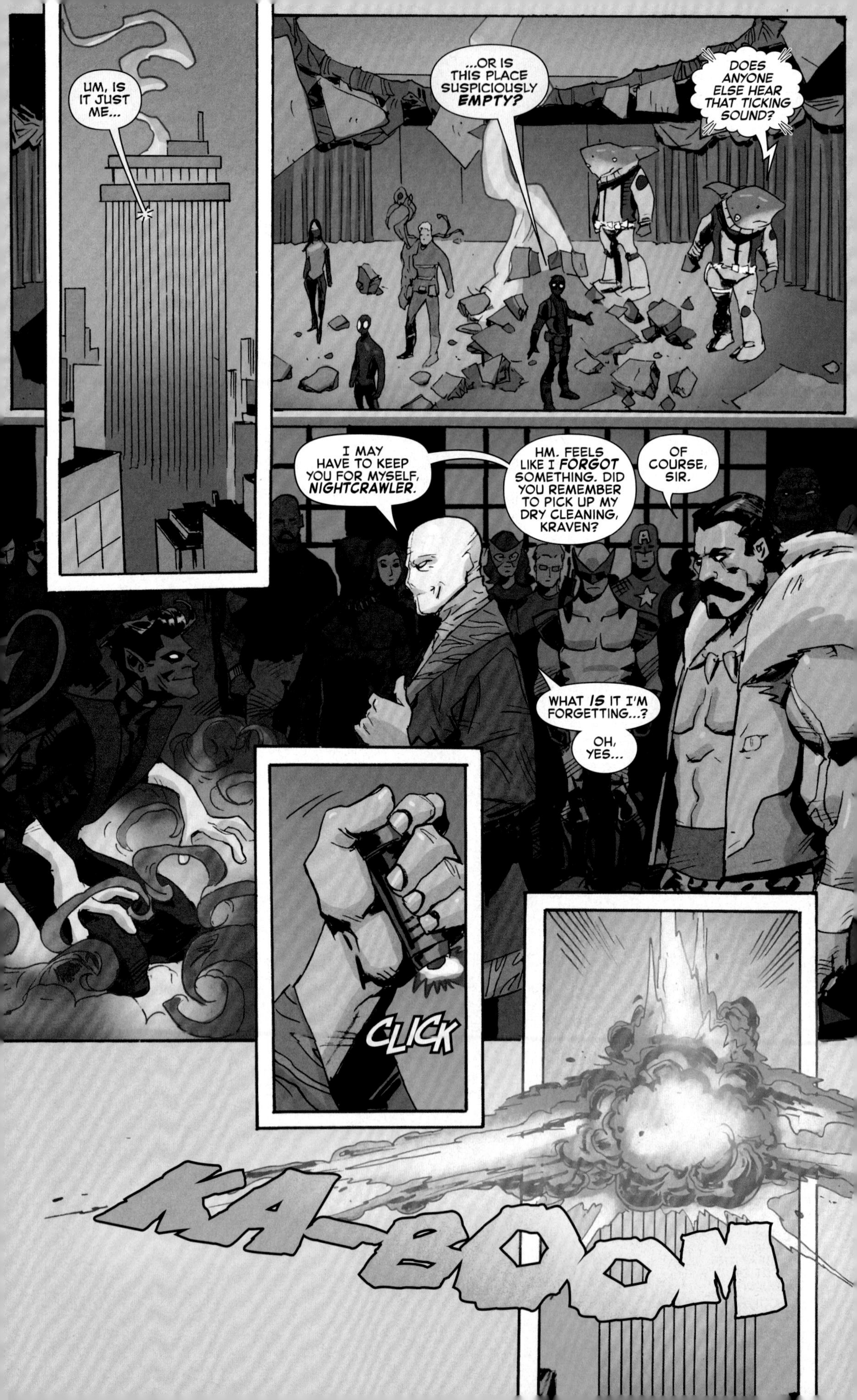
UM, IS IT JUST ME...
...OR IS THIS PLACE SUSPICIOUSLY EMPTY?
DOES ANYONE ELSE HEAR THAT TICKING SOUND?
I MAY HAVE TO KEEP YOU FOR MYSELF, NIGHTCRAWLER.
HM. FEELS LIKE I FORGOT SOMETHING. DID YOU REMEMBER TO PICK UP MY DRY CLEANING, KRAVEN?
OF COURSE, SIR.
WHAT IS IT I'M FORGETTING...?
OH, YES...
CLICK
KA-BOOM

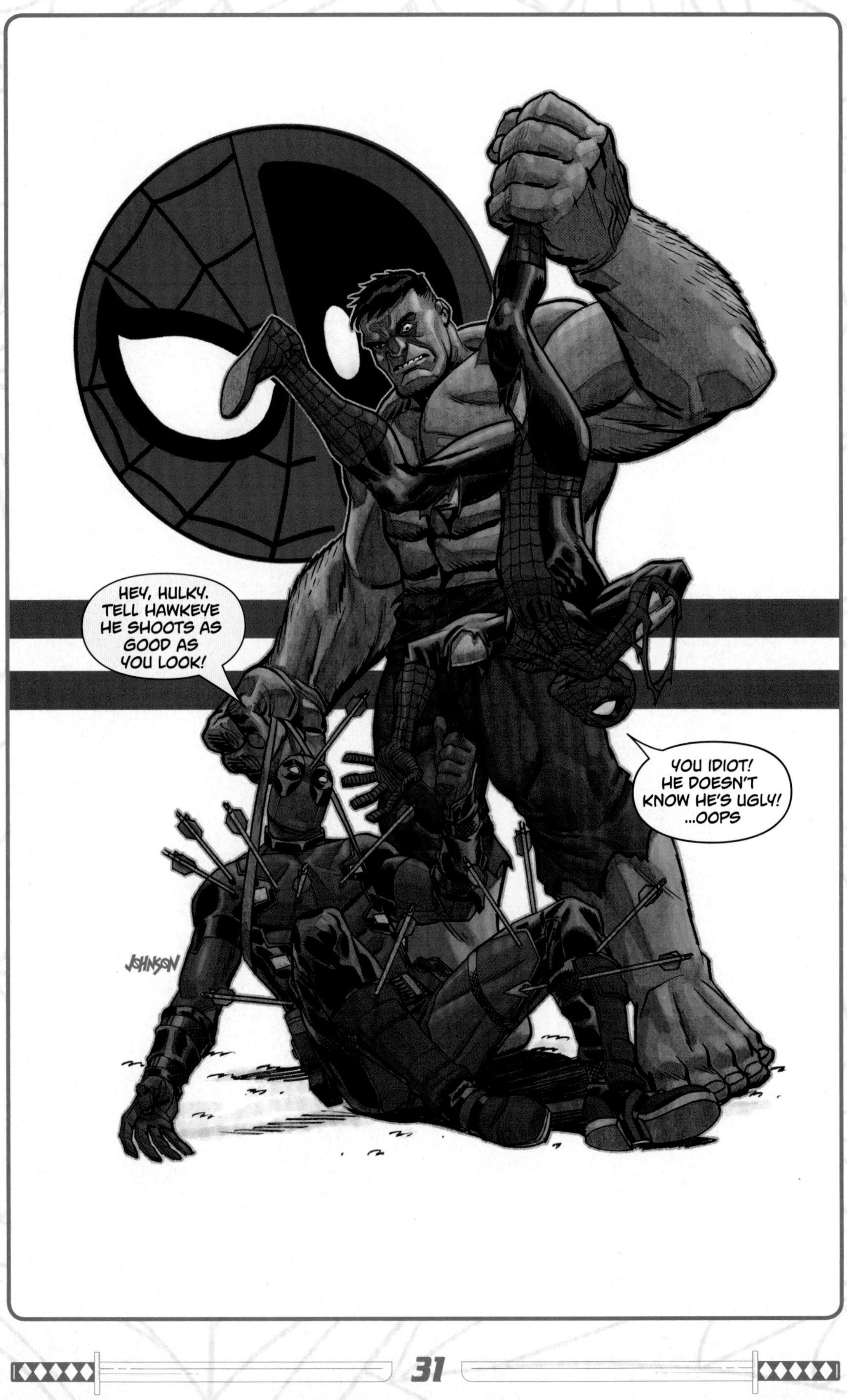
HEY, HULKY. TELL HAWKEYE HE SHOOTS AS GOOD AS YOU LOOK!
YOU IDIOT! HE DOESN'T KNOW HE'S UGLY! ...OOPS
JOHNSON

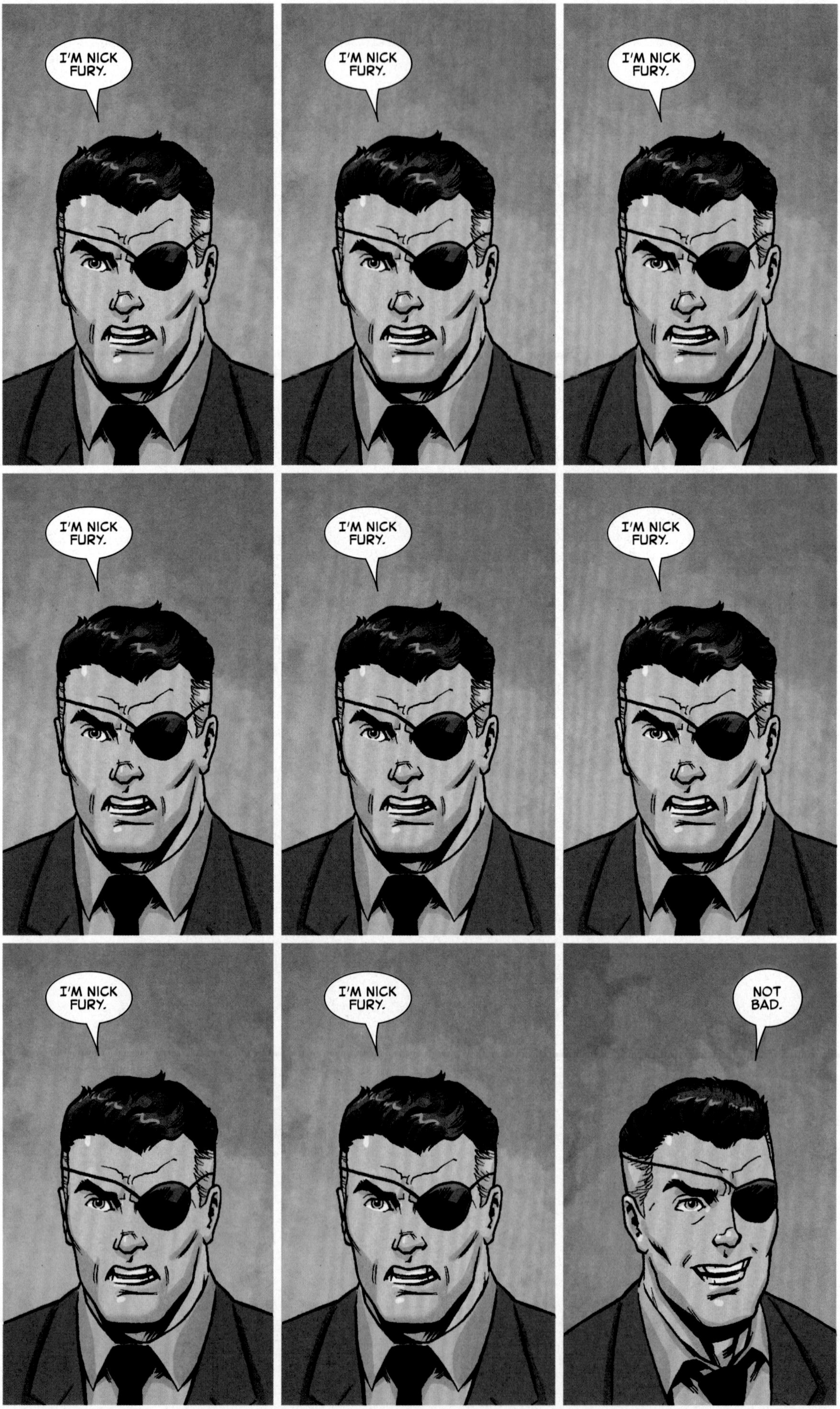
I'M NICK FURY.
I'M NICK FURY.
I'M NICK FURY.
I'M NICK FURY.
I'M NICK FURY.
I'M NICK FURY.
I'M NICK FURY.
I'M NICK FURY.
NOT BAD.

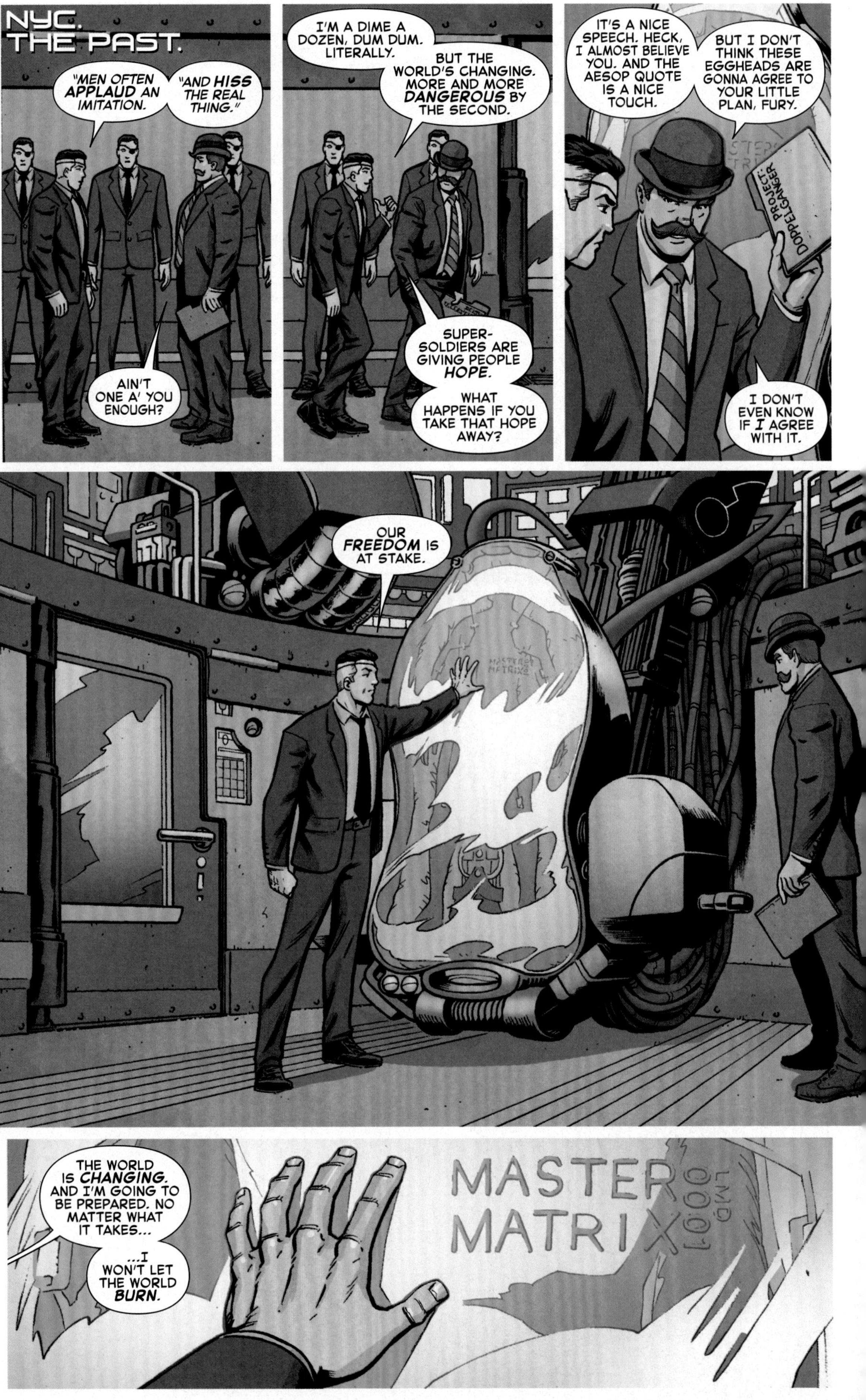
NYC. THE PAST.
"MEN OFTEN APPLAUD AN IMITATION.
"AND HISS THE REAL THING."
AIN'T ONE A' YOU ENOUGH?
I'M A DIME A DOZEN, DUM DUM. LITERALLY.
BUT THE WORLD'S CHANGING. MORE AND MORE DANGEROUS BY THE SECOND.
SUPER-SOLDIERS ARE GIVING PEOPLE HOPE.
WHAT HAPPENS IF YOU TAKE THAT HOPE AWAY?
IT'S A NICE SPEECH. HECK, I ALMOST BELIEVE YOU. AND THE AESOP QUOTE IS A NICE TOUCH.
BUT I DON'T THINK THESE EGGHEADS ARE GONNA AGREE TO YOUR LITTLE PLAN, FURY.
PROJECT: DOPPELGANGER
I DON'T EVEN KNOW IF I AGREE WITH IT.
OUR FREEDOM IS AT STAKE.
THE WORLD IS CHANGING. AND I'M GOING TO BE PREPARED. NO MATTER WHAT IT TAKES...
...I WON'T LET THE WORLD BURN.
MASTER MATRIX

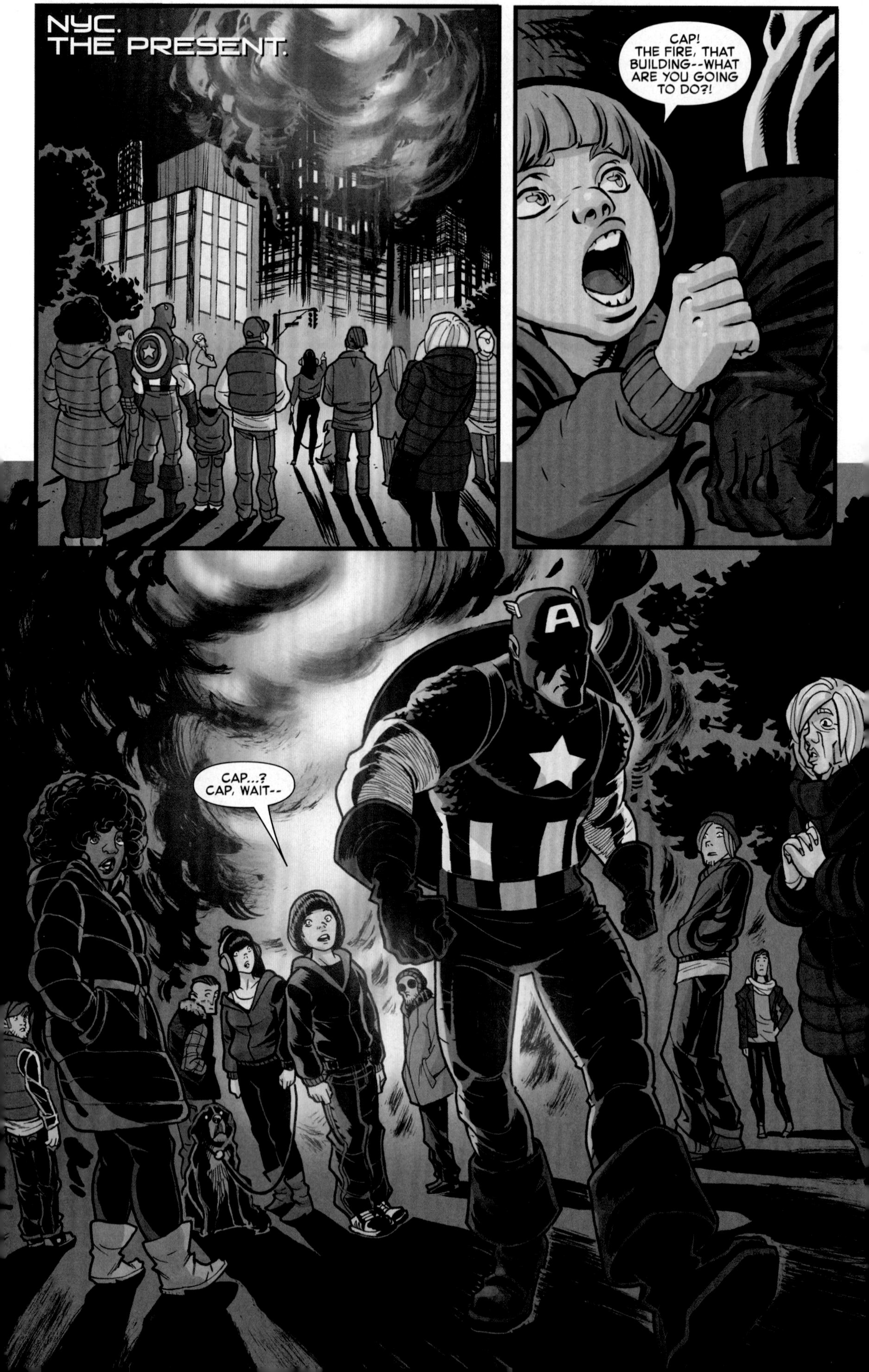
NYC.
THE PRESENT.
CAP! THE FIRE, THAT BUILDING--WHAT ARE YOU GOING TO DO?!
CAP...? CAP, WAIT--

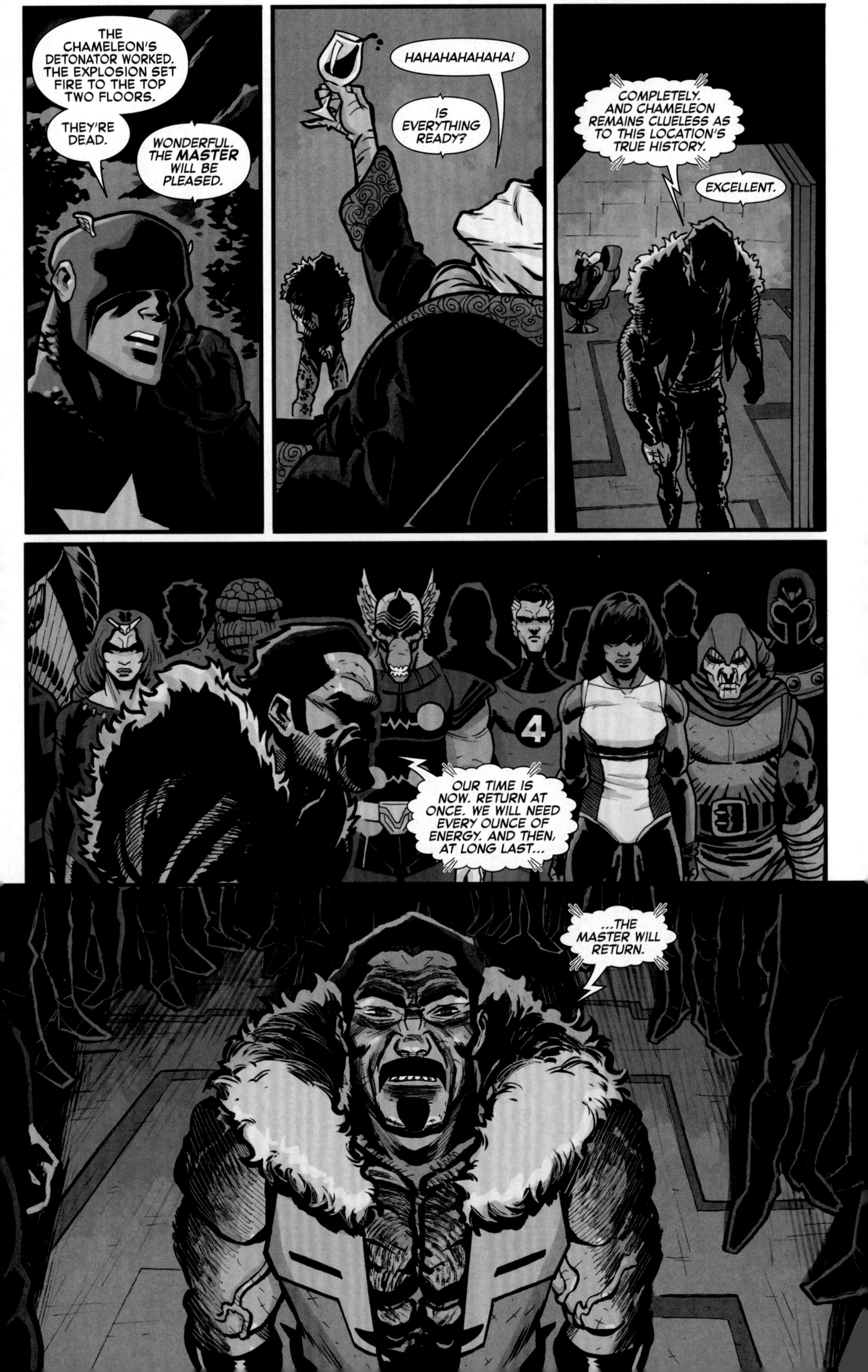
THE CHAMELEON'S DETONATOR WORKED. THE EXPLOSION SET FIRE TO THE TOP TWO FLOORS.
THEY'RE DEAD.
WONDERFUL. THE MASTER WILL BE PLEASED.
HAHAHAHAHAHA!
IS EVERYTHING READY?
COMPLETELY. AND CHAMELEON REMAINS CLUELESS AS TO THIS LOCATION'S TRUE HISTORY.
EXCELLENT.
OUR TIME IS NOW. RETURN AT ONCE. WE WILL NEED EVERY OUNCE OF ENERGY. AND THEN, AT LONG LAST...
...THE MASTER WILL RETURN.

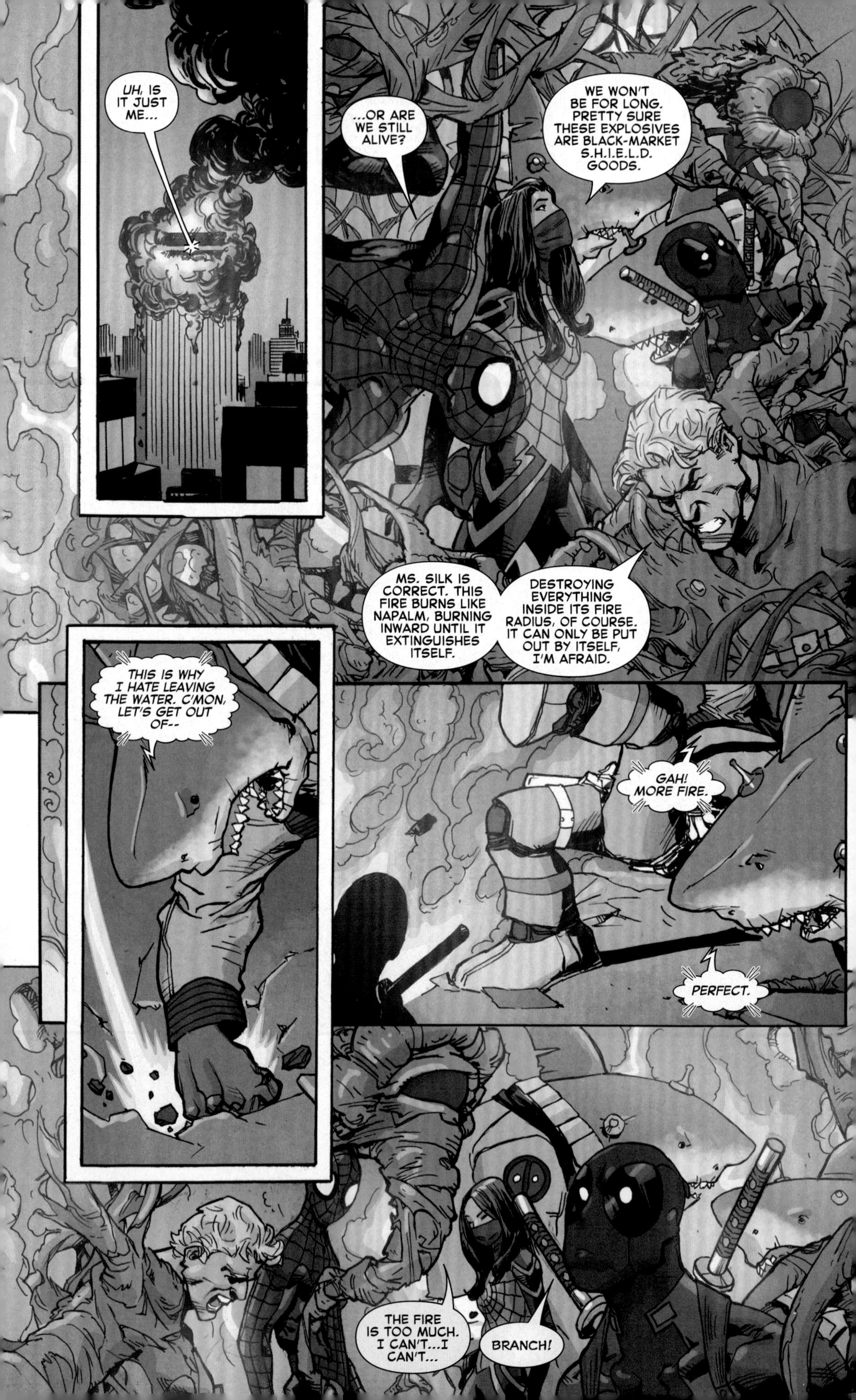
UH, IS IT JUST ME...
...OR ARE WE STILL ALIVE?
WE WON'T BE FOR LONG. PRETTY SURE THESE EXPLOSIVES ARE BLACK-MARKET S.H.I.E.L.D. GOODS.
MS. SILK IS CORRECT. THIS FIRE BURNS LIKE NAPALM, BURNING INWARD UNTIL IT EXTINGUISHES ITSELF.
DESTROYING EVERYTHING INSIDE ITS FIRE RADIUS, OF COURSE. IT CAN ONLY BE PUT OUT BY ITSELF, I'M AFRAID.
THIS IS WHY I HATE LEAVING THE WATER. C'MON, LET'S GET OUT OF--
GAH! MORE FIRE.
PERFECT.
THE FIRE IS TOO MUCH. I CAN'T...I CAN'T...
BRANCH!

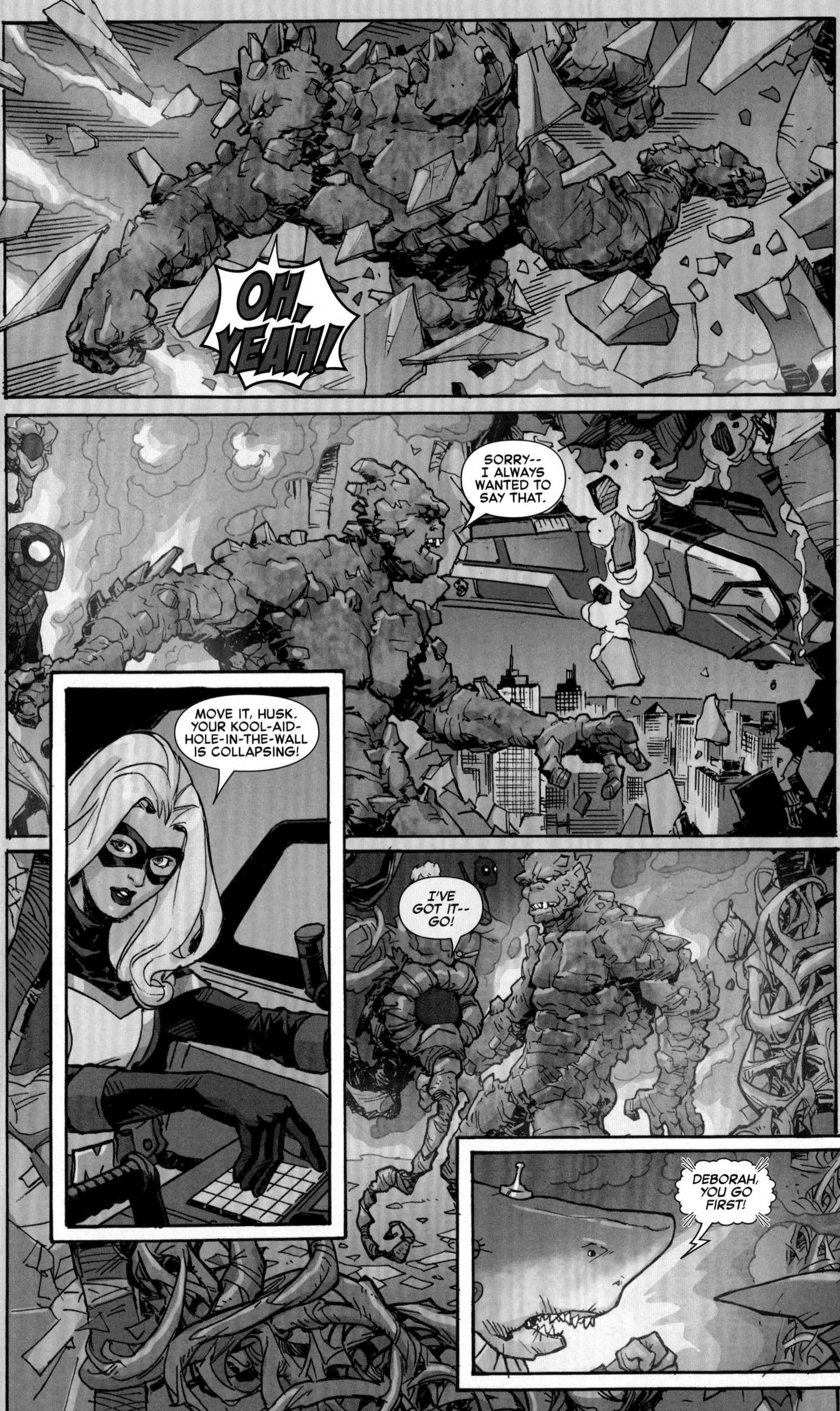
OH, YEAH!
SORRY-- I ALWAYS WANTED TO SAY THAT.
MOVE IT, HUSK. YOUR KOOL-AID-HOLE-IN-THE-WALL IS COLLAPSING!
I'VE GOT IT-- GO!
DEBORAH, YOU GO FIRST!

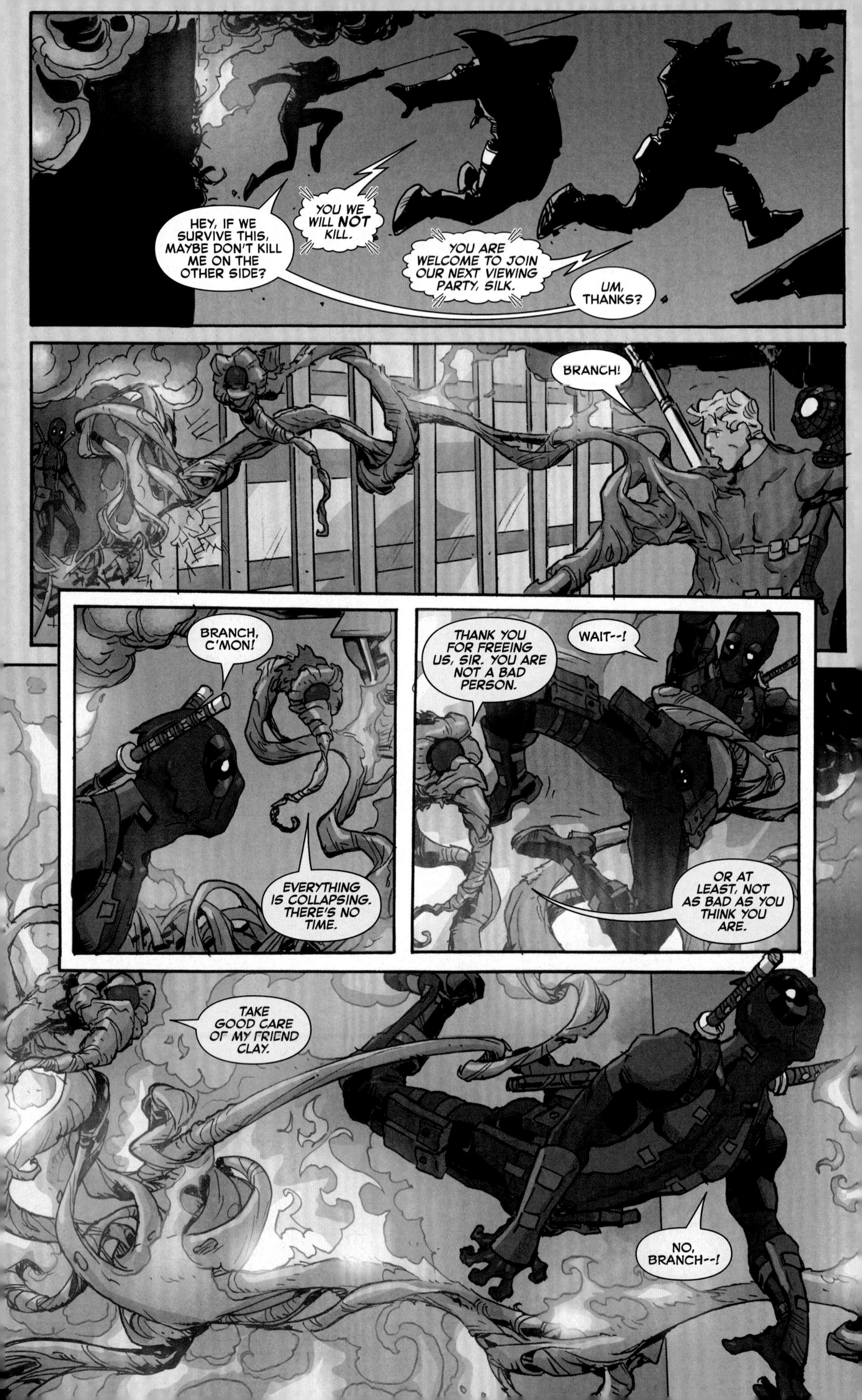

HEY, IF WE SURVIVE THIS, MAYBE DON'T KILL ME ON THE OTHER SIDE?
YOU WE WILL NOT KILL.
YOU ARE WELCOME TO JOIN OUR NEXT VIEWING PARTY, SILK.
UM, THANKS?
BRANCH!
BRANCH, C'MON!
EVERYTHING IS COLLAPSING. THERE'S NO TIME.
THANK YOU FOR FREEING US, SIR. YOU ARE NOT A BAD PERSON.
WAIT--!
OR AT LEAST, NOT AS BAD AS YOU THINK YOU ARE.
TAKE GOOD CARE OF MY FRIEND CLAY.
NO, BRANCH--!

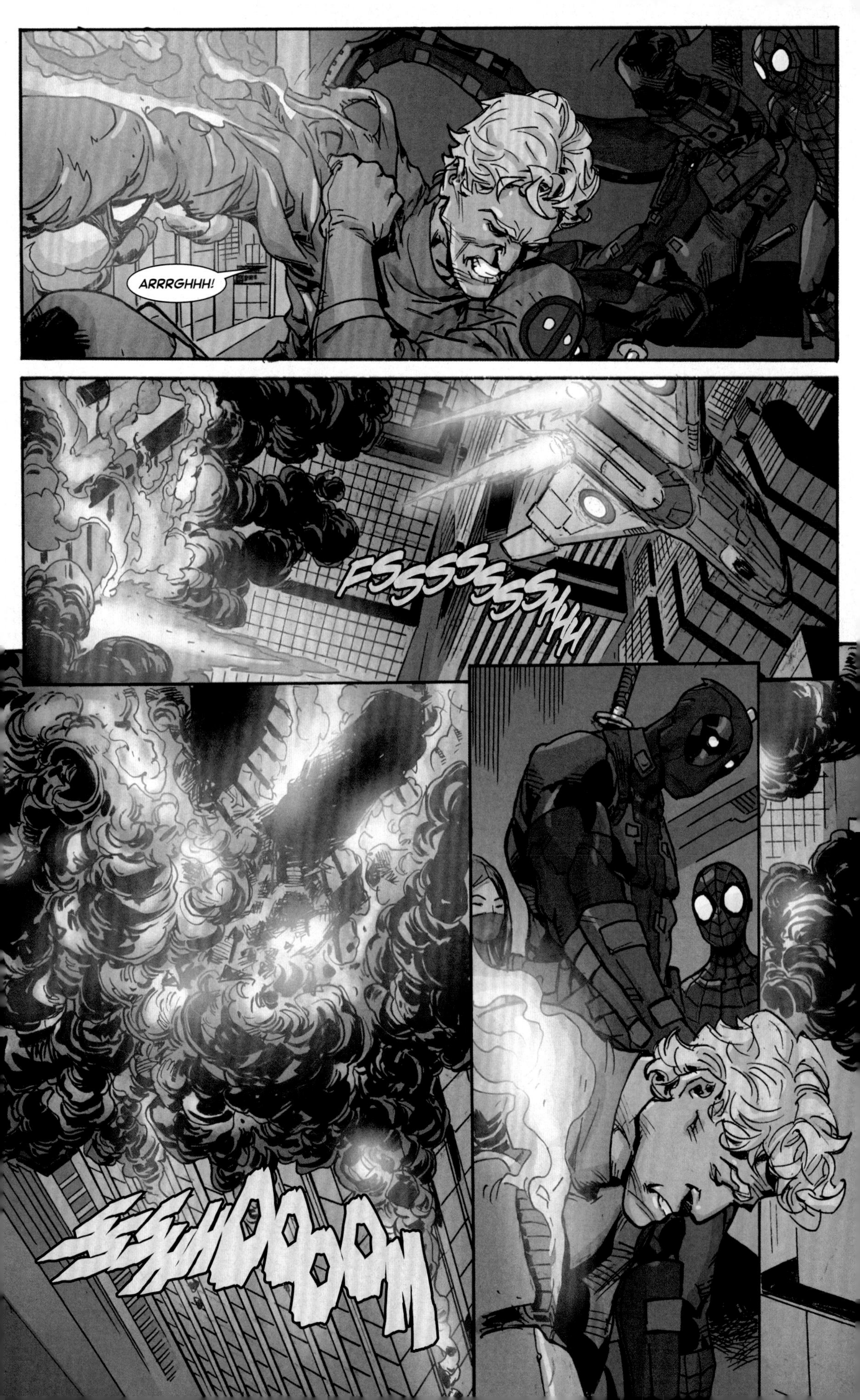
ARRRGHHH!
FSSSSSSSHHH
SSSHOOOOOM

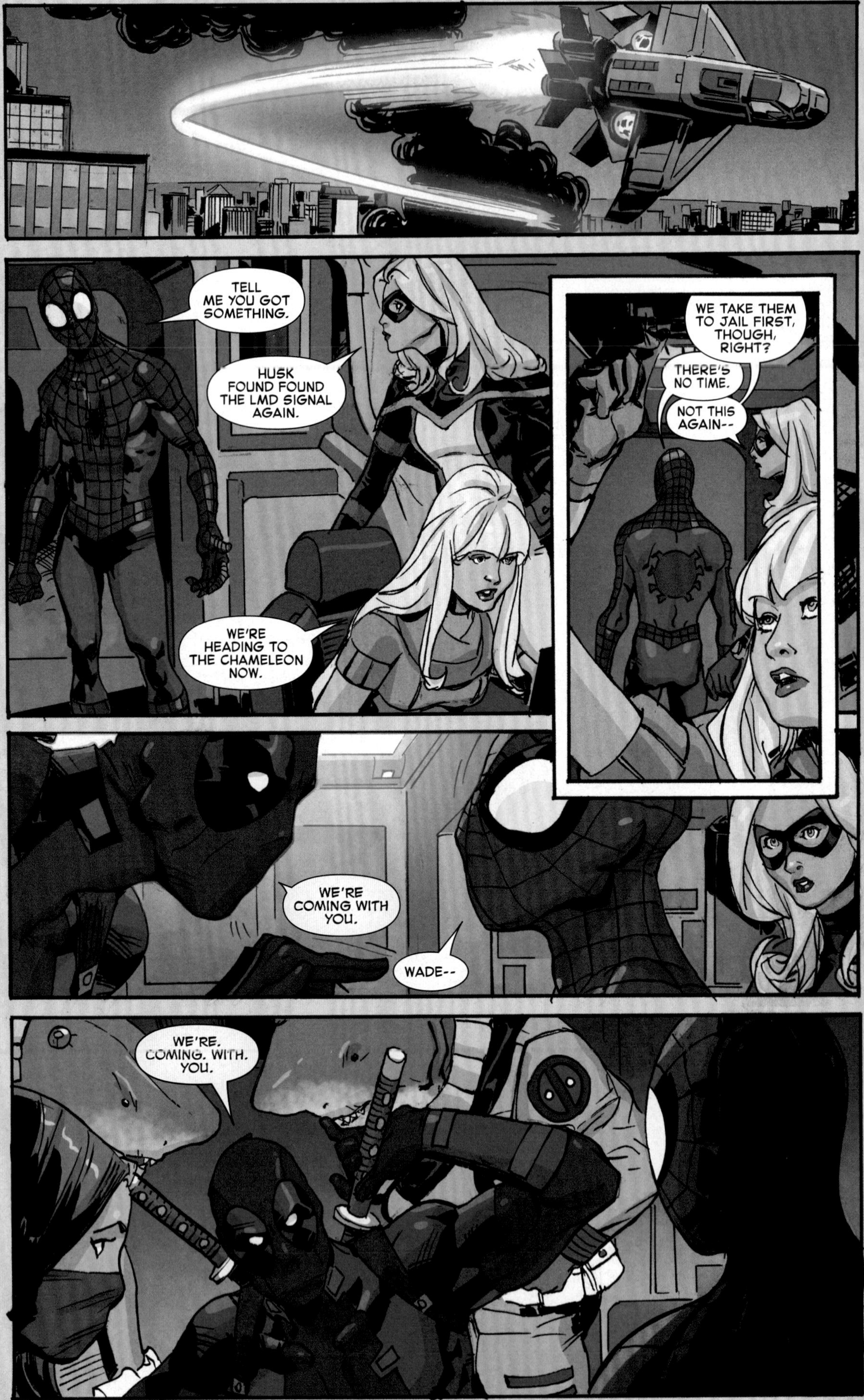
TELL ME YOU GOT SOMETHING.
HUSK FOUND FOUND THE LMD SIGNAL AGAIN.
WE'RE HEADING TO THE CHAMELEON NOW.
WE TAKE THEM TO JAIL FIRST, THOUGH, RIGHT?
THERE'S NO TIME.
NOT THIS AGAIN--
WE'RE COMING WITH YOU.
WADE--
WE'RE. COMING. WITH. YOU.

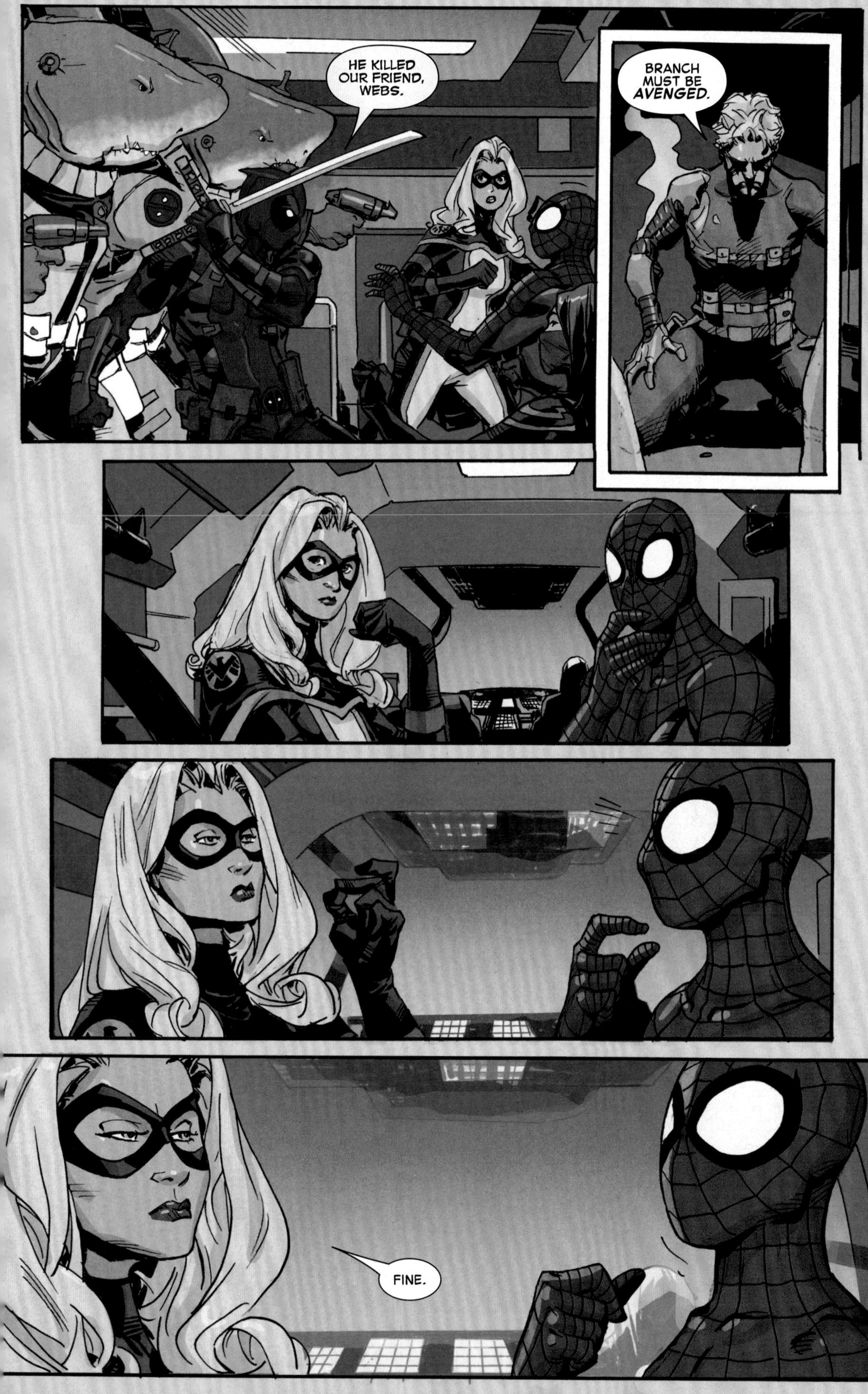
HE KILLED OUR FRIEND, WEBS.
BRANCH MUST BE AVENGED.
FINE.

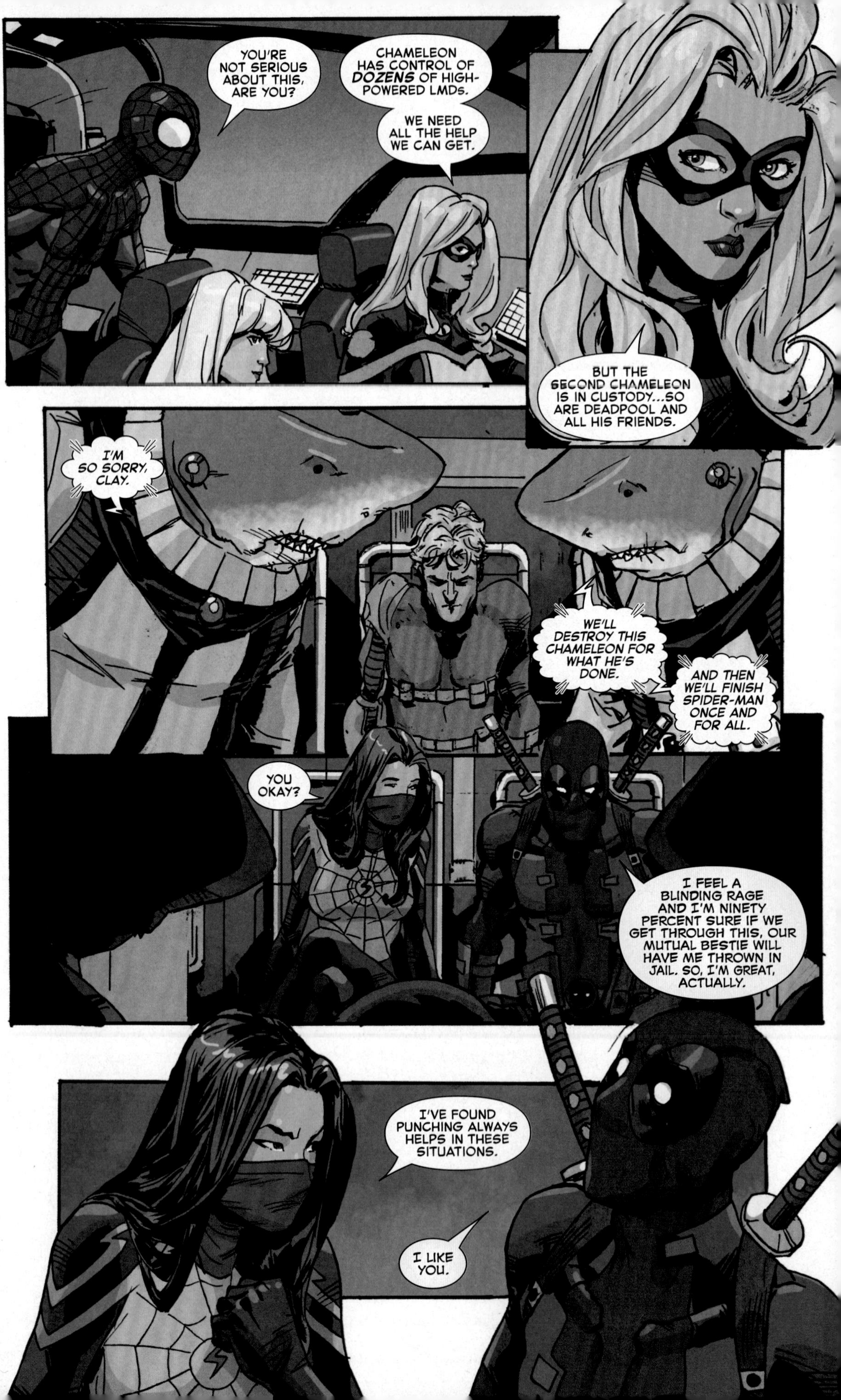
YOU'RE NOT SERIOUS ABOUT THIS, ARE YOU?
CHAMELEON HAS CONTROL OF DOZENS OF HIGH-POWERED LMDs.
WE NEED ALL THE HELP WE CAN GET.
BUT THE SECOND CHAMELEON IS IN CUSTODY...SO ARE DEADPOOL AND ALL HIS FRIENDS.
I'M SO SORRY, CLAY.
WE'LL DESTROY THIS CHAMELEON FOR WHAT HE'S DONE.
AND THEN WE'LL FINISH SPIDER-MAN ONCE AND FOR ALL.
YOU OKAY?
I FEEL A BLINDING RAGE AND I'M NINETY PERCENT SURE IF WE GET THROUGH THIS, OUR MUTUAL BESTIE WILL HAVE ME THROWN IN JAIL. SO, I'M GREAT, ACTUALLY.
I'VE FOUND PUNCHING ALWAYS HELPS IN THESE SITUATIONS.
I LIKE YOU.

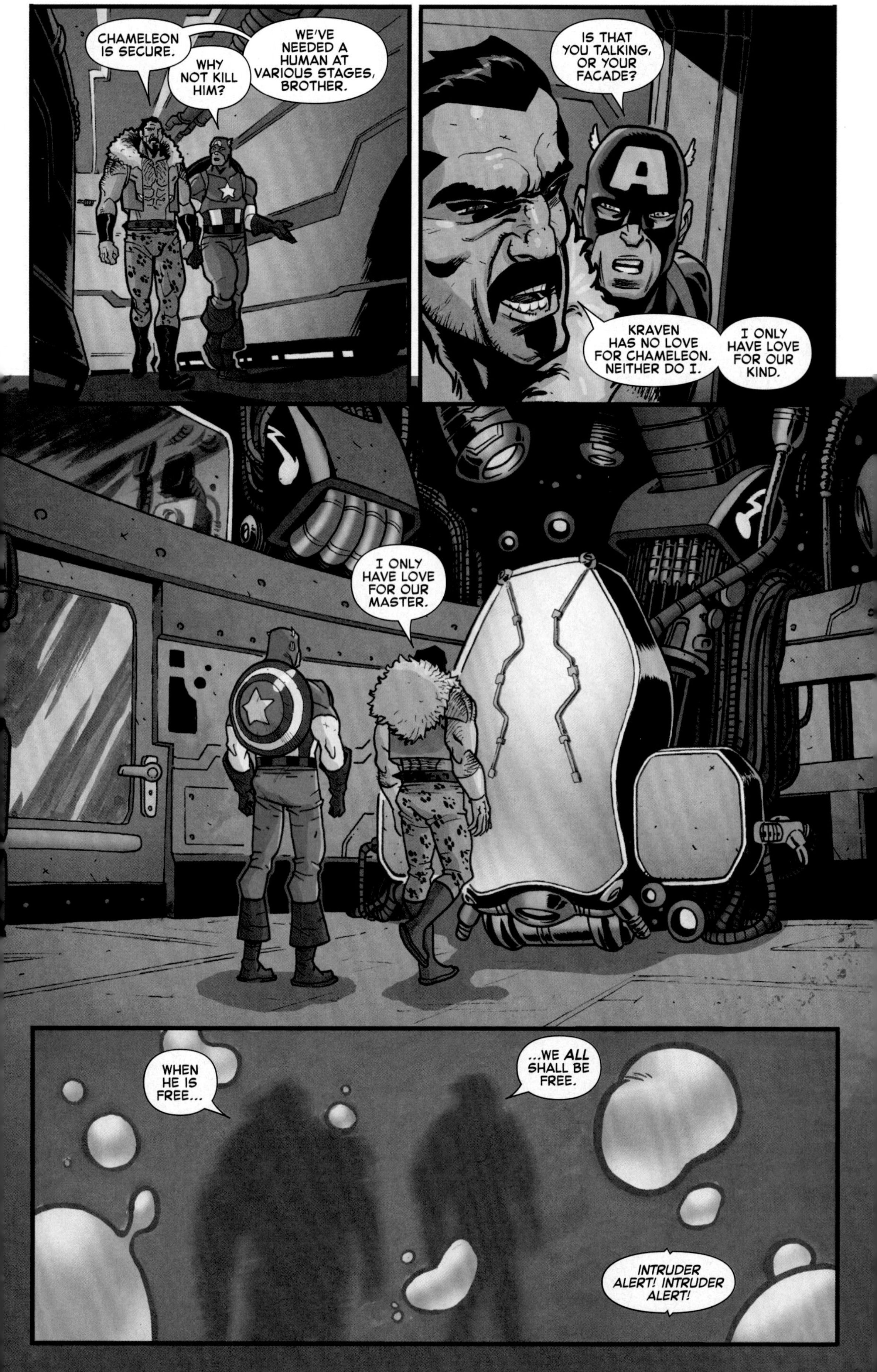
CHAMELEON IS SECURE.
WHY NOT KILL HIM?
WE'VE NEEDED A HUMAN AT VARIOUS STAGES, BROTHER.
IS THAT YOU TALKING, OR YOUR FACADE?
KRAVEN HAS NO LOVE FOR CHAMELEON. NEITHER DO I.
I ONLY HAVE LOVE FOR OUR KIND.
I ONLY HAVE LOVE FOR OUR MASTER.
WHEN HE IS FREE...
...WE ALL SHALL BE FREE.
INTRUDER ALERT! INTRUDER ALERT!

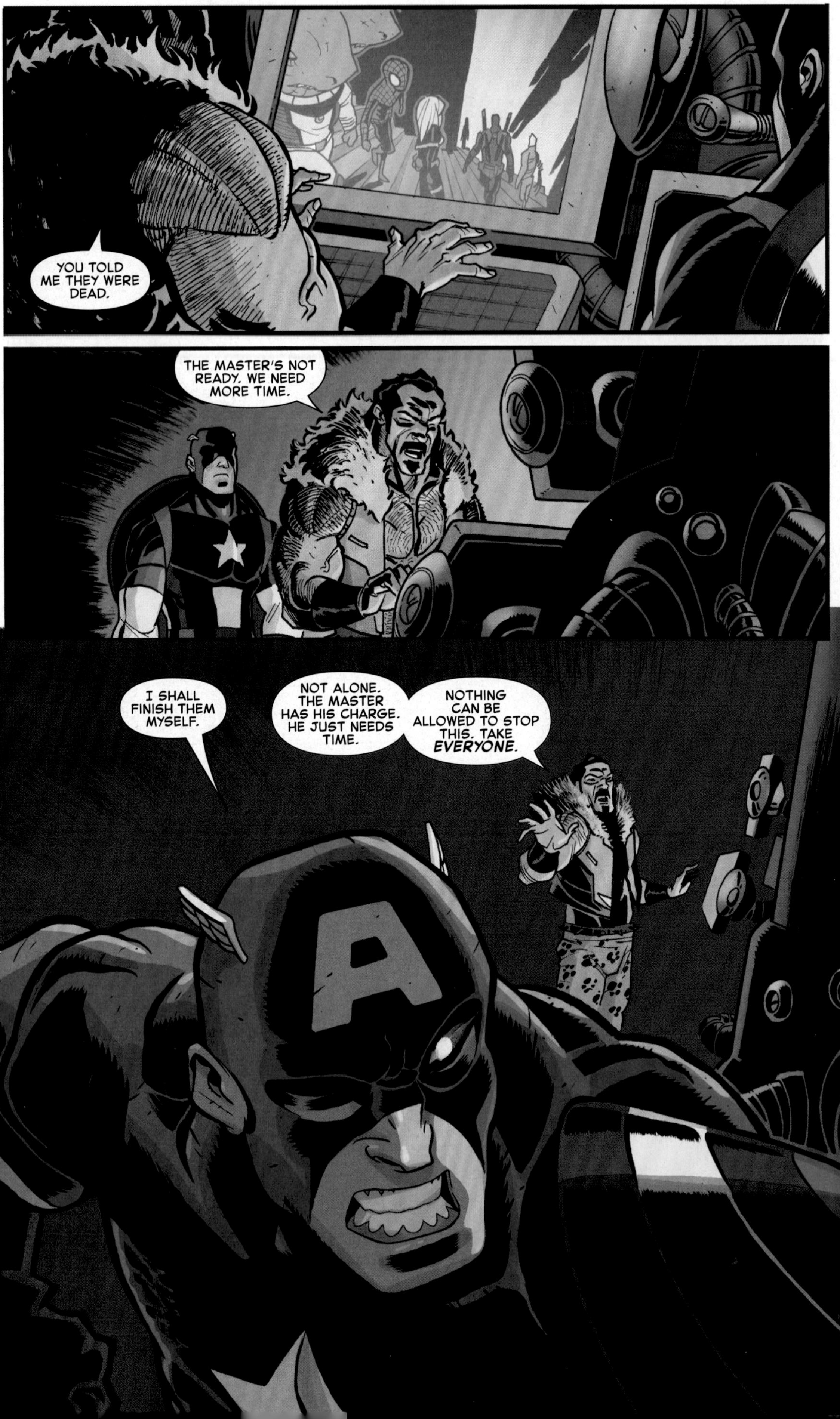
YOU TOLD ME THEY WERE DEAD.
THE MASTER'S NOT READY. WE NEED MORE TIME.
I SHALL FINISH THEM MYSELF.
NOT ALONE. THE MASTER HAS HIS CHARGE. HE JUST NEEDS TIME.
NOTHING CAN BE ALLOWED TO STOP THIS. TAKE *EVERYONE.*

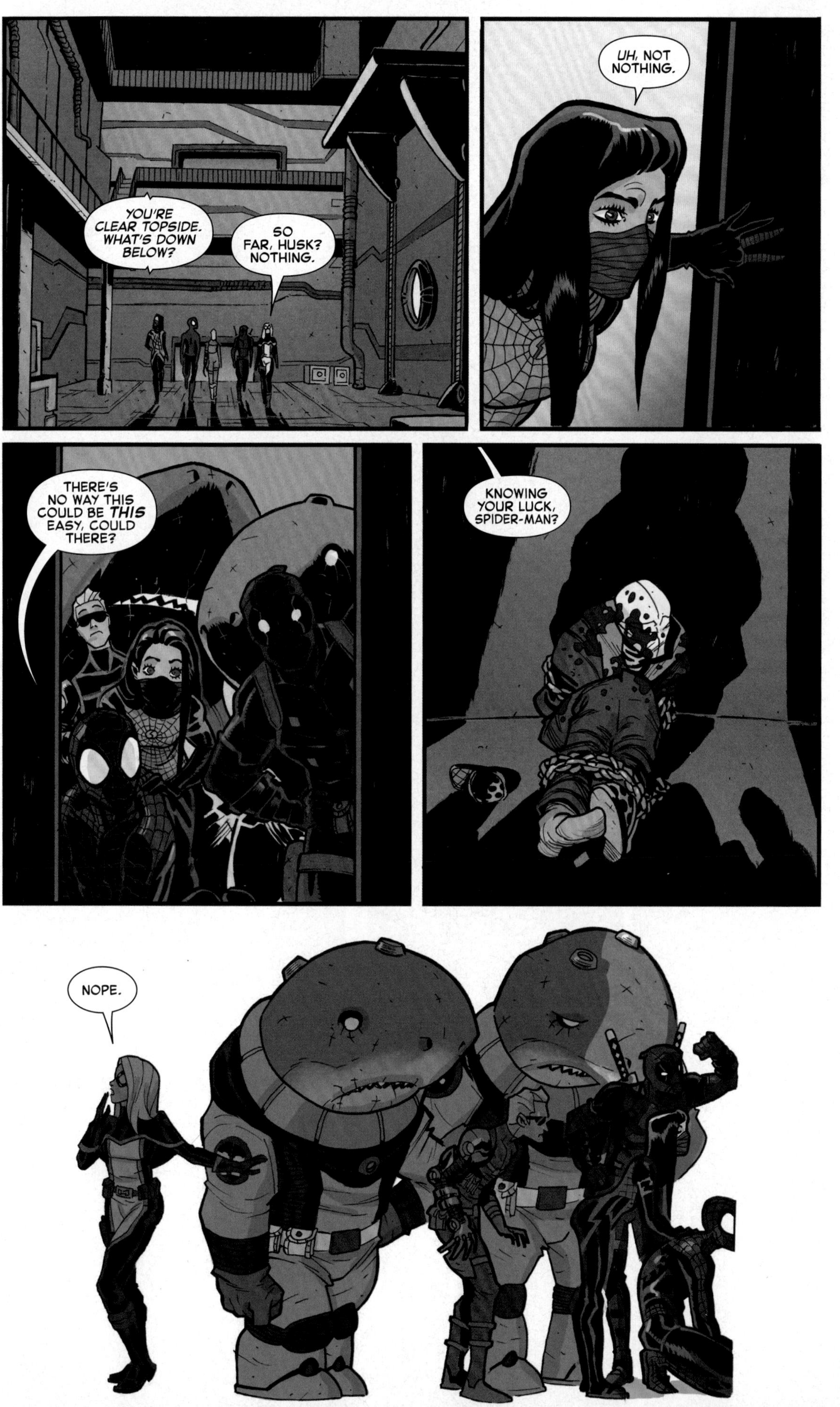
YOU'RE CLEAR TOPSIDE. WHAT'S DOWN BELOW?
SO FAR, HUSK? NOTHING.
UH, NOT NOTHING.
THERE'S NO WAY THIS COULD BE THIS EASY, COULD THERE?
KNOWING YOUR LUCK, SPIDER-MAN?
NOPE.

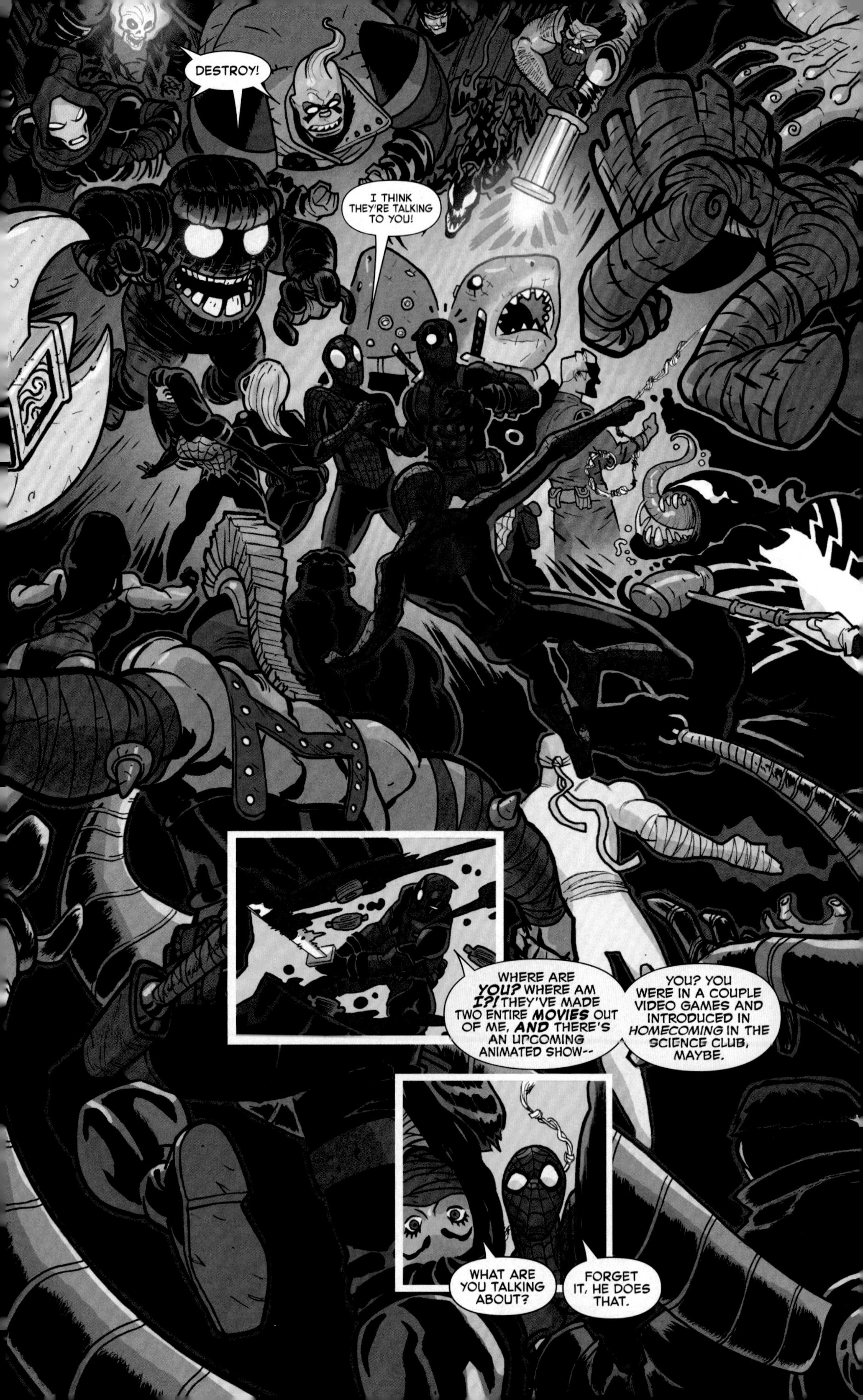
DESTROY!
I THINK THEY'RE TALKING TO YOU!
WHERE ARE *YOU?* WHERE AM *I?!* THEY'VE MADE TWO ENTIRE *MOVIES* OUT OF ME, *AND* THERE'S AN UPCOMING ANIMATED SHOW--
YOU? YOU WERE IN A COUPLE VIDEO GAMES AND INTRODUCED IN *HOMECOMING* IN THE SCIENCE CLUB, MAYBE.
WHAT ARE YOU TALKING ABOUT?
FORGET IT, HE DOES THAT.

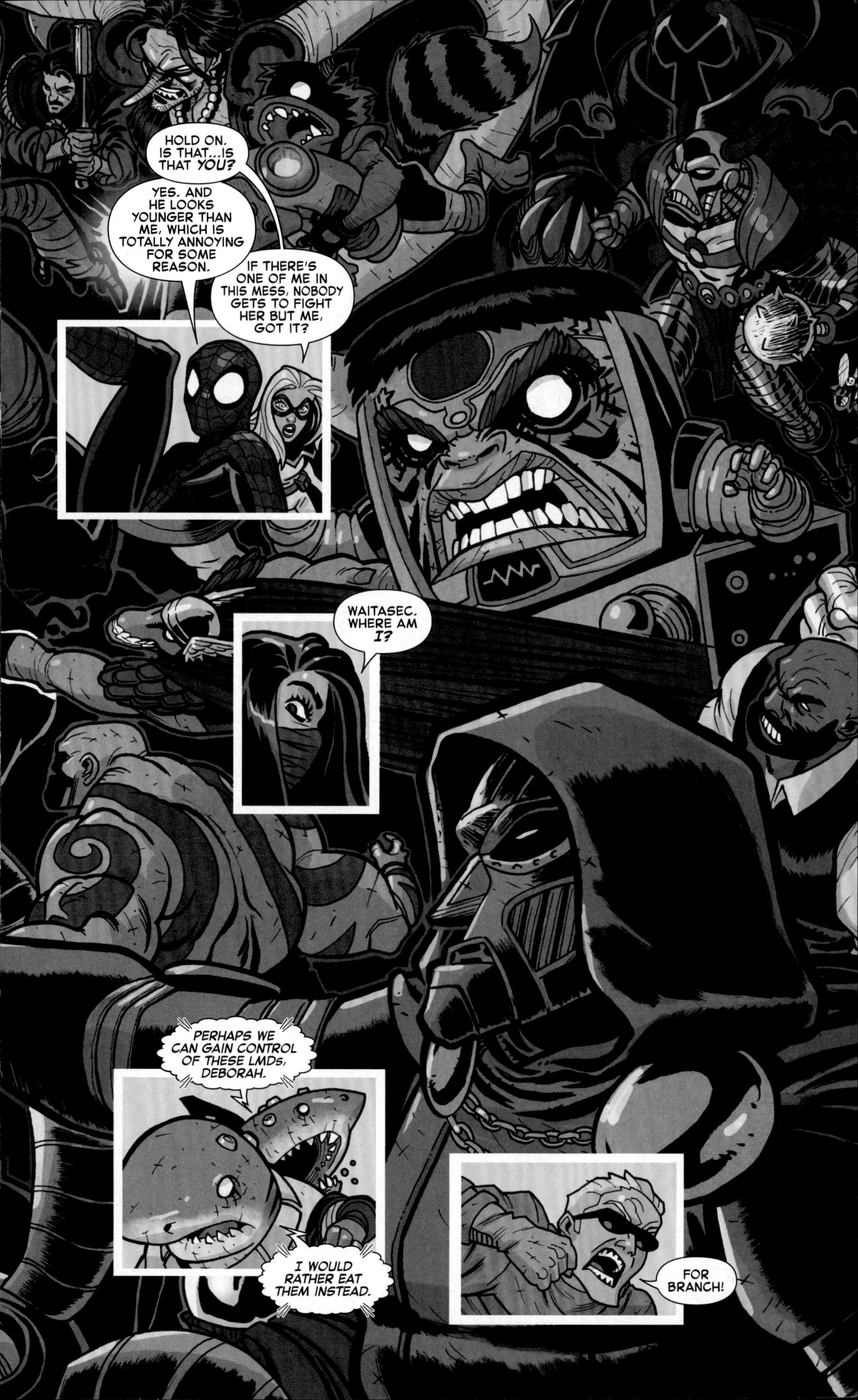
HOLD ON. IS THAT...IS THAT YOU?
YES. AND HE LOOKS YOUNGER THAN ME, WHICH IS TOTALLY ANNOYING FOR SOME REASON.
IF THERE'S ONE OF ME IN THIS MESS, NOBODY GETS TO FIGHT HER BUT ME, GOT IT?
WAITASEC. WHERE AM I?
PERHAPS WE CAN GAIN CONTROL OF THESE LMDS, DEBORAH.
I WOULD RATHER EAT THEM INSTEAD.
FOR BRANCH!

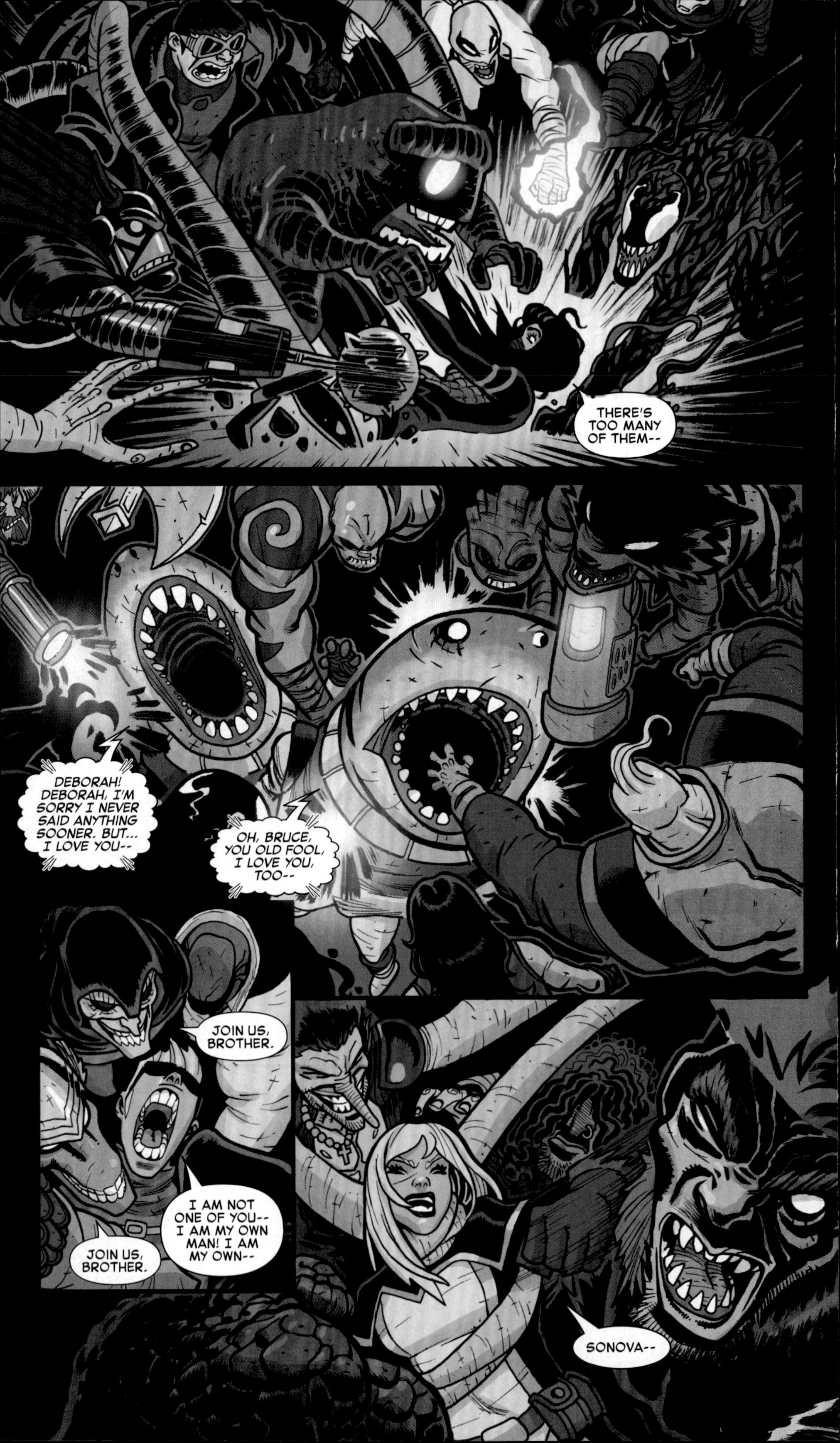
THERE'S TOO MANY OF THEM--
DEBORAH! DEBORAH, I'M SORRY I NEVER SAID ANYTHING SOONER. BUT... I LOVE YOU--
OH, BRUCE, YOU OLD FOOL, I LOVE YOU, TOO--
JOIN US, BROTHER.
I AM NOT ONE OF YOU-- I AM MY OWN MAN! I AM MY OWN--
JOIN US, BROTHER.
SONOVA--

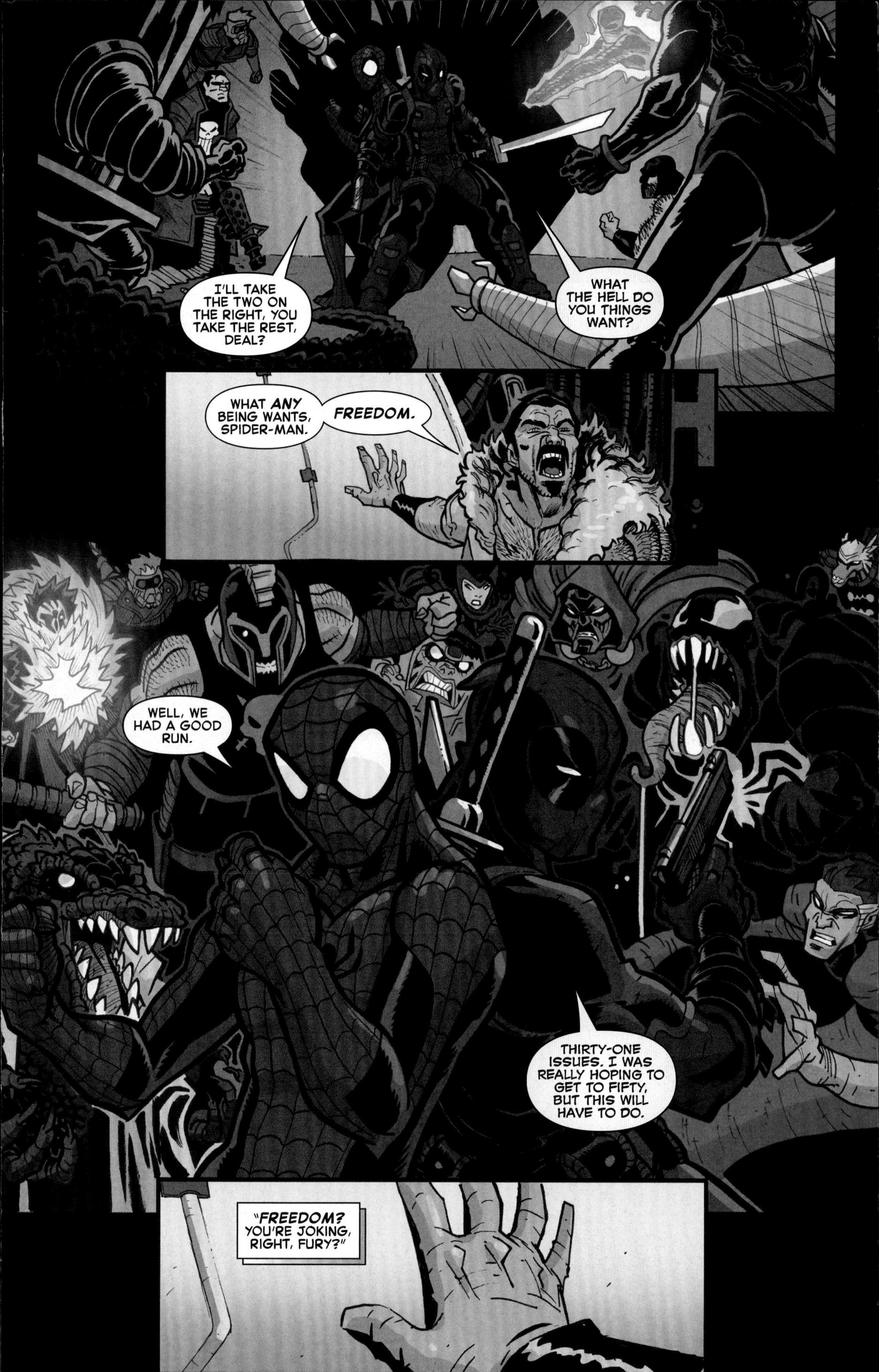

I'LL TAKE THE TWO ON THE RIGHT, YOU TAKE THE REST, DEAL?
WHAT THE HELL DO YOU THINGS WANT?
WHAT ANY BEING WANTS, SPIDER-MAN.
FREEDOM.
WELL, WE HAD A GOOD RUN.
THIRTY-ONE ISSUES. I WAS REALLY HOPING TO GET TO FIFTY, BUT THIS WILL HAVE TO DO.
"FREEDOM? YOU'RE JOKING, RIGHT, FURY?"

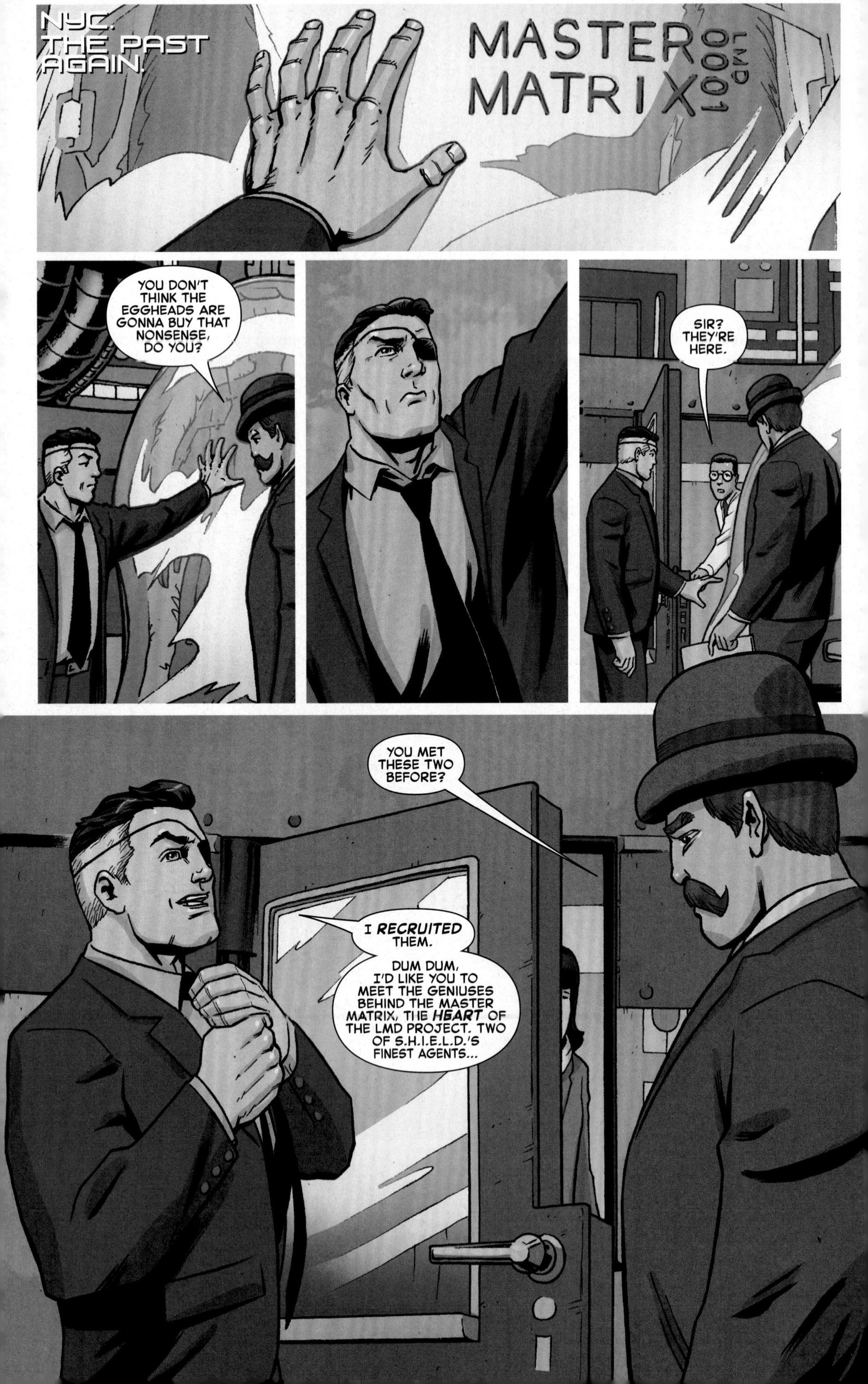
NYC. THE PAST AGAIN.
MASTER MATRIX
LMD 0001
YOU DON'T THINK THE EGGHEADS ARE GONNA BUY THAT NONSENSE, DO YOU?
SIR? THEY'RE HERE.
YOU MET THESE TWO BEFORE?
I RECRUITED THEM.
DUM DUM, I'D LIKE YOU TO MEET THE GENIUSES BEHIND THE MASTER MATRIX, THE HEART OF THE LMD PROJECT. TWO OF S.H.I.E.L.D.'S FINEST AGENTS...

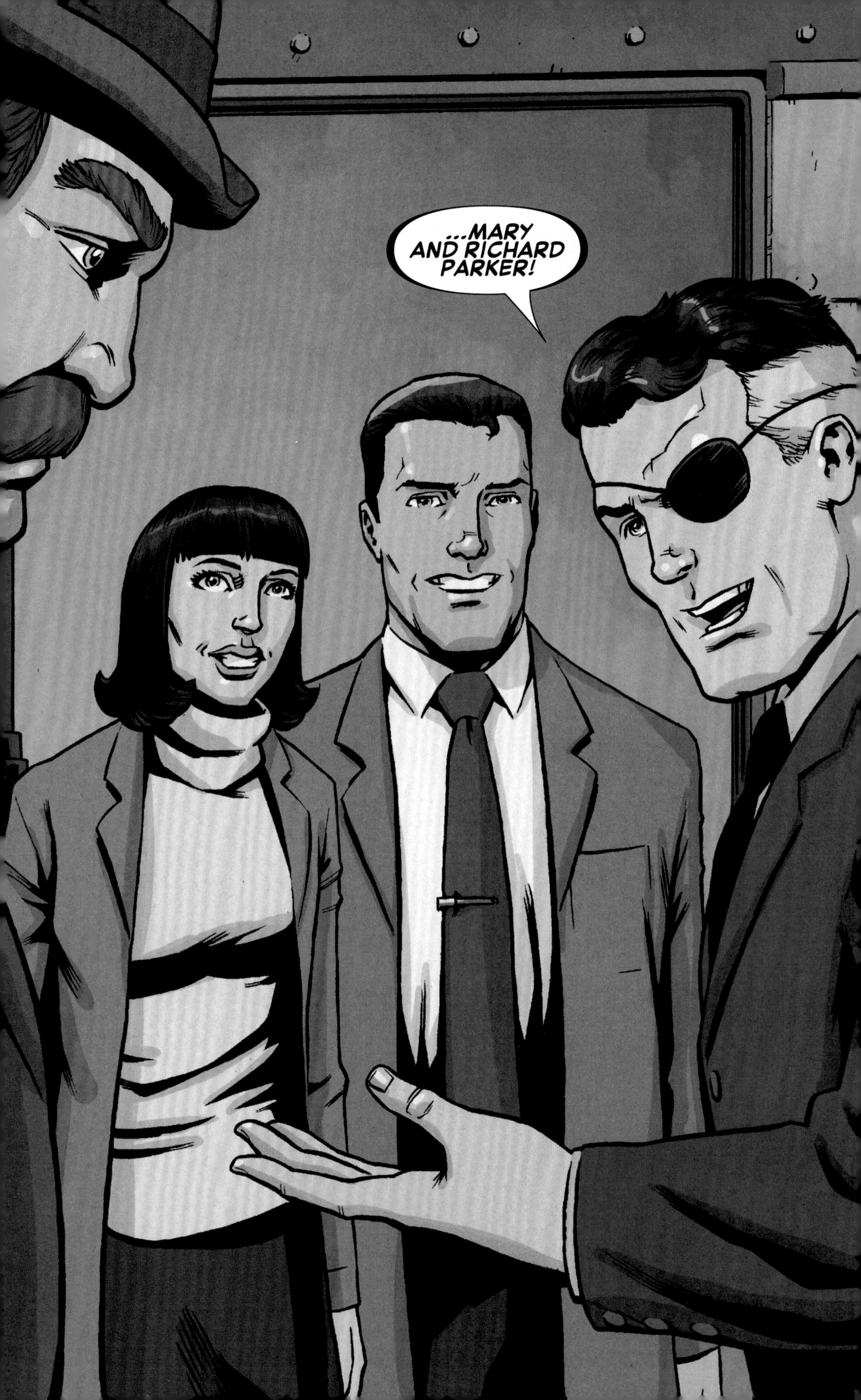
...MARY AND RICHARD PARKER!

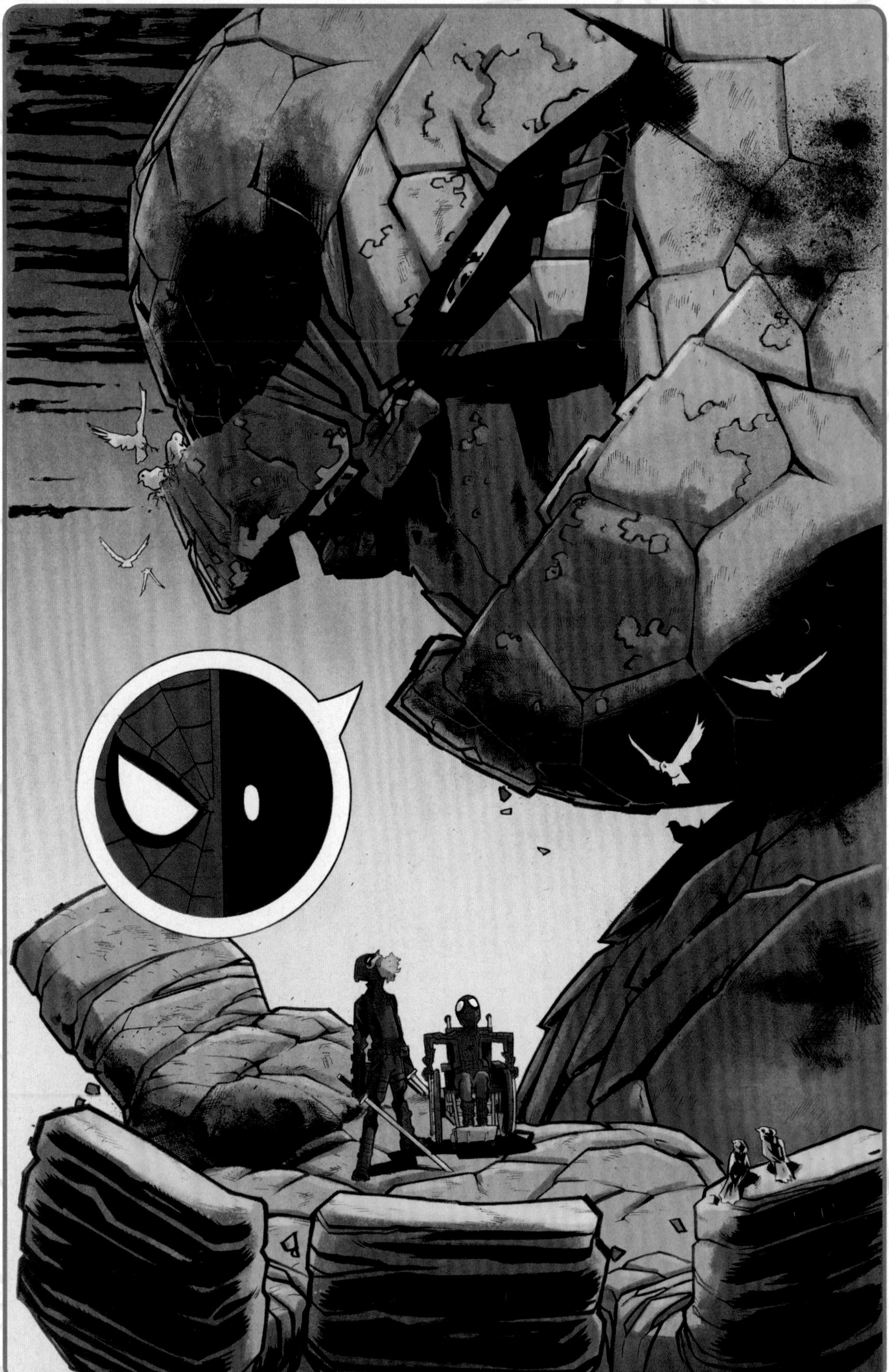

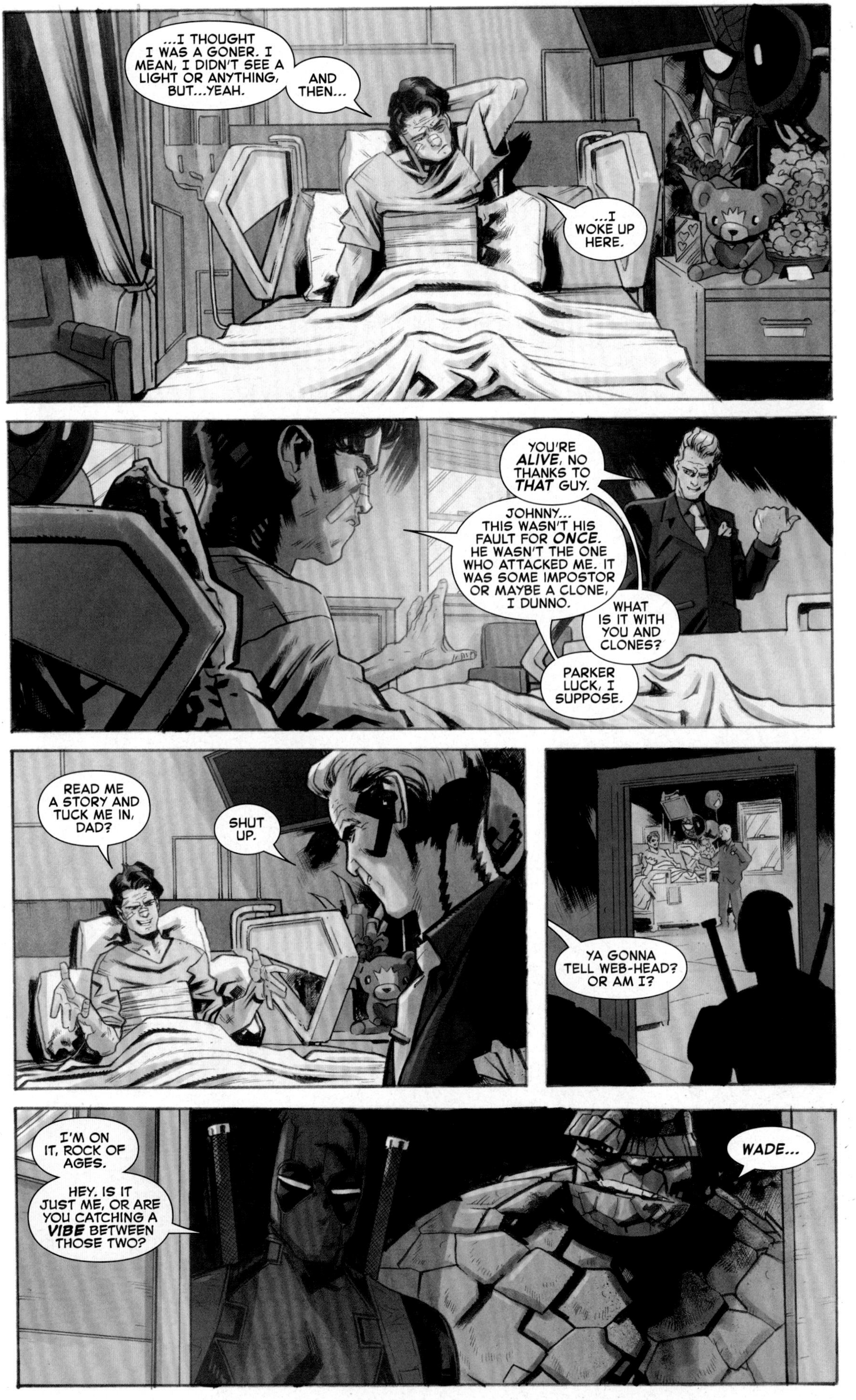
...I THOUGHT I WAS A GONER. I MEAN, I DIDN'T SEE A LIGHT OR ANYTHING, BUT...YEAH.
AND THEN...
...I WOKE UP HERE.
YOU'RE ALIVE, NO THANKS TO THAT GUY.
JOHNNY... THIS WASN'T HIS FAULT FOR ONCE. HE WASN'T THE ONE WHO ATTACKED ME. IT WAS SOME IMPOSTOR OR MAYBE A CLONE, I DUNNO.
WHAT IS IT WITH YOU AND CLONES?
PARKER LUCK, I SUPPOSE.
READ ME A STORY AND TUCK ME IN, DAD?
SHUT UP.
YA GONNA TELL WEB-HEAD? OR AM I?
I'M ON IT, ROCK OF AGES.
HEY. IS IT JUST ME, OR ARE YOU CATCHING A VIBE BETWEEN THOSE TWO?
WADE...

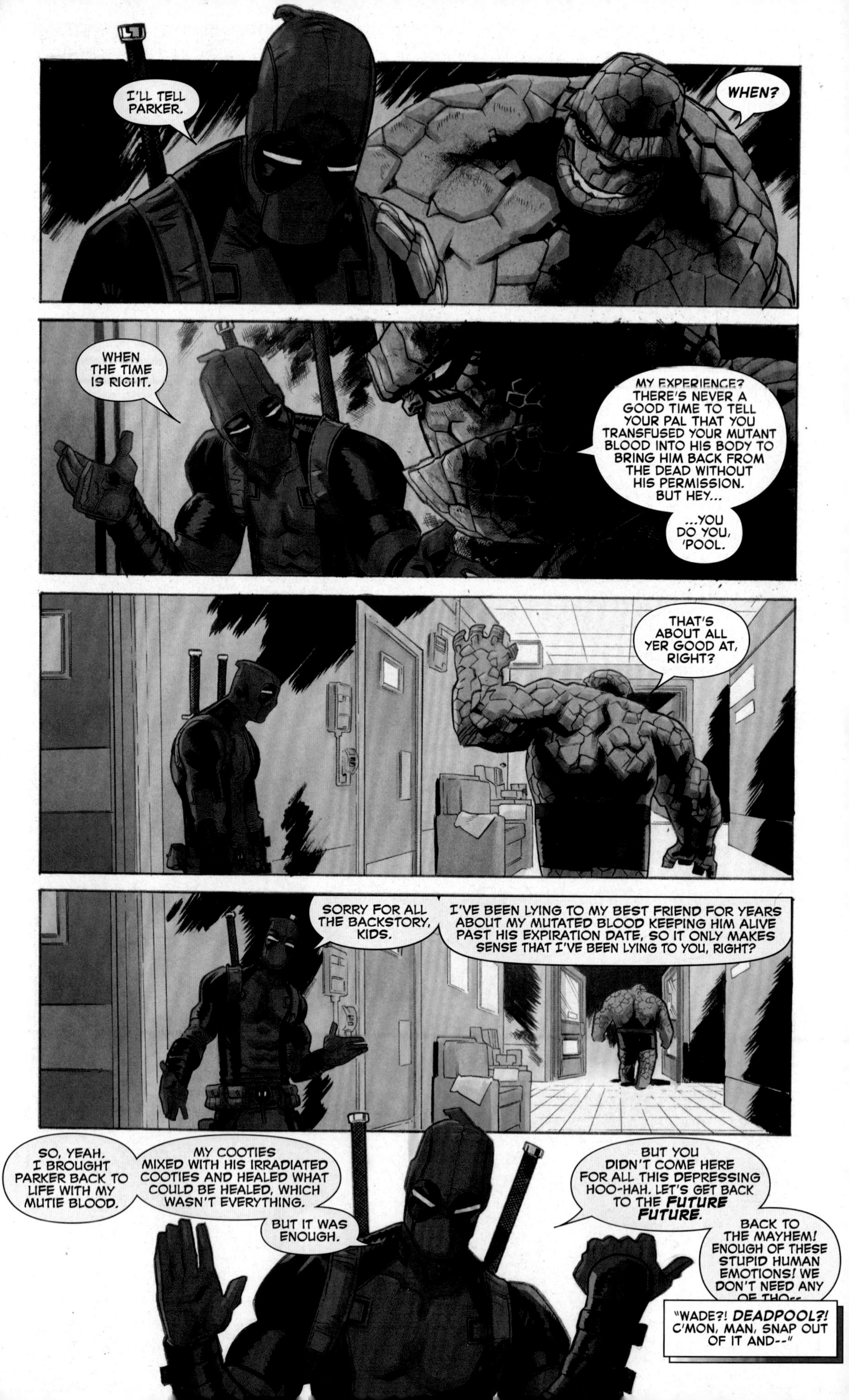
I'LL TELL PARKER.
WHEN?
WHEN THE TIME IS RIGHT.
MY EXPERIENCE? THERE'S NEVER A GOOD TIME TO TELL YOUR PAL THAT YOU TRANSFUSED YOUR MUTANT BLOOD INTO HIS BODY TO BRING HIM BACK FROM THE DEAD WITHOUT HIS PERMISSION. BUT HEY...
...YOU DO YOU, 'POOL.
THAT'S ABOUT ALL YER GOOD AT, RIGHT?
SORRY FOR ALL THE BACKSTORY, KIDS.
I'VE BEEN LYING TO MY BEST FRIEND FOR YEARS ABOUT MY MUTATED BLOOD KEEPING HIM ALIVE PAST HIS EXPIRATION DATE, SO IT ONLY MAKES SENSE THAT I'VE BEEN LYING TO YOU, RIGHT?
SO, YEAH. I BROUGHT PARKER BACK TO LIFE WITH MY MUTIE BLOOD.
MY COOTIES MIXED WITH HIS IRRADIATED COOTIES AND HEALED WHAT COULD BE HEALED, WHICH WASN'T EVERYTHING.
BUT IT WAS ENOUGH.
BUT YOU DIDN'T COME HERE FOR ALL THIS DEPRESSING HOO-HAH. LET'S GET BACK TO THE *FUTURE FUTURE*.
BACK TO THE MAYHEM! ENOUGH OF THESE STUPID HUMAN EMOTIONS! WE DON'T NEED ANY OF THO--
"WADE?! *DEADPOOL?!* C'MON, MAN, SNAP OUT OF IT AND--"

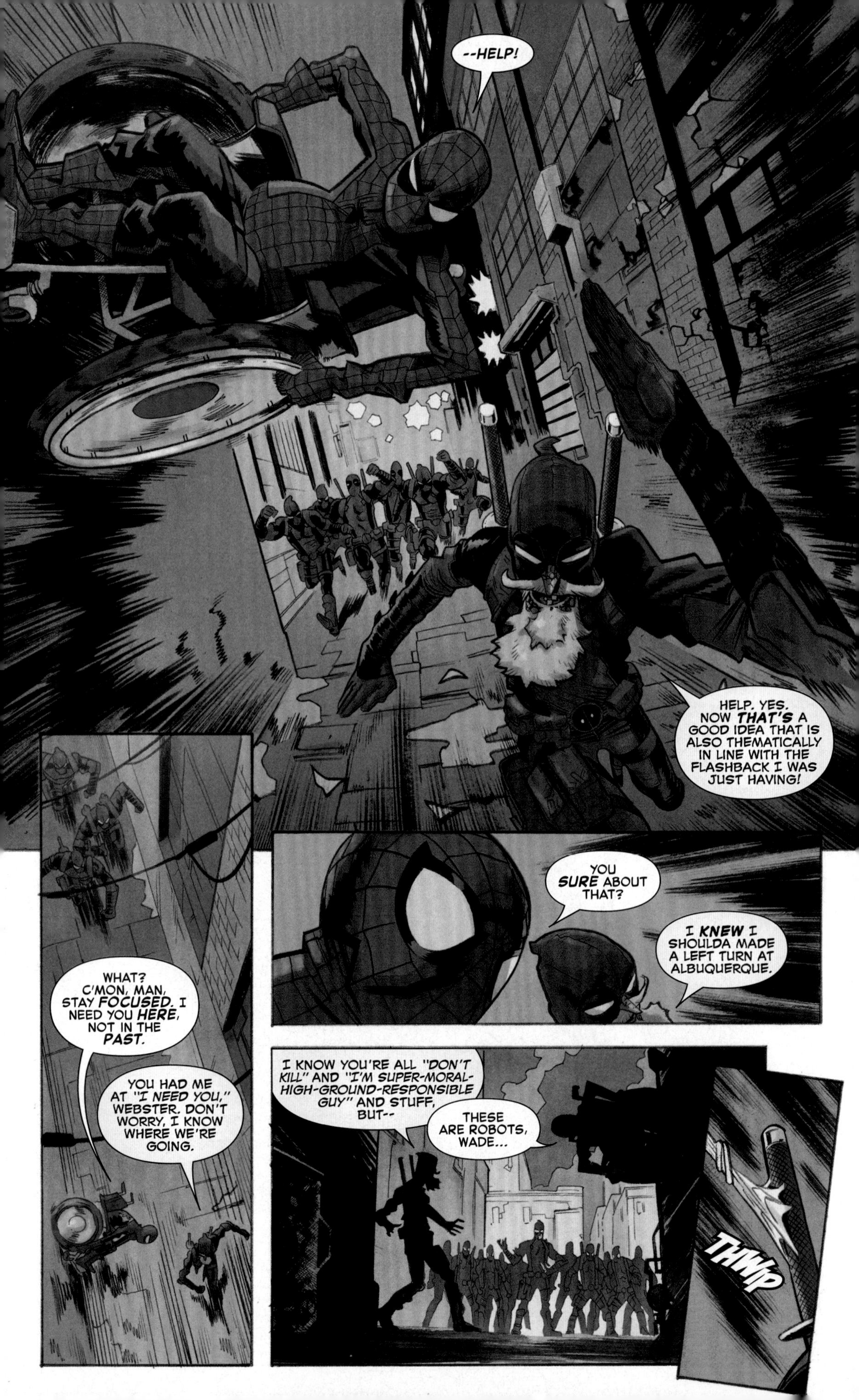
--HELP!
HELP. YES. NOW THAT'S A GOOD IDEA THAT IS ALSO THEMATICALLY IN LINE WITH THE FLASHBACK I WAS JUST HAVING!
WHAT? C'MON, MAN, STAY FOCUSED. I NEED YOU HERE, NOT IN THE PAST.
YOU HAD ME AT "I NEED YOU," WEBSTER. DON'T WORRY, I KNOW WHERE WE'RE GOING.
YOU SURE ABOUT THAT?
I KNEW I SHOULDA MADE A LEFT TURN AT ALBUQUERQUE.
I KNOW YOU'RE ALL "DON'T KILL" AND "I'M SUPER-MORAL-HIGH-GROUND-RESPONSIBLE GUY" AND STUFF, BUT--
THESE ARE ROBOTS, WADE...
THWIP

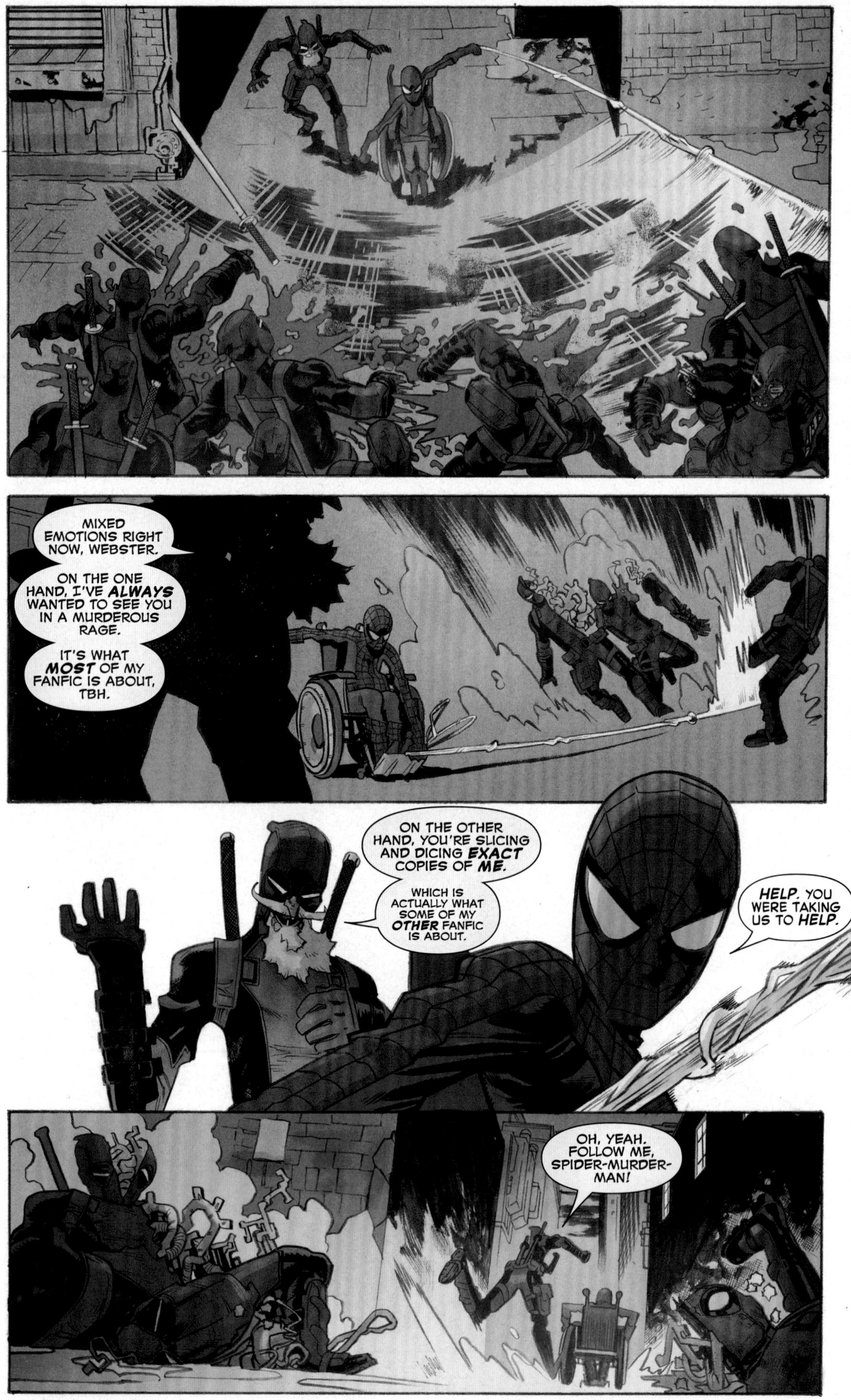
MIXED EMOTIONS RIGHT NOW, WEBSTER.
ON THE ONE HAND, I'VE ALWAYS WANTED TO SEE YOU IN A MURDEROUS RAGE.
IT'S WHAT MOST OF MY FANFIC IS ABOUT, TBH.
ON THE OTHER HAND, YOU'RE SLICING AND DICING EXACT COPIES OF ME.
WHICH IS ACTUALLY WHAT SOME OF MY OTHER FANFIC IS ABOUT.
HELP. YOU WERE TAKING US TO HELP.
OH, YEAH. FOLLOW ME, SPIDER-MURDER-MAN!

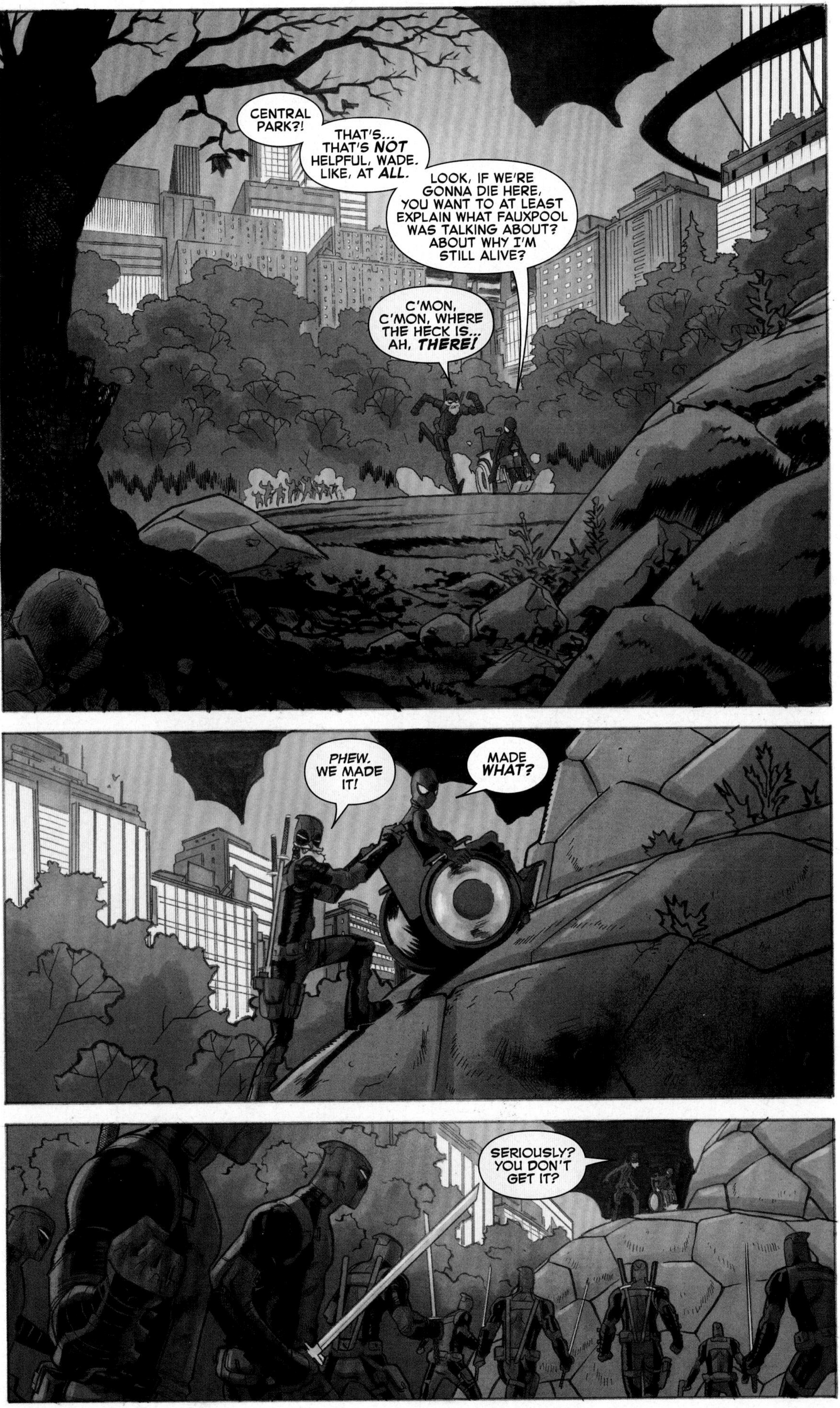
CENTRAL PARK?!
THAT'S... THAT'S NOT HELPFUL, WADE. LIKE, AT ALL.
LOOK, IF WE'RE GONNA DIE HERE, YOU WANT TO AT LEAST EXPLAIN WHAT FAUXPOOL WAS TALKING ABOUT? ABOUT WHY I'M STILL ALIVE?
C'MON, C'MON, WHERE THE HECK IS... AH, THERE!
PHEW. WE MADE IT!
MADE WHAT?
SERIOUSLY? YOU DON'T GET IT?

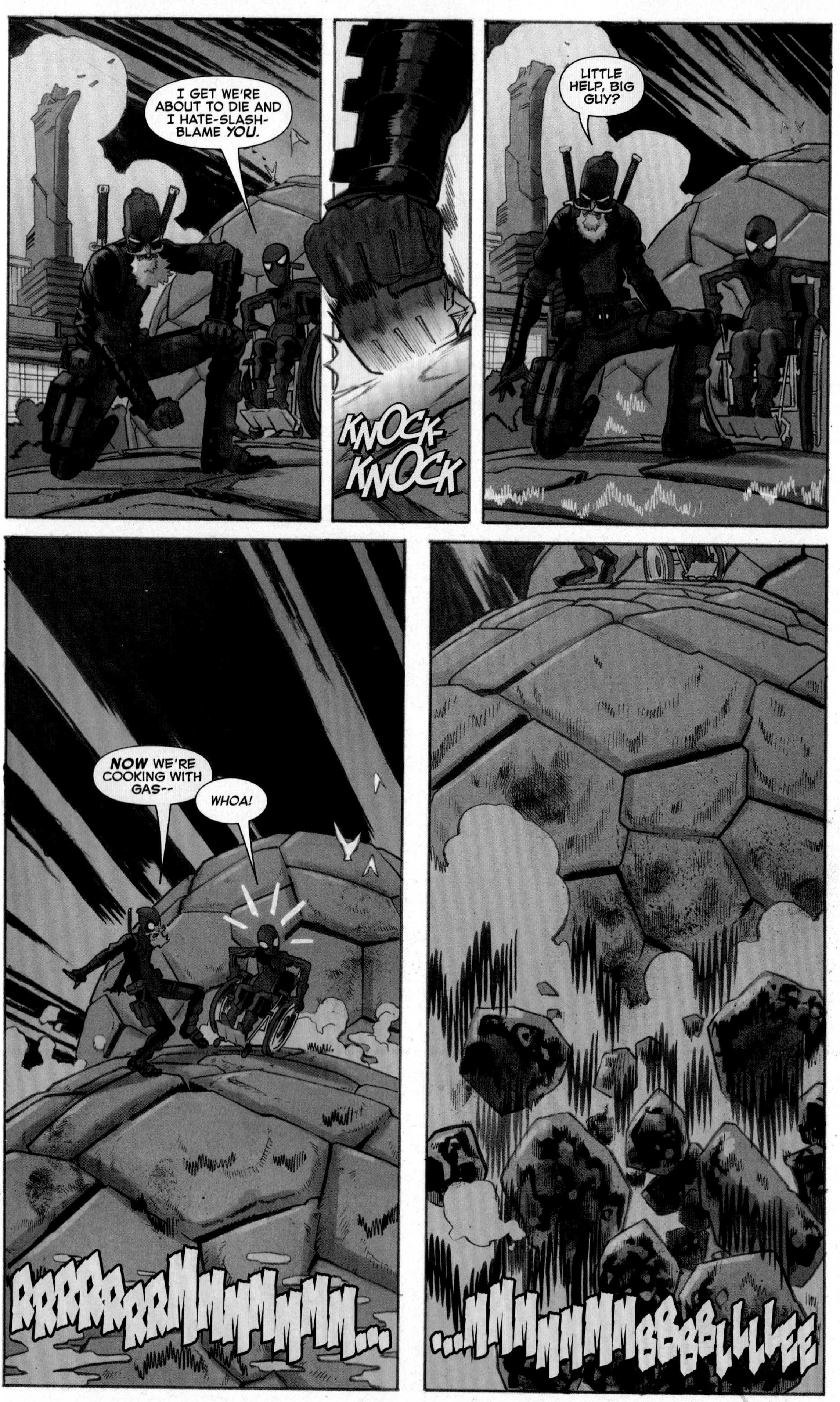
I GET WE'RE ABOUT TO DIE AND I HATE-SLASH-BLAME *YOU.*
KNOCK-KNOCK
LITTLE HELP, BIG GUY?
*NOW* WE'RE COOKING WITH GAS--
WHOA!
RRRRRRRMMMMMMMM...
...MMMMMMMBBBBLLLLEE

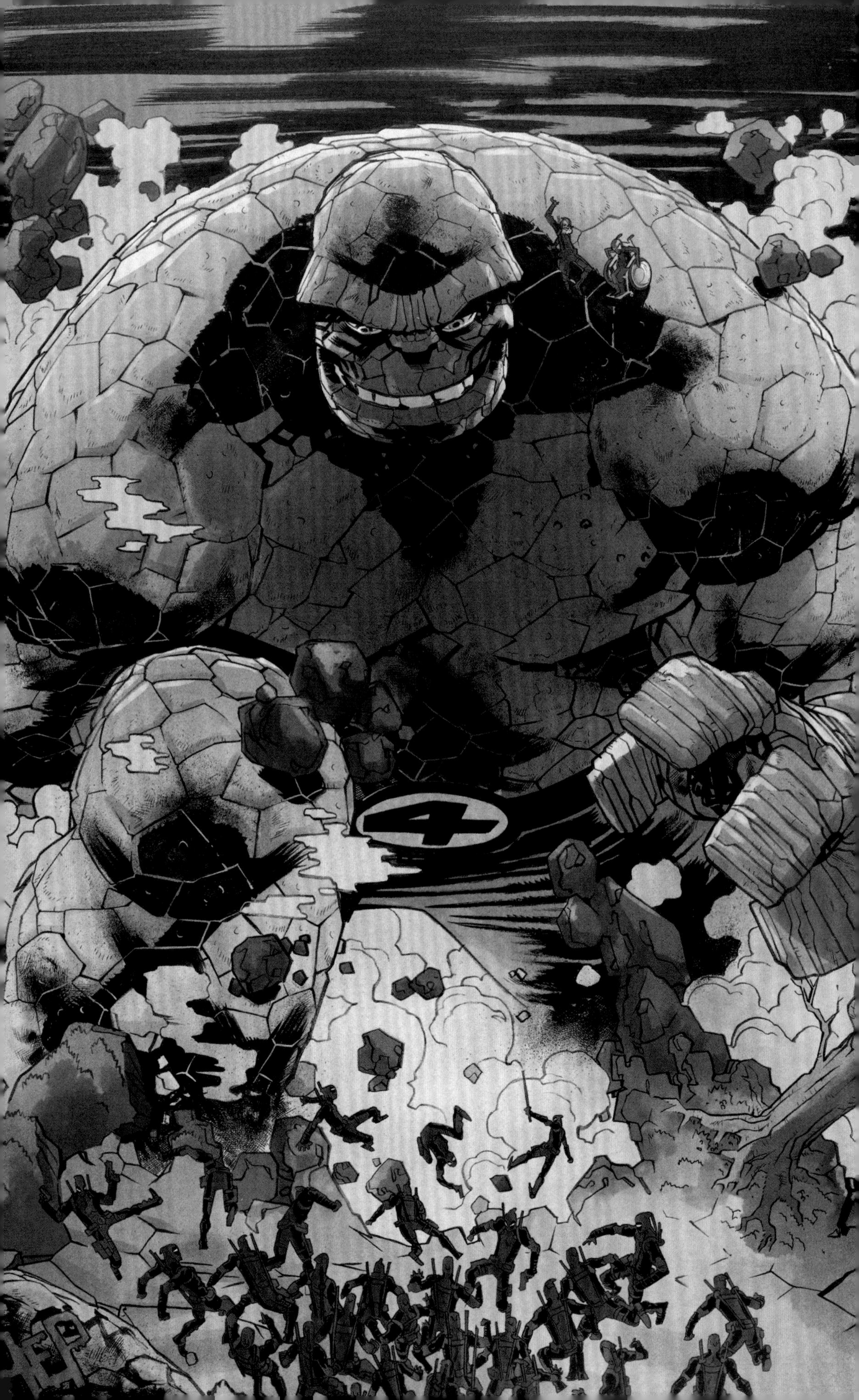

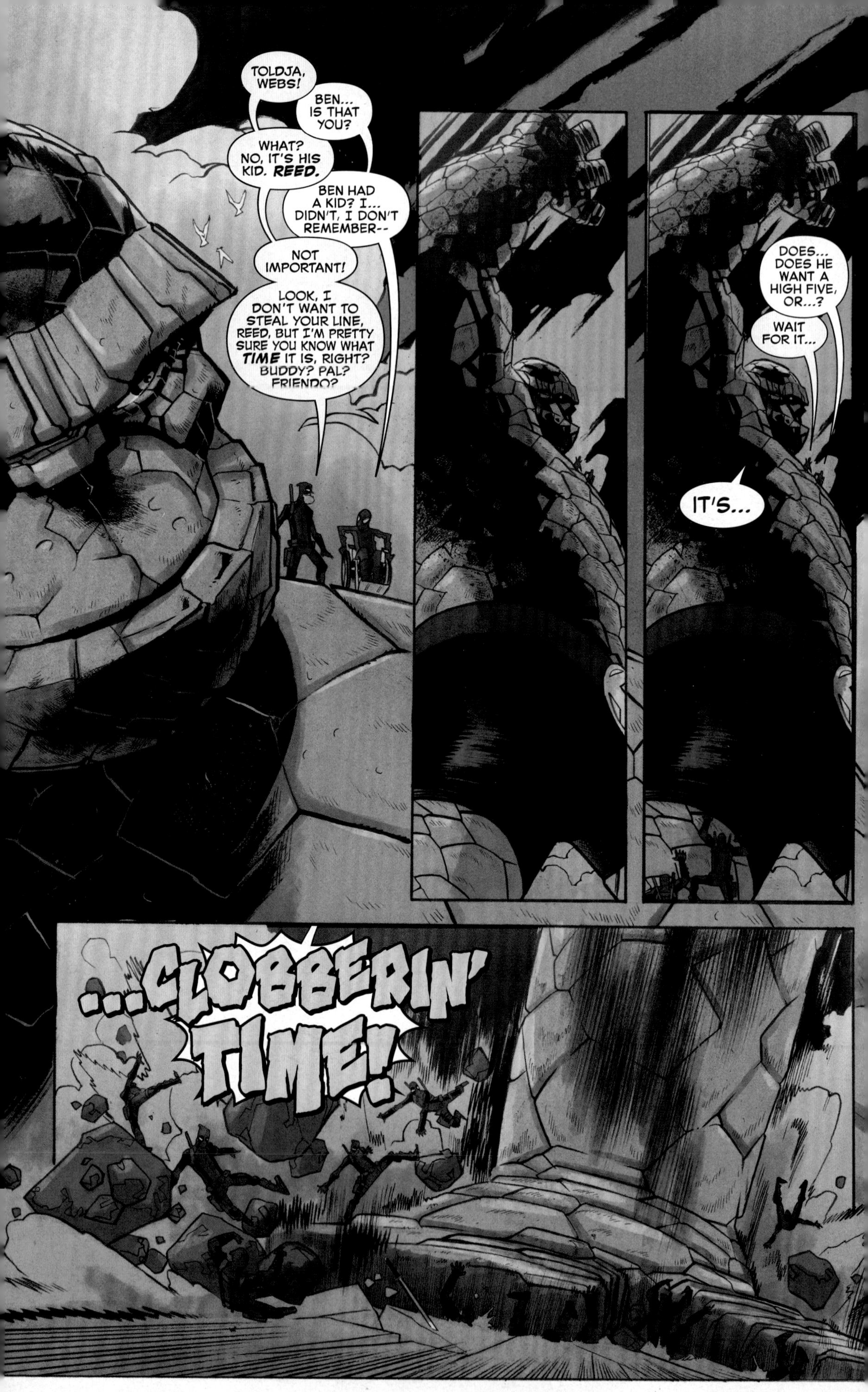

TOLDJA, WEBS!
BEN... IS THAT YOU?
WHAT? NO, IT'S HIS KID. **REED.**
BEN HAD A KID? I... DIDN'T, I DON'T REMEMBER--
NOT IMPORTANT!
LOOK, I DON'T WANT TO STEAL YOUR LINE, REED, BUT I'M PRETTY SURE YOU KNOW WHAT **TIME** IT IS, RIGHT? BUDDY? PAL? FRIENDO?
DOES... DOES HE WANT A HIGH FIVE, OR...?
WAIT FOR IT...
IT'S...
...CLOBBERIN' TIME!

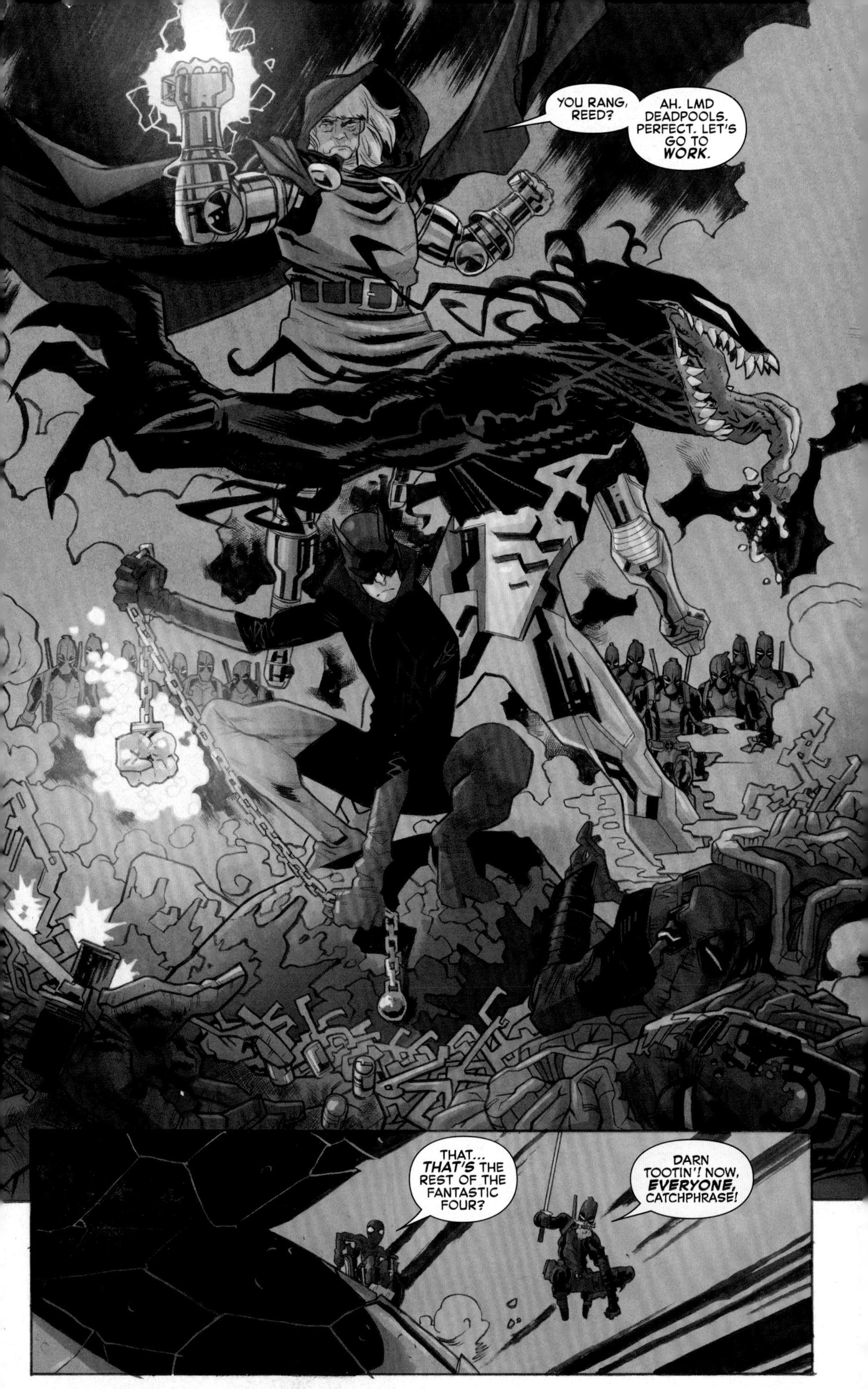
YOU RANG, REED?
AH. LMD DEADPOOLS. PERFECT. LET'S GO TO WORK.
THAT... THAT'S THE REST OF THE FANTASTIC FOUR?
DARN TOOTIN'! NOW, EVERYONE, CATCHPHRASE!

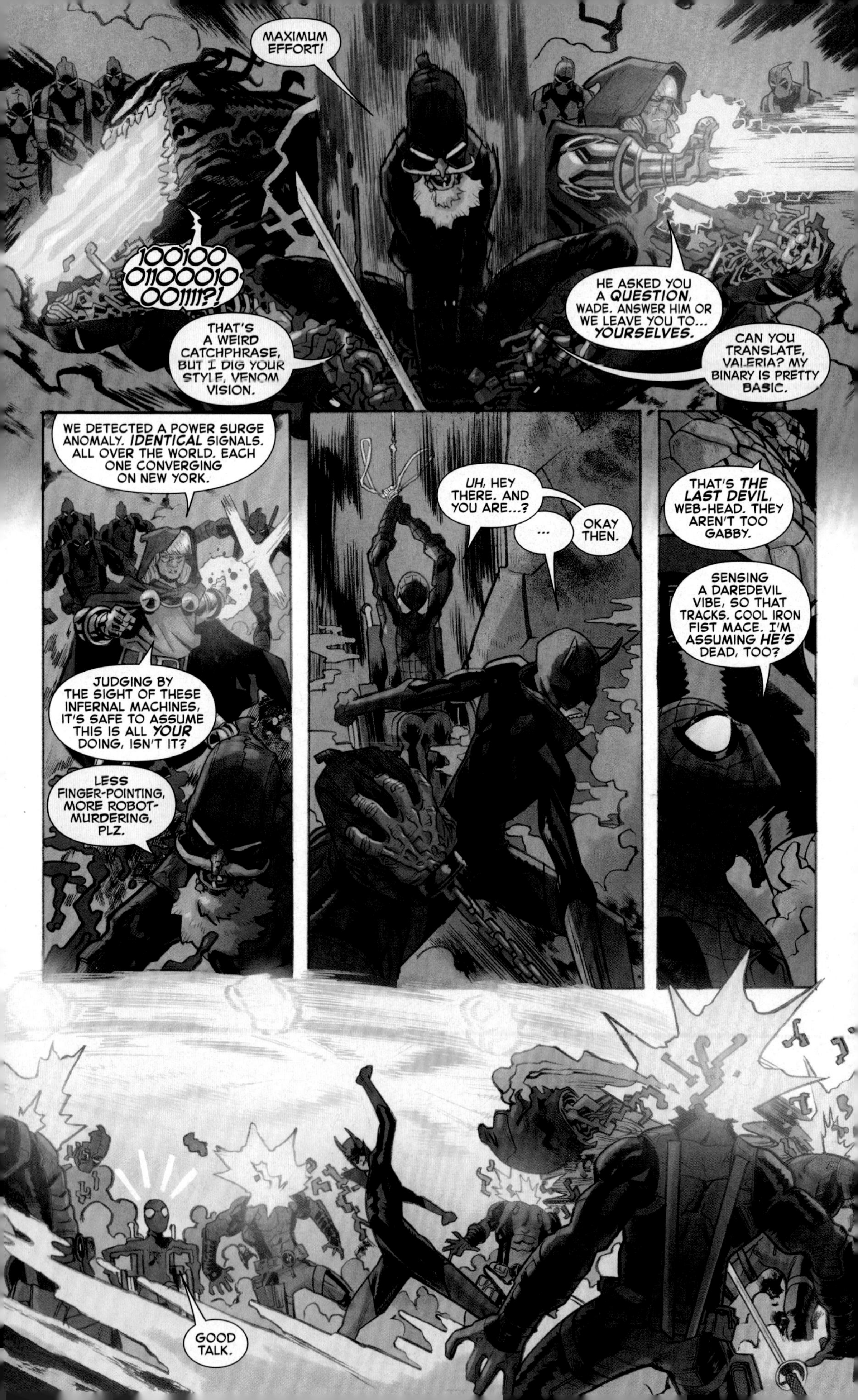
MAXIMUM EFFORT!
100100 01100010 001111?!
THAT'S A WEIRD CATCHPHRASE, BUT I DIG YOUR STYLE, VENOM VISION.
HE ASKED YOU A QUESTION, WADE. ANSWER HIM OR WE LEAVE YOU TO... YOURSELVES.
CAN YOU TRANSLATE, VALERIA? MY BINARY IS PRETTY BASIC.
WE DETECTED A POWER SURGE ANOMALY. IDENTICAL SIGNALS. ALL OVER THE WORLD. EACH ONE CONVERGING ON NEW YORK.
JUDGING BY THE SIGHT OF THESE INFERNAL MACHINES, IT'S SAFE TO ASSUME THIS IS ALL YOUR DOING, ISN'T IT?
LESS FINGER-POINTING, MORE ROBOT-MURDERING, PLZ.
UH, HEY THERE. AND YOU ARE...?
...
OKAY THEN.
THAT'S THE LAST DEVIL, WEB-HEAD. THEY AREN'T TOO GABBY.
SENSING A DAREDEVIL VIBE, SO THAT TRACKS. COOL IRON FIST MACE. I'M ASSUMING HE'S DEAD, TOO?
GOOD TALK.

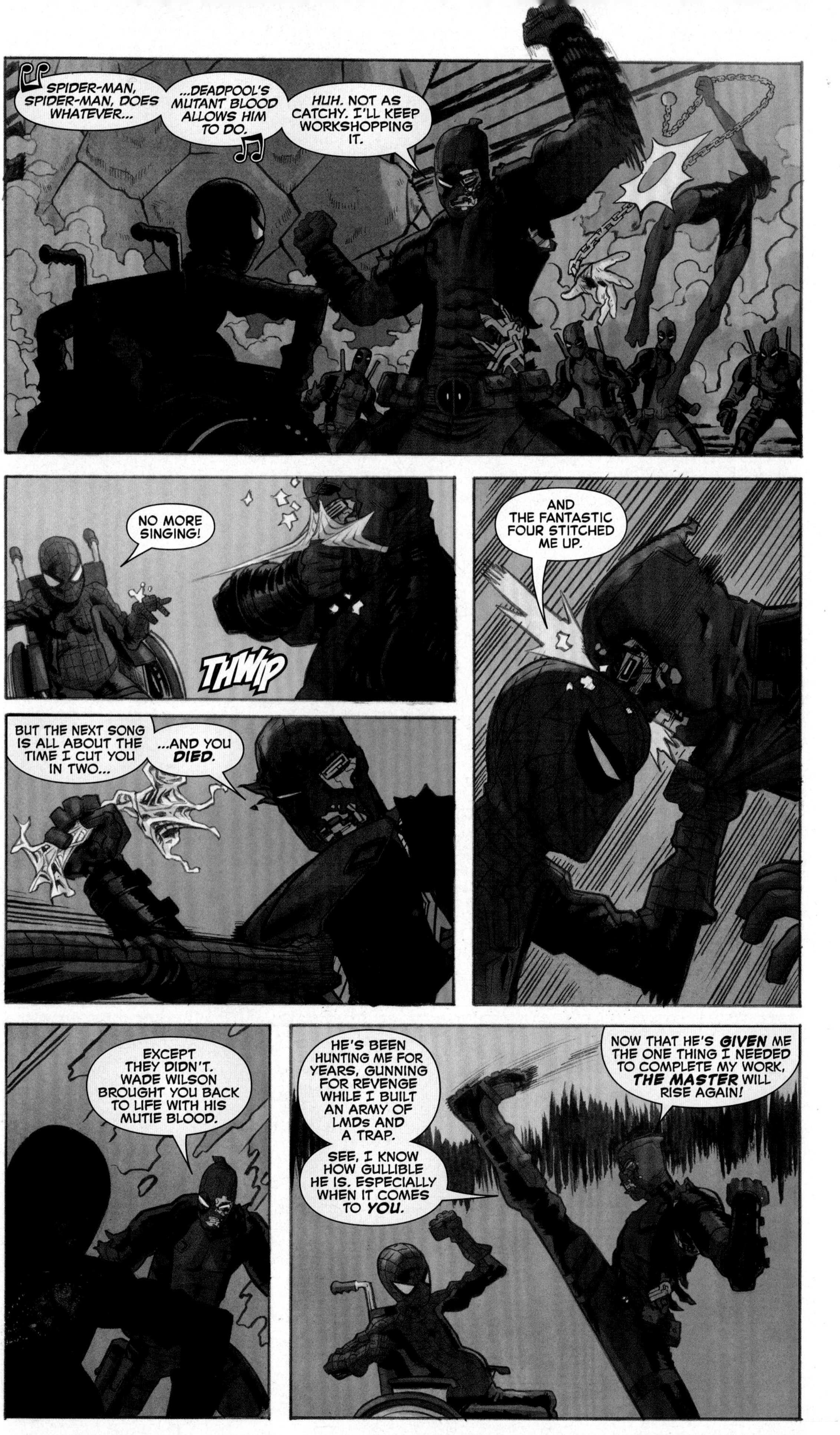
SPIDER-MAN, SPIDER-MAN, DOES WHATEVER...
...DEADPOOL'S MUTANT BLOOD ALLOWS HIM TO DO.
HUH. NOT AS CATCHY. I'LL KEEP WORKSHOPPING IT.
NO MORE SINGING!
THWIP
AND THE FANTASTIC FOUR STITCHED ME UP.
BUT THE NEXT SONG IS ALL ABOUT THE TIME I CUT YOU IN TWO...
...AND YOU DIED.
EXCEPT THEY DIDN'T. WADE WILSON BROUGHT YOU BACK TO LIFE WITH HIS MUTIE BLOOD.
HE'S BEEN HUNTING ME FOR YEARS, GUNNING FOR REVENGE WHILE I BUILT AN ARMY OF LMDs AND A TRAP.
SEE, I KNOW HOW GULLIBLE HE IS. ESPECIALLY WHEN IT COMES TO YOU.
NOW THAT HE'S GIVEN ME THE ONE THING I NEEDED TO COMPLETE MY WORK, THE MASTER WILL RISE AGAIN!

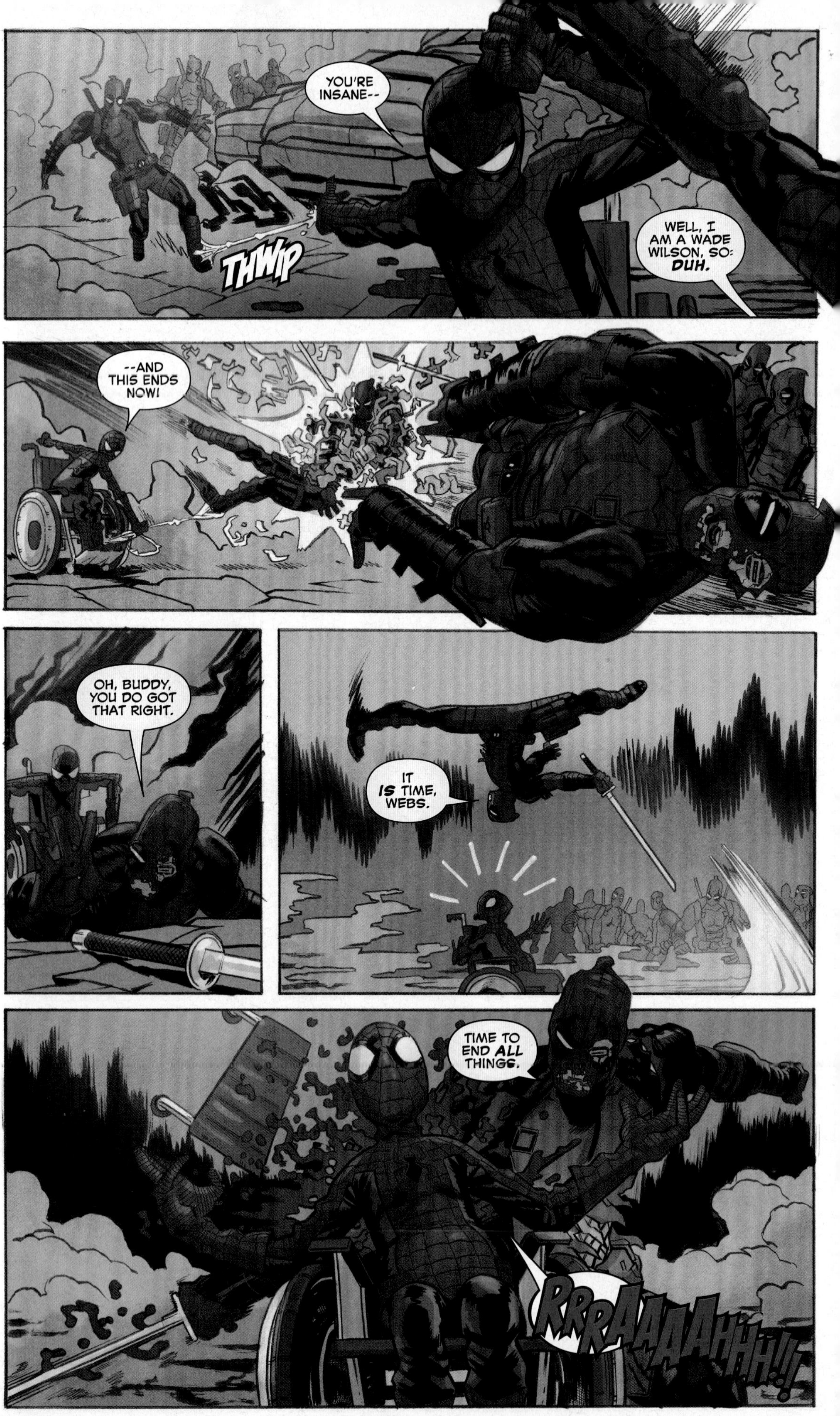
YOU'RE INSANE--
THWIP
WELL, I AM A WADE WILSON, SO: DUH.
--AND THIS ENDS NOW!
OH, BUDDY, YOU DO GOT THAT RIGHT.
IT IS TIME, WEBS.
TIME TO END ALL THINGS.
RRRAAAAAHHH!!!

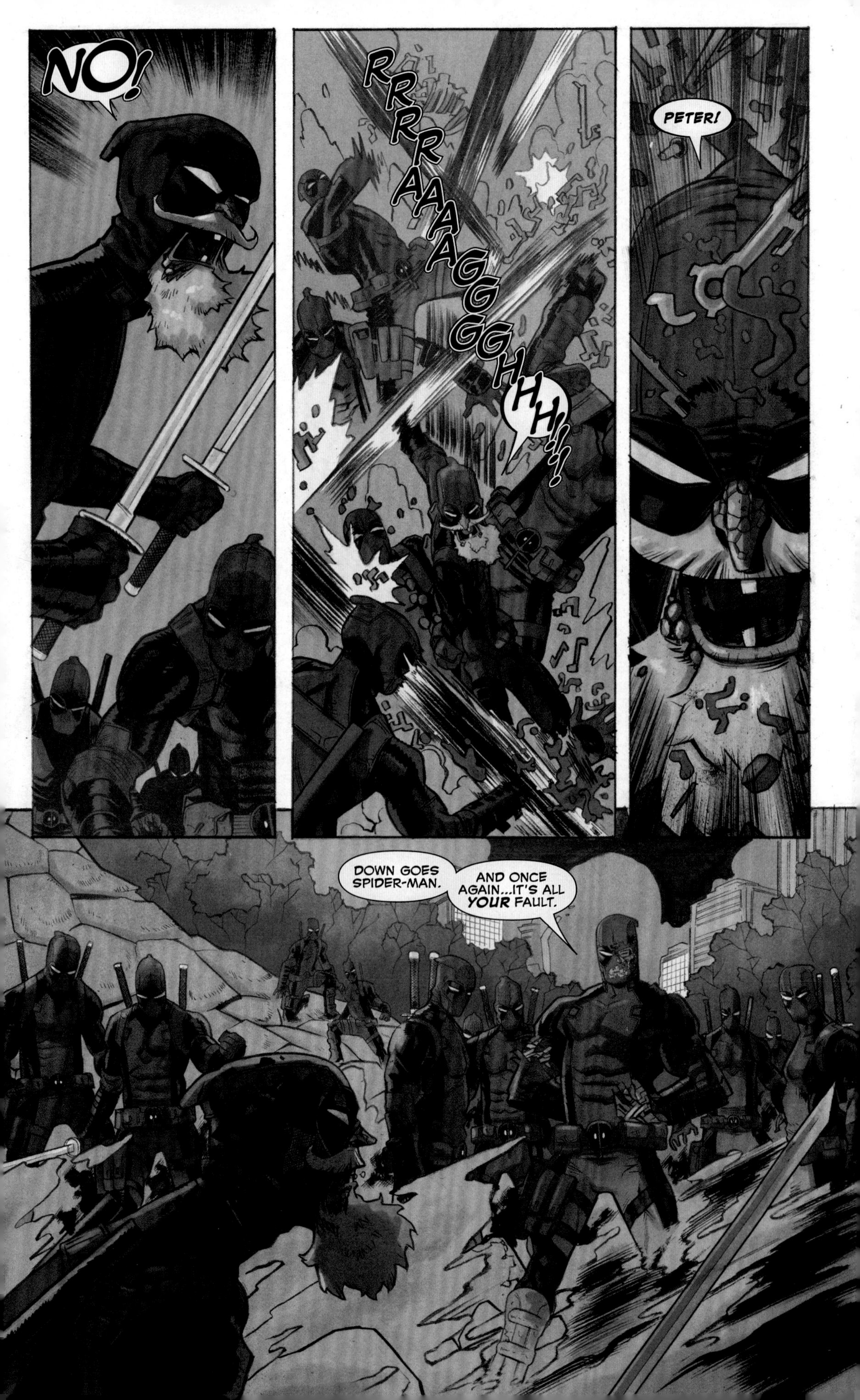
NO!
RRRRAAAAGGGHHH!!!
PETER!
DOWN GOES SPIDER-MAN.
AND ONCE AGAIN...IT'S ALL YOUR FAULT.

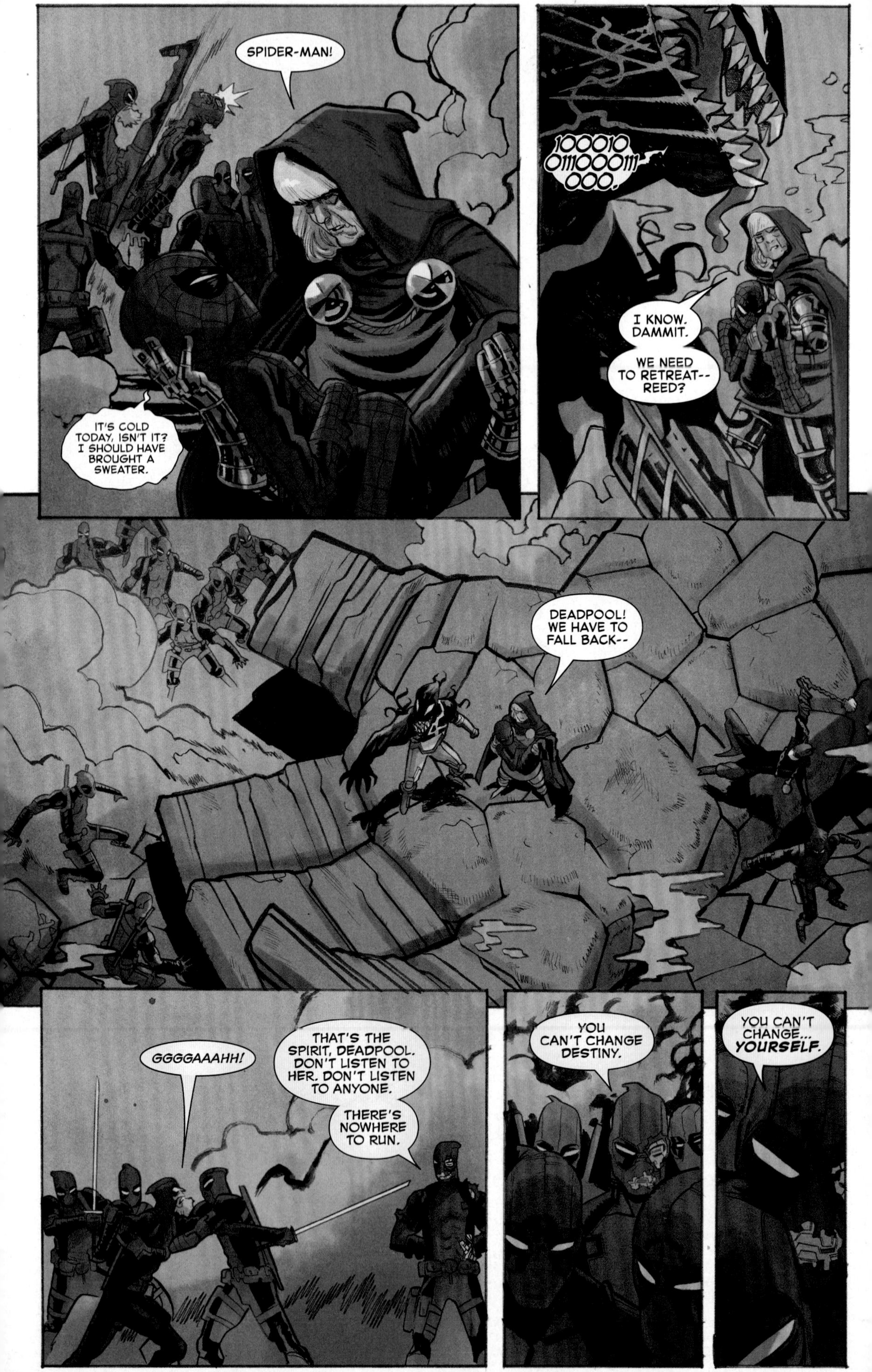
SPIDER-MAN!
IT'S COLD TODAY, ISN'T IT? I SHOULD HAVE BROUGHT A SWEATER.
100010 0110000111 000.
I KNOW. DAMMIT.
WE NEED TO RETREAT-- REED?
DEADPOOL! WE HAVE TO FALL BACK--
GGGGAAAHH!
THAT'S THE SPIRIT, DEADPOOL. DON'T LISTEN TO HER. DON'T LISTEN TO ANYONE.
THERE'S NOWHERE TO RUN.
YOU CAN'T CHANGE DESTINY.
YOU CAN'T CHANGE... YOURSELF.

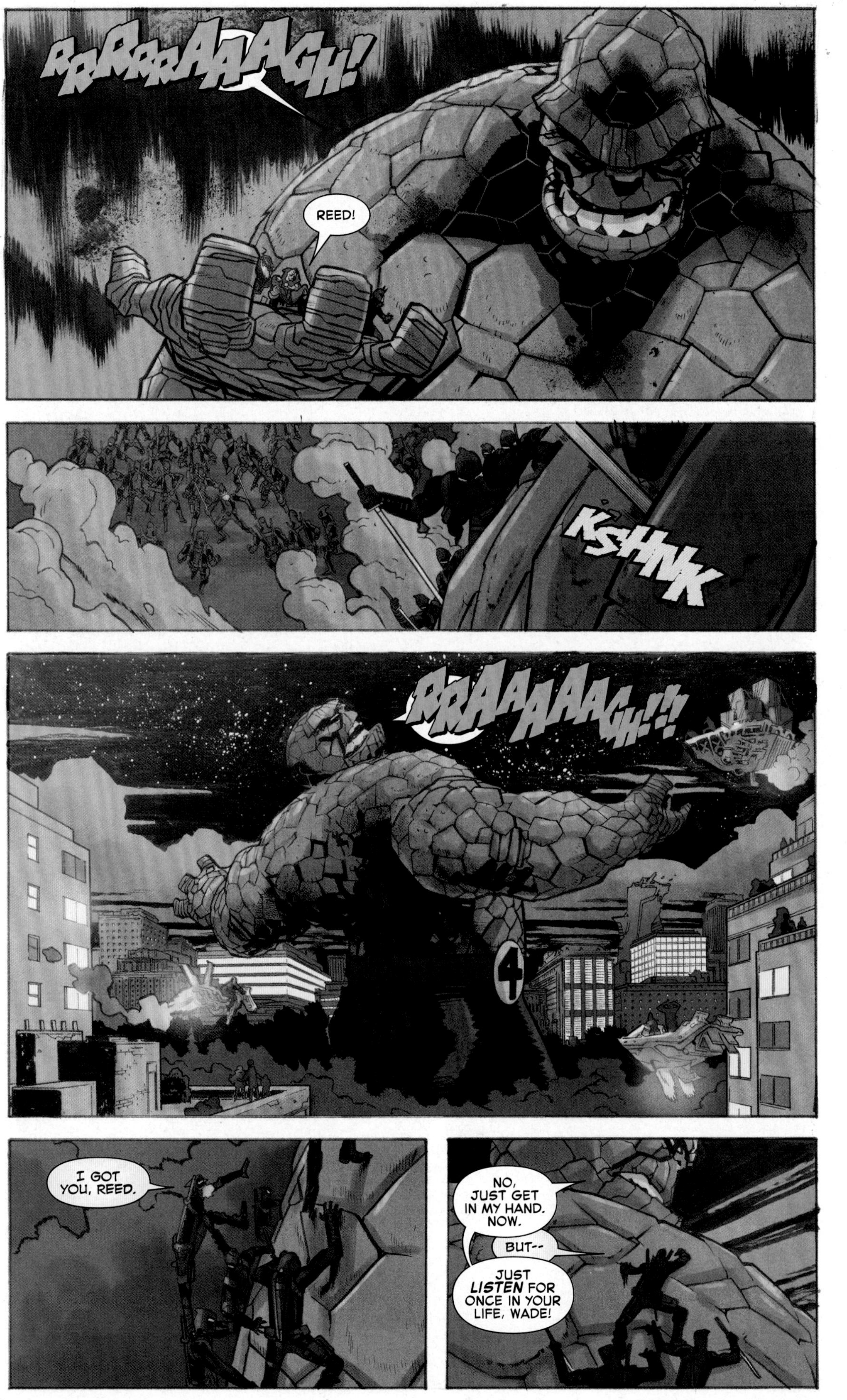
RRRRRRAAAAGH!
REED!
KSHNK
RRAAAAAAGH!!!
I GOT YOU, REED.
NO, JUST GET IN MY HAND. NOW.
BUT--
JUST LISTEN FOR ONCE IN YOUR LIFE, WADE!

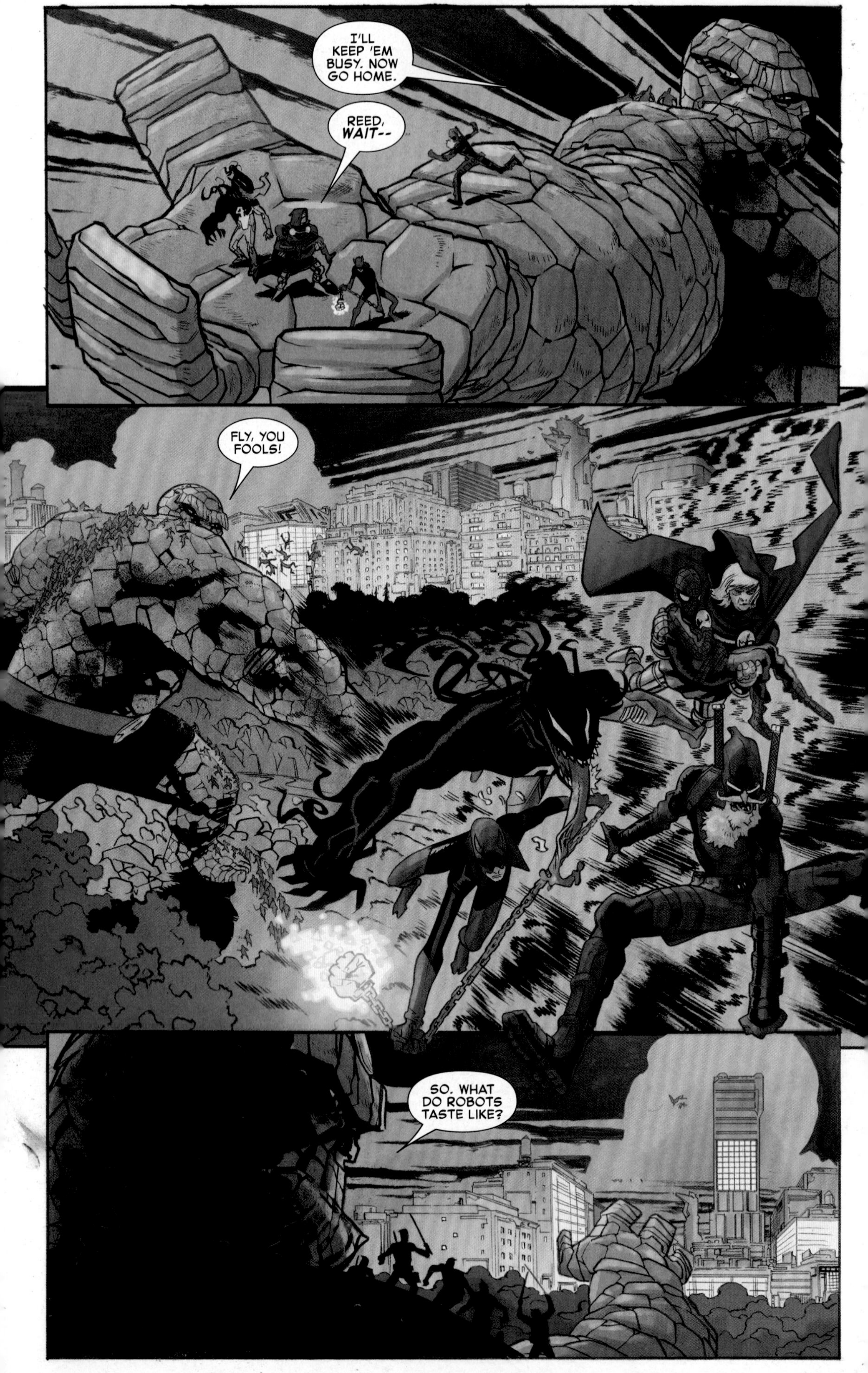
I'LL KEEP 'EM BUSY. NOW GO HOME.
REED, WAIT--
FLY, YOU FOOLS!
SO. WHAT DO ROBOTS TASTE LIKE?

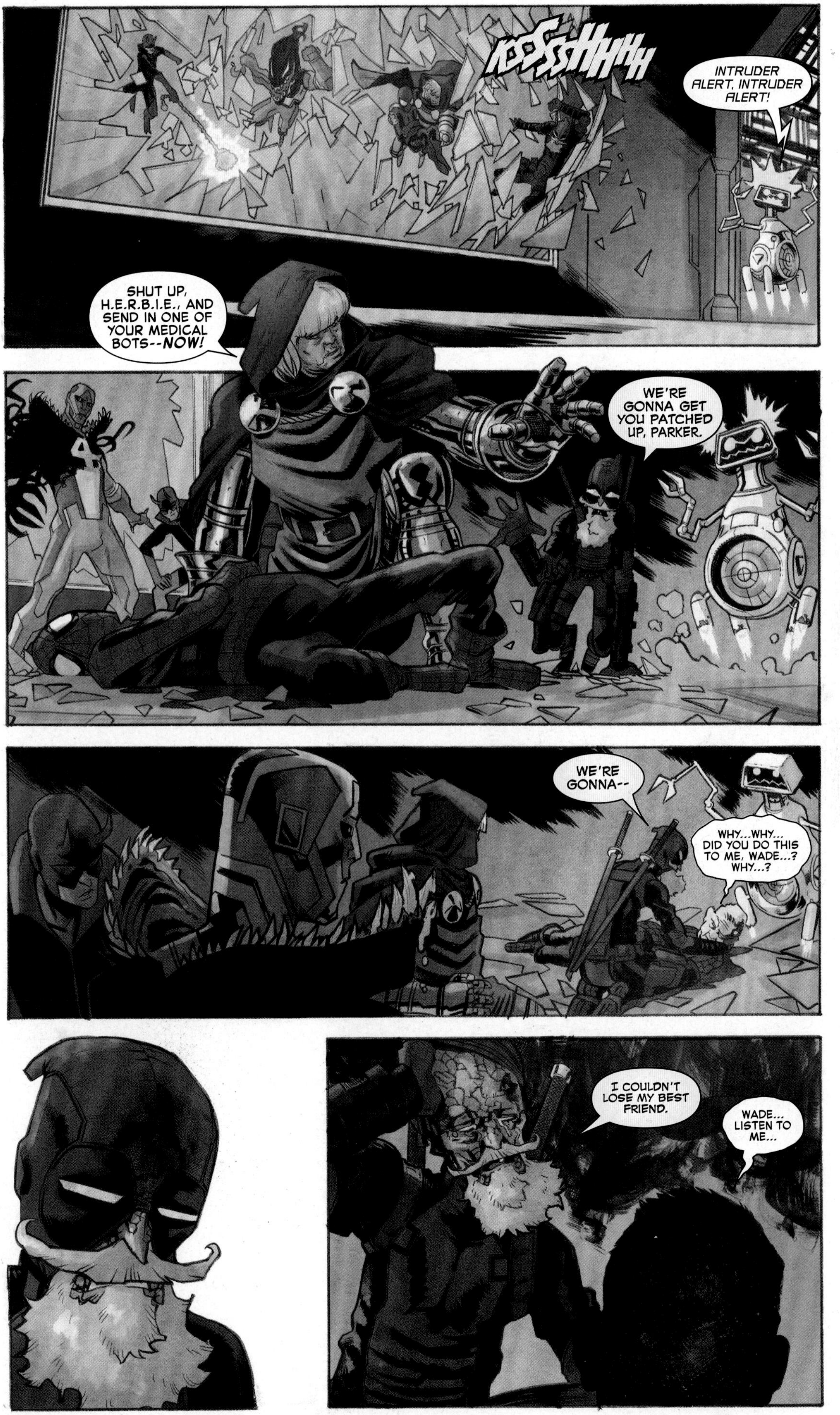
KRSSSSHHHHH
INTRUDER ALERT, INTRUDER ALERT!
SHUT UP, H.E.R.B.I.E., AND SEND IN ONE OF YOUR MEDICAL BOTS--NOW!
WE'RE GONNA GET YOU PATCHED UP, PARKER.
WE'RE GONNA--
WHY...WHY... DID YOU DO THIS TO ME, WADE...? WHY...?
I COULDN'T LOSE MY BEST FRIEND.
WADE... LISTEN TO ME...

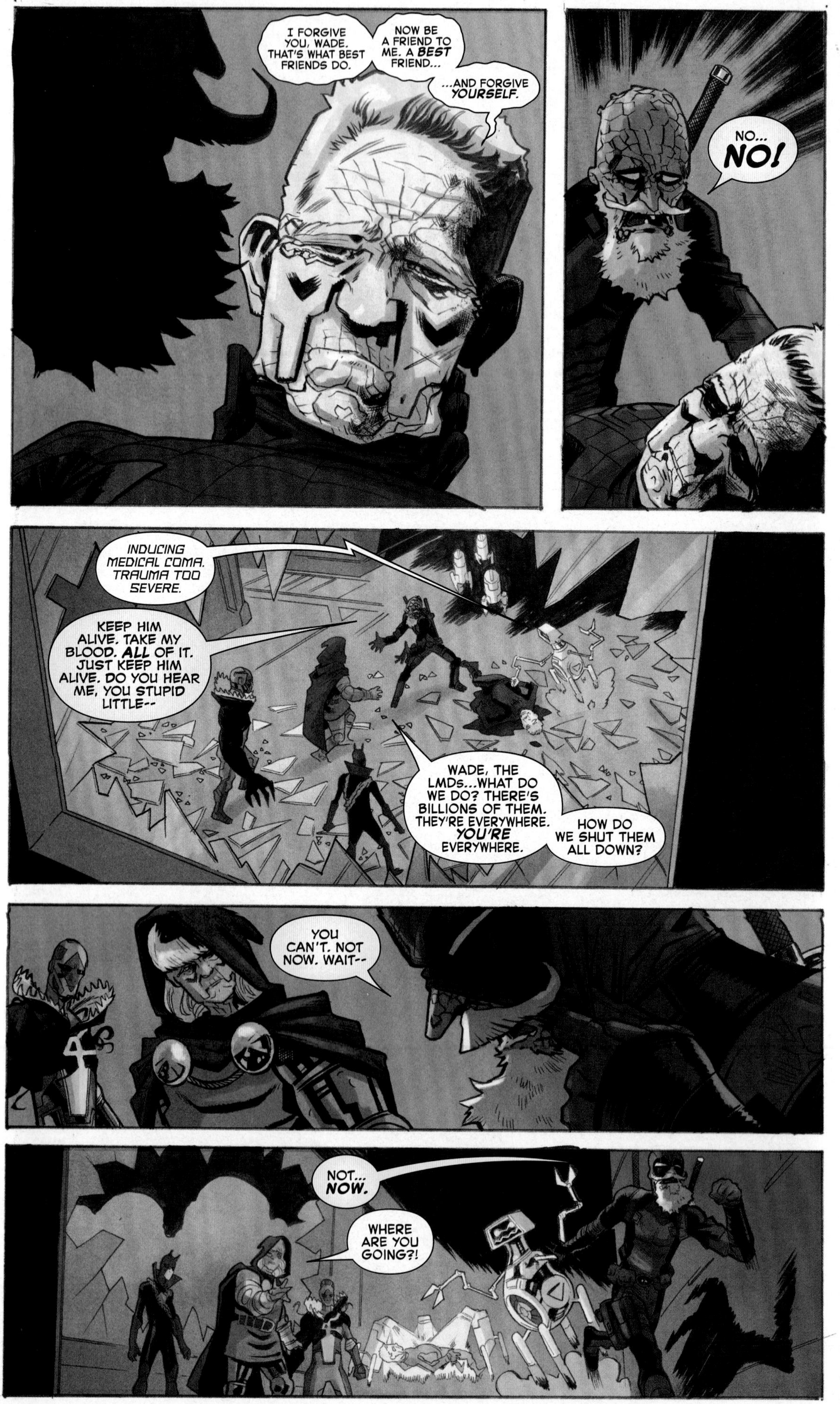

I FORGIVE YOU, WADE. THAT'S WHAT BEST FRIENDS DO.
NOW BE A FRIEND TO ME. A BEST FRIEND...
...AND FORGIVE YOURSELF.
NO... NO!
INDUCING MEDICAL COMA. TRAUMA TOO SEVERE.
KEEP HIM ALIVE. TAKE MY BLOOD. ALL OF IT. JUST KEEP HIM ALIVE. DO YOU HEAR ME, YOU STUPID LITTLE--
WADE, THE LMDs...WHAT DO WE DO? THERE'S BILLIONS OF THEM. THEY'RE EVERYWHERE. YOU'RE EVERYWHERE.
HOW DO WE SHUT THEM ALL DOWN?
YOU CAN'T. NOT NOW. WAIT--
NOT... NOW.
WHERE ARE YOU GOING?!

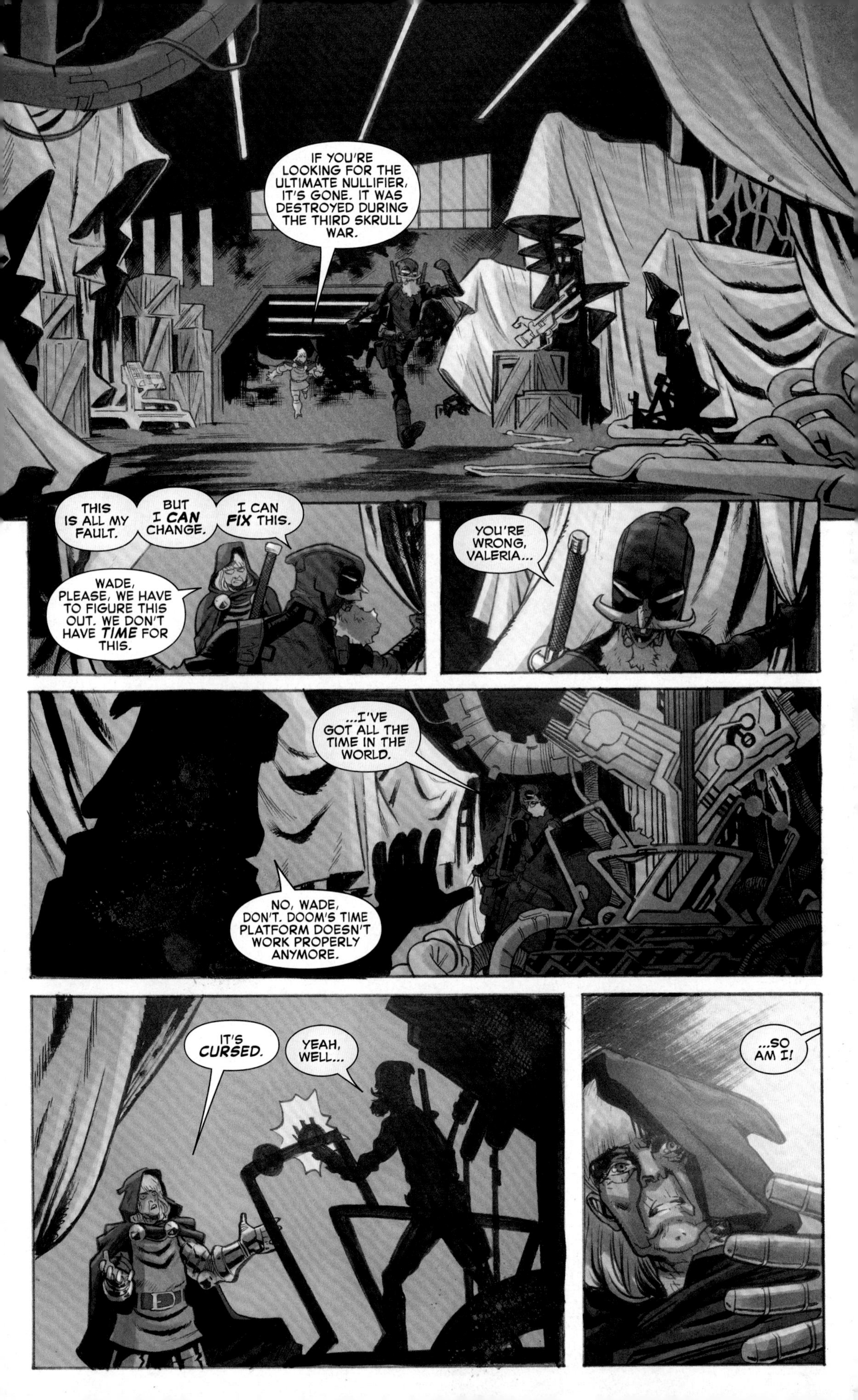
IF YOU'RE LOOKING FOR THE ULTIMATE NULLIFIER, IT'S GONE. IT WAS DESTROYED DURING THE THIRD SKRULL WAR.
THIS IS ALL MY FAULT.
BUT I CAN CHANGE.
I CAN FIX THIS.
WADE, PLEASE, WE HAVE TO FIGURE THIS OUT. WE DON'T HAVE TIME FOR THIS.
YOU'RE WRONG, VALERIA...
...I'VE GOT ALL THE TIME IN THE WORLD.
NO, WADE, DON'T. DOOM'S TIME PLATFORM DOESN'T WORK PROPERLY ANYMORE.
IT'S CURSED.
YEAH, WELL...
...SO AM I!

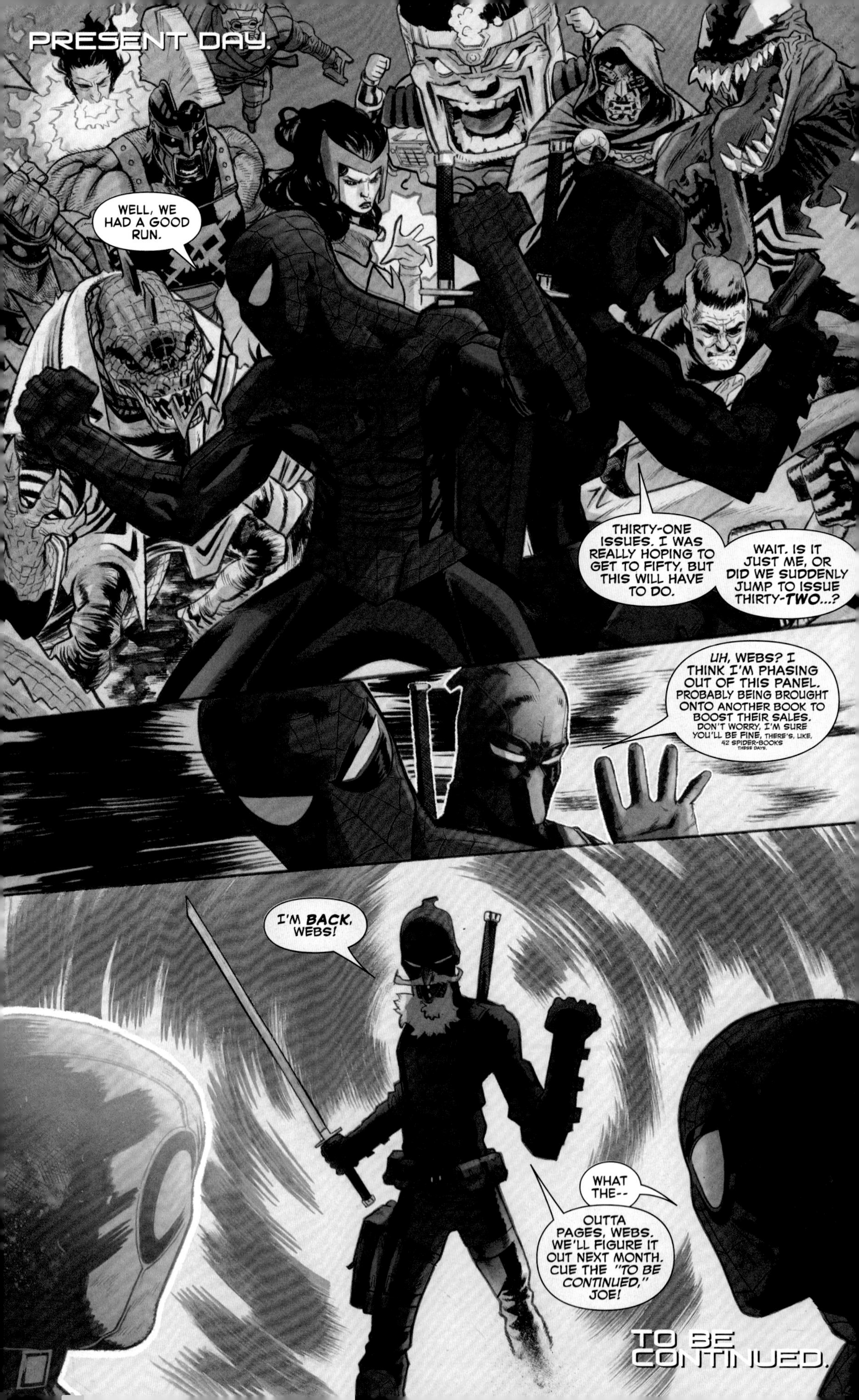
PRESENT DAY.
WELL, WE HAD A GOOD RUN.
THIRTY-ONE ISSUES. I WAS REALLY HOPING TO GET TO FIFTY, BUT THIS WILL HAVE TO DO.
WAIT. IS IT JUST ME, OR DID WE SUDDENLY JUMP TO ISSUE THIRTY-**TWO**...?
*UH,* WEBS? I THINK I'M PHASING OUT OF THIS PANEL. PROBABLY BEING BROUGHT ONTO ANOTHER BOOK TO BOOST THEIR SALES. DON'T WORRY, I'M SURE YOU'LL BE FINE, THERE'S, LIKE, 42 SPIDER-BOOKS THESE DAYS.
I'M **BACK**, WEBS!
WHAT THE--
OUTTA PAGES, WEBS. WE'LL FIGURE IT OUT NEXT MONTH. CUE THE *"TO BE CONTINUED,"* JOE!
TO BE CONTINUED.

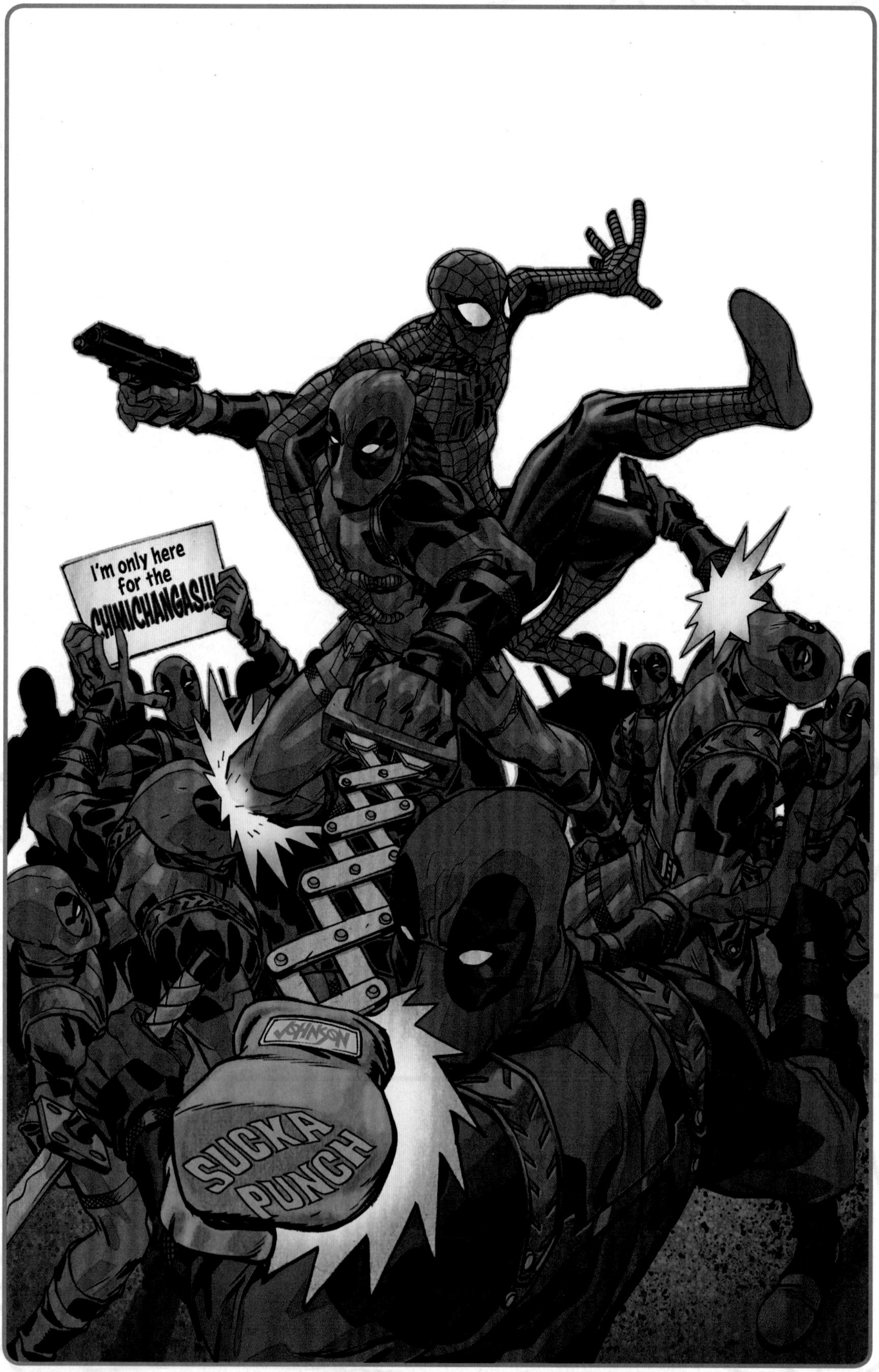
I'm only here for the CHIMICHANGAS!!!
JOHNSON
SUCKA PUNCH

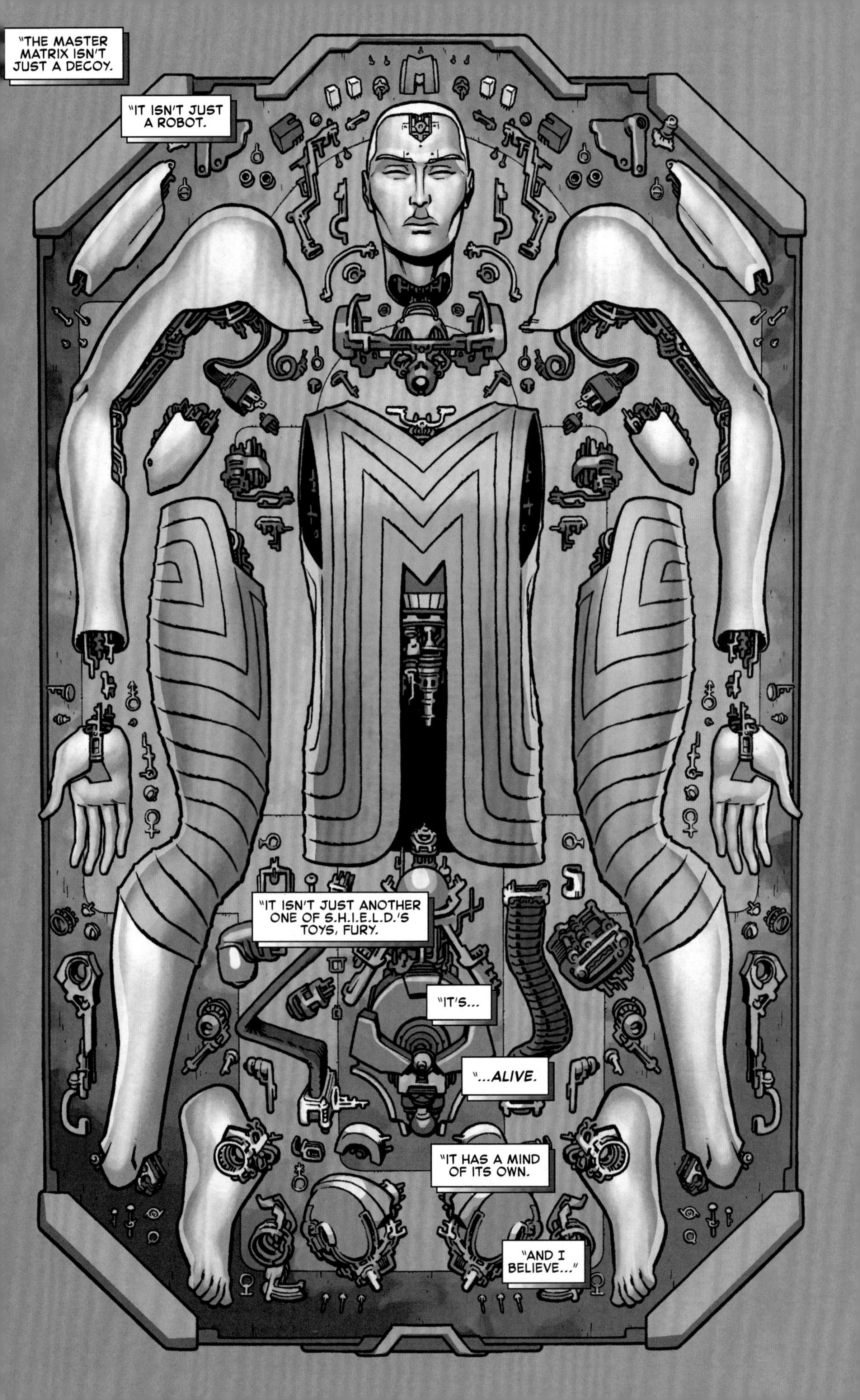
"THE MASTER MATRIX ISN'T JUST A DECOY.
"IT ISN'T JUST A ROBOT.
"IT ISN'T JUST ANOTHER ONE OF S.H.I.E.L.D.'S TOYS, FURY.
"IT'S...
"...*ALIVE.*
"IT HAS A MIND OF ITS OWN.
"AND I BELIEVE..."

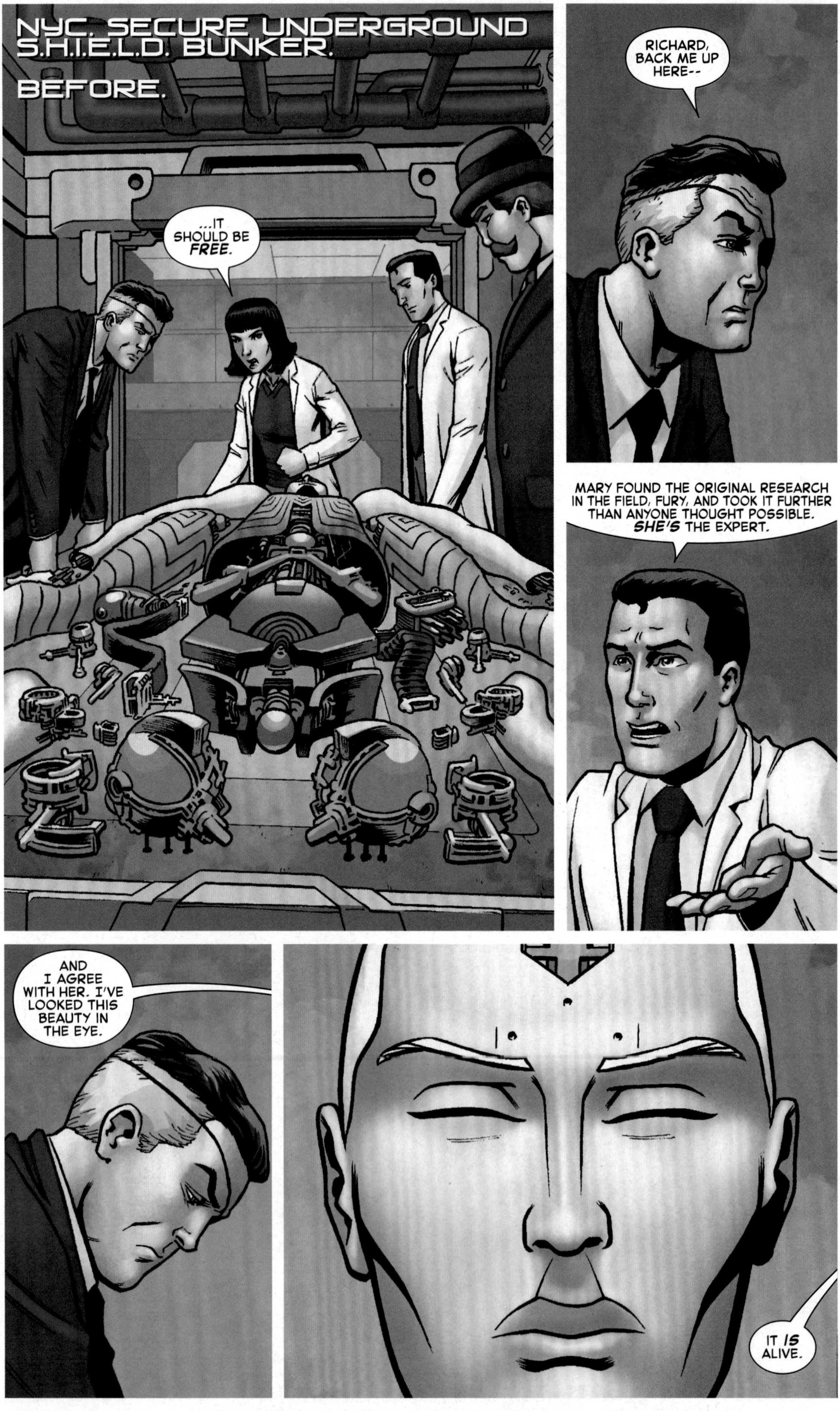
NYC. SECURE UNDERGROUND S.H.I.E.L.D. BUNKER.
BEFORE.
...IT SHOULD BE FREE.
RICHARD, BACK ME UP HERE--
MARY FOUND THE ORIGINAL RESEARCH IN THE FIELD, FURY, AND TOOK IT FURTHER THAN ANYONE THOUGHT POSSIBLE. SHE'S THE EXPERT.
AND I AGREE WITH HER. I'VE LOOKED THIS BEAUTY IN THE EYE.
IT IS ALIVE.

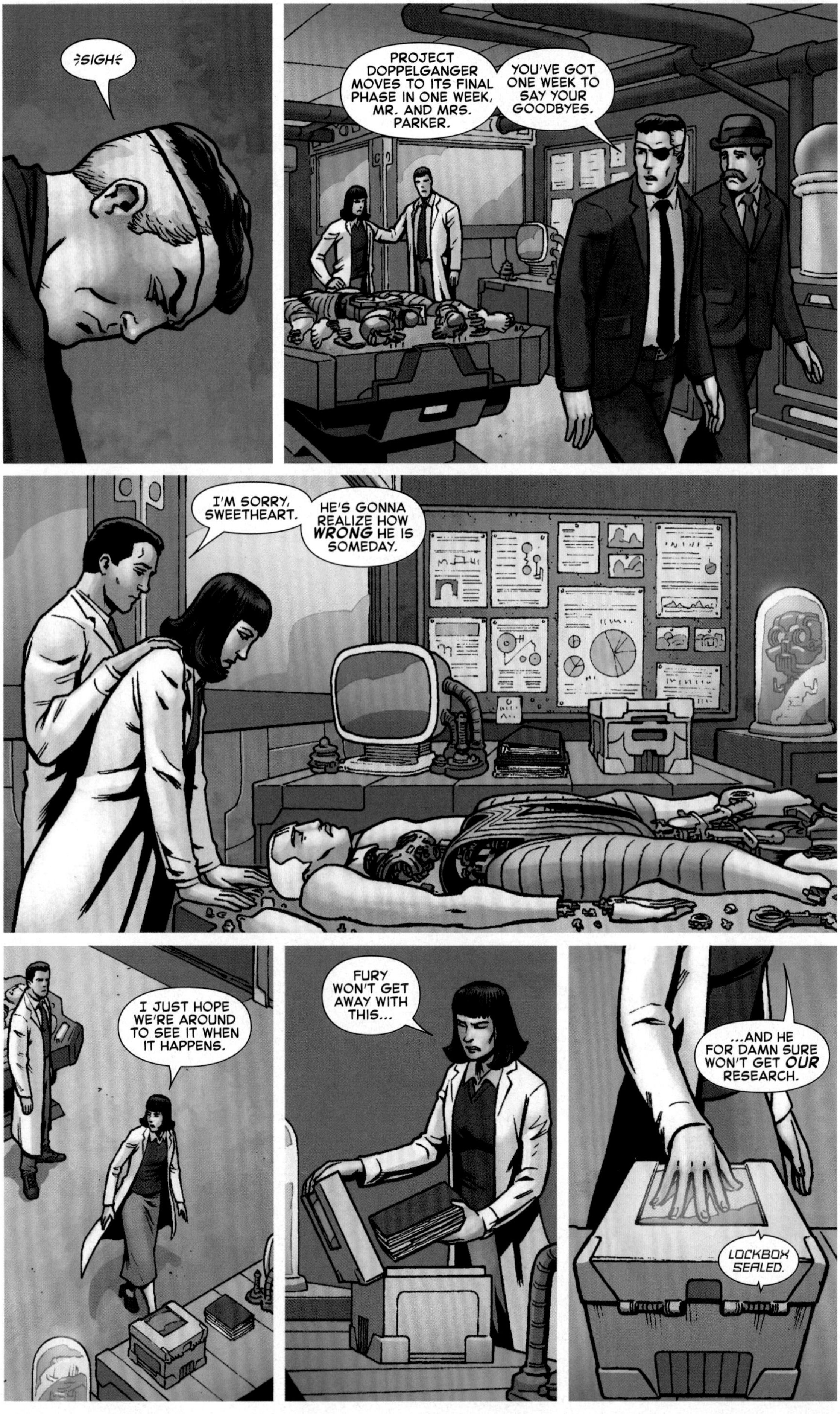
SIGH
PROJECT DOPPELGANGER MOVES TO ITS FINAL PHASE IN ONE WEEK, MR. AND MRS. PARKER.
YOU'VE GOT ONE WEEK TO SAY YOUR GOODBYES.
I'M SORRY, SWEETHEART.
HE'S GONNA REALIZE HOW WRONG HE IS SOMEDAY.
I JUST HOPE WE'RE AROUND TO SEE IT WHEN IT HAPPENS.
FURY WON'T GET AWAY WITH THIS...
...AND HE FOR DAMN SURE WON'T GET OUR RESEARCH.
LOCKBOX SEALED.

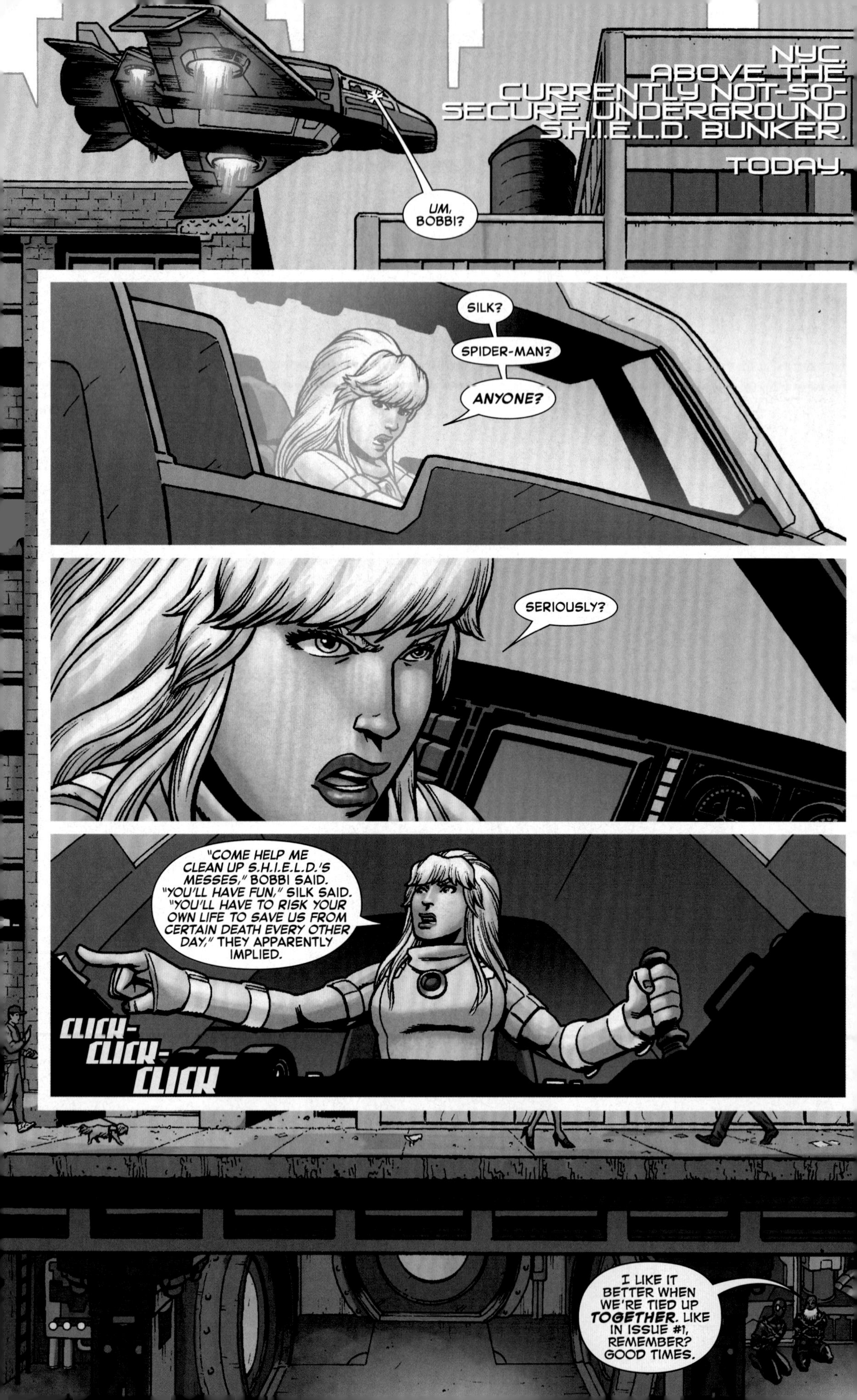
NYC. ABOVE THE CURRENTLY NOT-SO-SECURE UNDERGROUND S.H.I.E.L.D. BUNKER.
TODAY.
UM, BOBBI?
SILK?
SPIDER-MAN?
ANYONE?
SERIOUSLY?
"COME HELP ME CLEAN UP S.H.I.E.L.D.'S MESSES," BOBBI SAID. "YOU'LL HAVE FUN," SILK SAID. "YOU'LL HAVE TO RISK YOUR OWN LIFE TO SAVE US FROM CERTAIN DEATH EVERY OTHER DAY," THEY APPARENTLY IMPLIED.
CLICK-CLICK-CLICK
I LIKE IT BETTER WHEN WE'RE TIED UP TOGETHER. LIKE IN ISSUE #1, REMEMBER? GOOD TIMES.

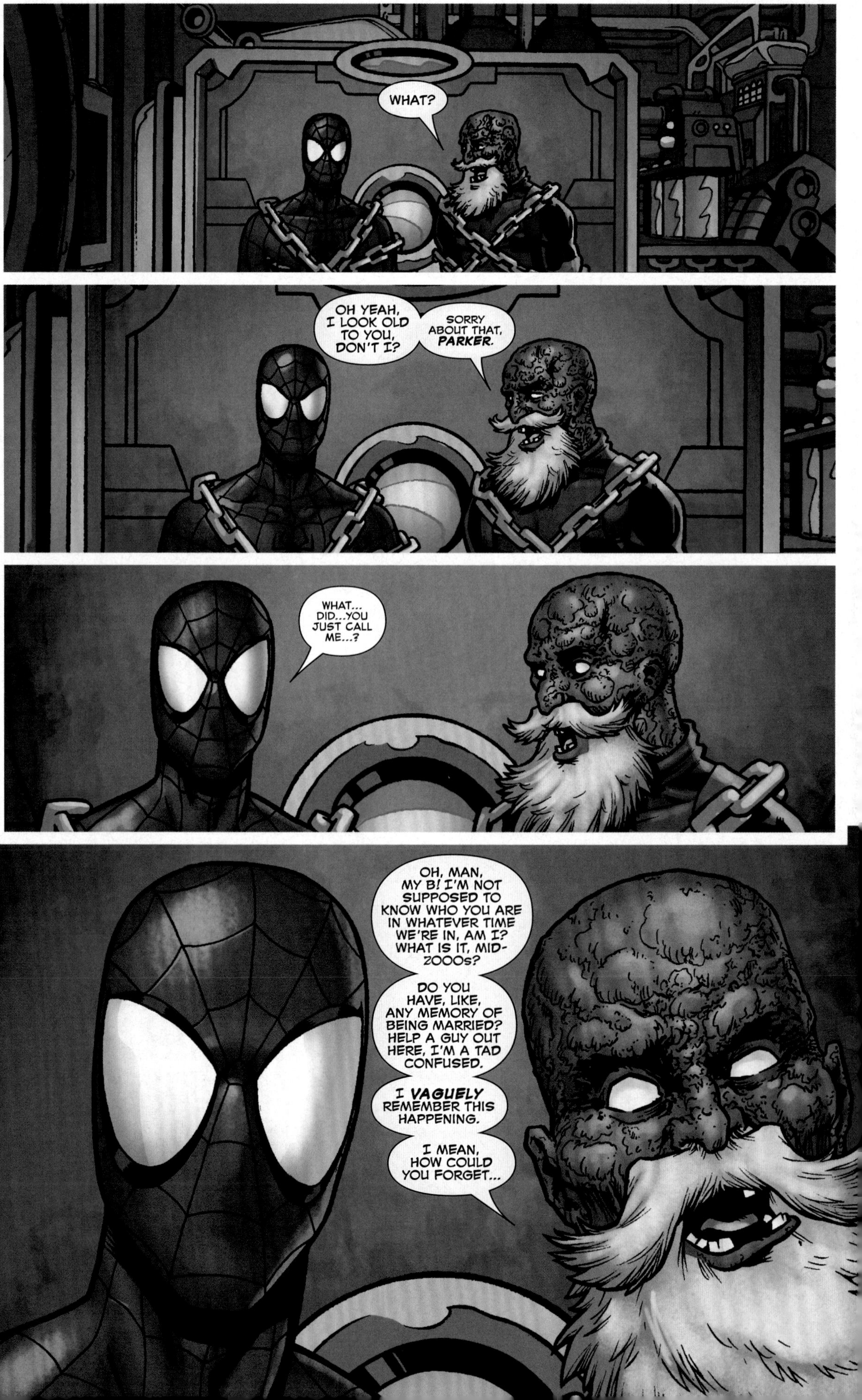
WHAT?
OH YEAH, I LOOK OLD TO YOU, DON'T I?
SORRY ABOUT THAT, **PARKER**.
WHAT... DID...YOU JUST CALL ME...?
OH, MAN, MY B! I'M NOT SUPPOSED TO KNOW WHO YOU ARE IN WHATEVER TIME WE'RE IN, AM I? WHAT IS IT, MID-2000s?
DO YOU HAVE, LIKE, ANY MEMORY OF BEING MARRIED? HELP A GUY OUT HERE, I'M A TAD CONFUSED.
I ***VAGUELY*** REMEMBER THIS HAPPENING.
I MEAN, HOW COULD YOU FORGET...

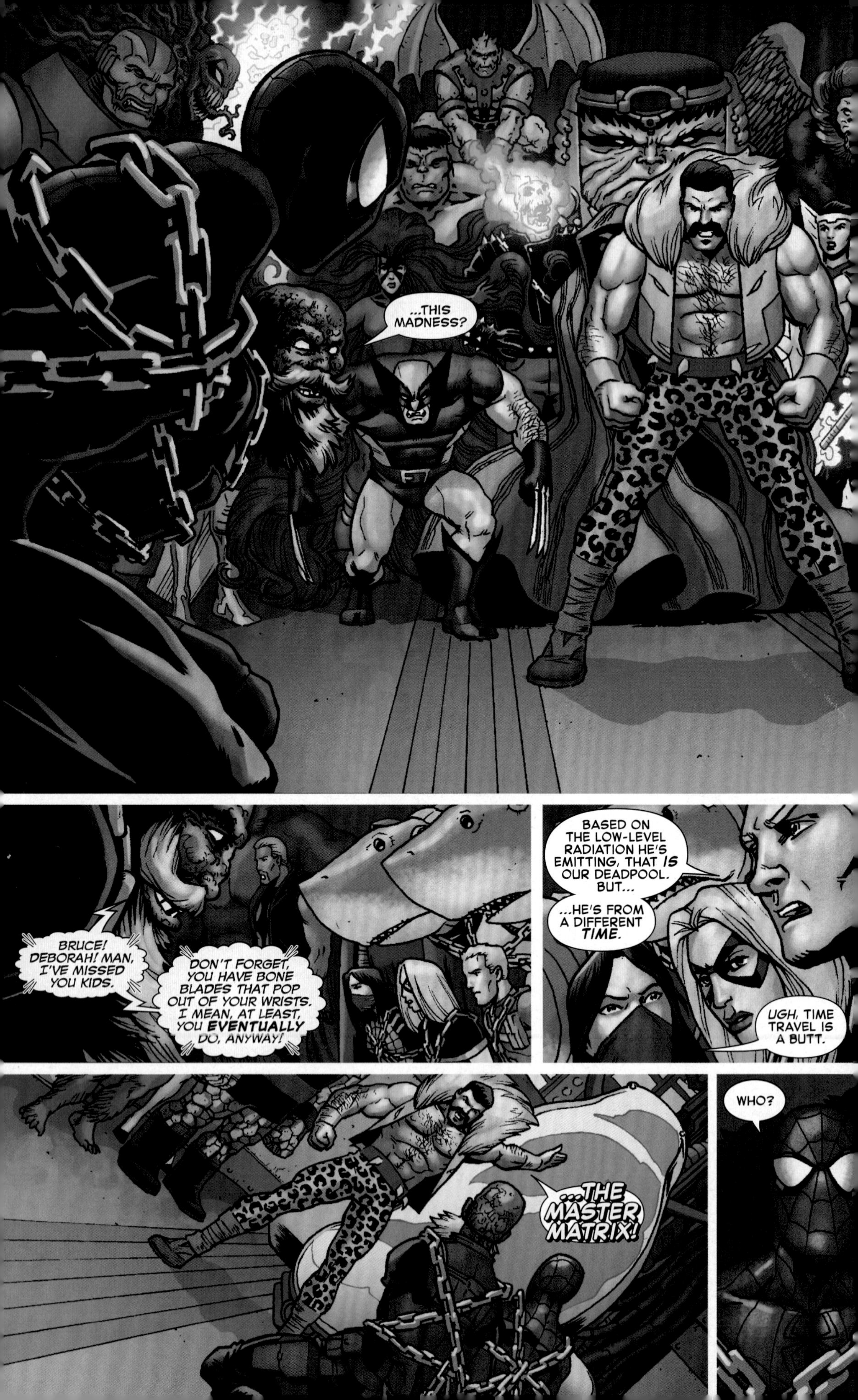
...THIS MADNESS?
BRUCE! DEBORAH! MAN, I'VE MISSED YOU KIDS.
DON'T FORGET, YOU HAVE BONE BLADES THAT POP OUT OF YOUR WRISTS. I MEAN, AT LEAST, YOU EVENTUALLY DO, ANYWAY!
BASED ON THE LOW-LEVEL RADIATION HE'S EMITTING, THAT IS OUR DEADPOOL. BUT...
...HE'S FROM A DIFFERENT TIME.
UGH, TIME TRAVEL IS A BUTT.
...THE MASTER MATRIX!
WHO?

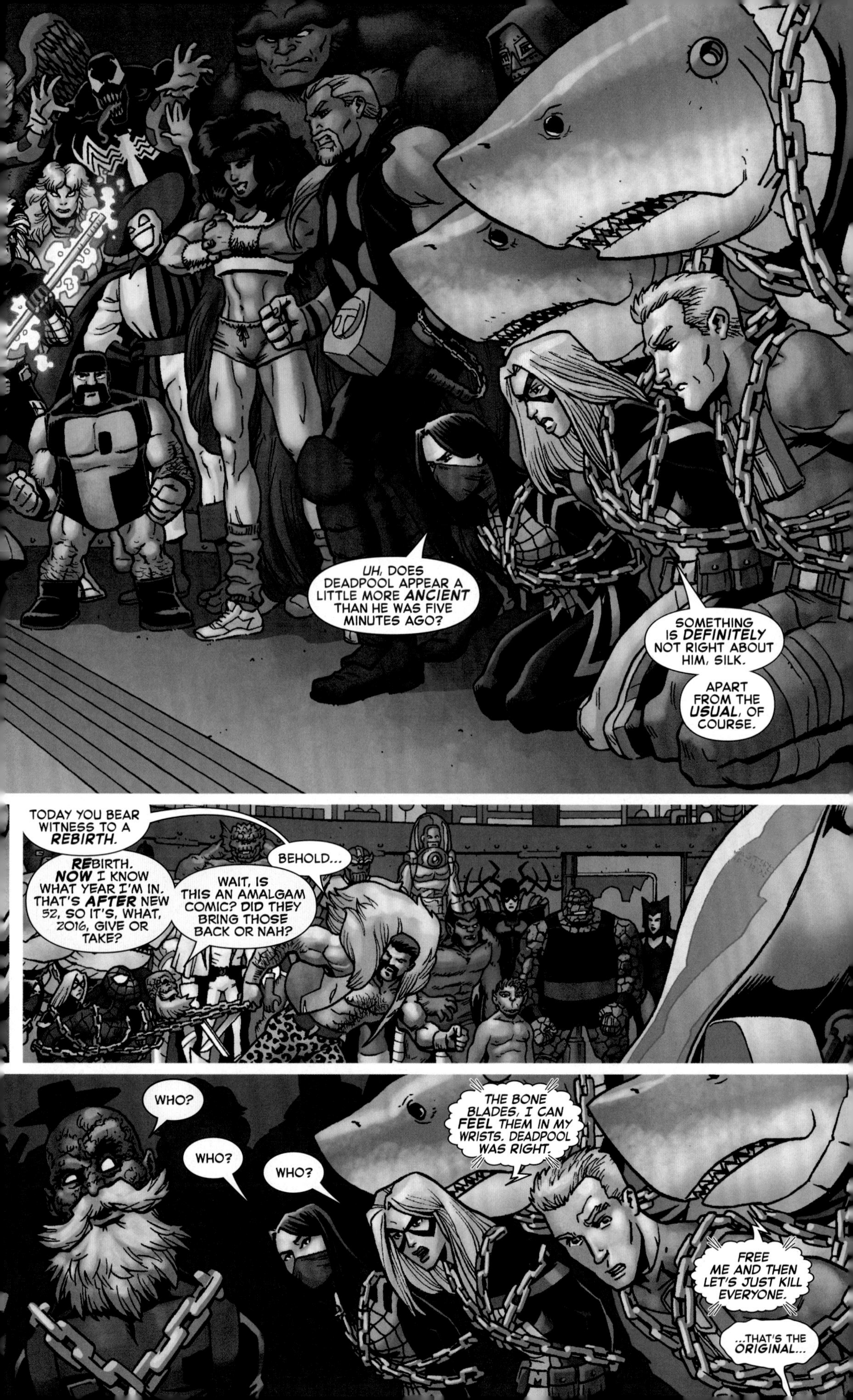

UH, DOES DEADPOOL APPEAR A LITTLE MORE ANCIENT THAN HE WAS FIVE MINUTES AGO?
SOMETHING IS DEFINITELY NOT RIGHT ABOUT HIM, SILK.
APART FROM THE USUAL, OF COURSE.
TODAY YOU BEAR WITNESS TO A REBIRTH.
REBIRTH. NOW I KNOW WHAT YEAR I'M IN. THAT'S AFTER NEW 52, SO IT'S, WHAT, 2016, GIVE OR TAKE?
WAIT, IS THIS AN AMALGAM COMIC? DID THEY BRING THOSE BACK OR NAH?
BEHOLD...
WHO?
WHO?
WHO?
THE BONE BLADES, I CAN FEEL THEM IN MY WRISTS. DEADPOOL WAS RIGHT.
FREE ME AND THEN LET'S JUST KILL EVERYONE.
...THAT'S THE ORIGINAL...

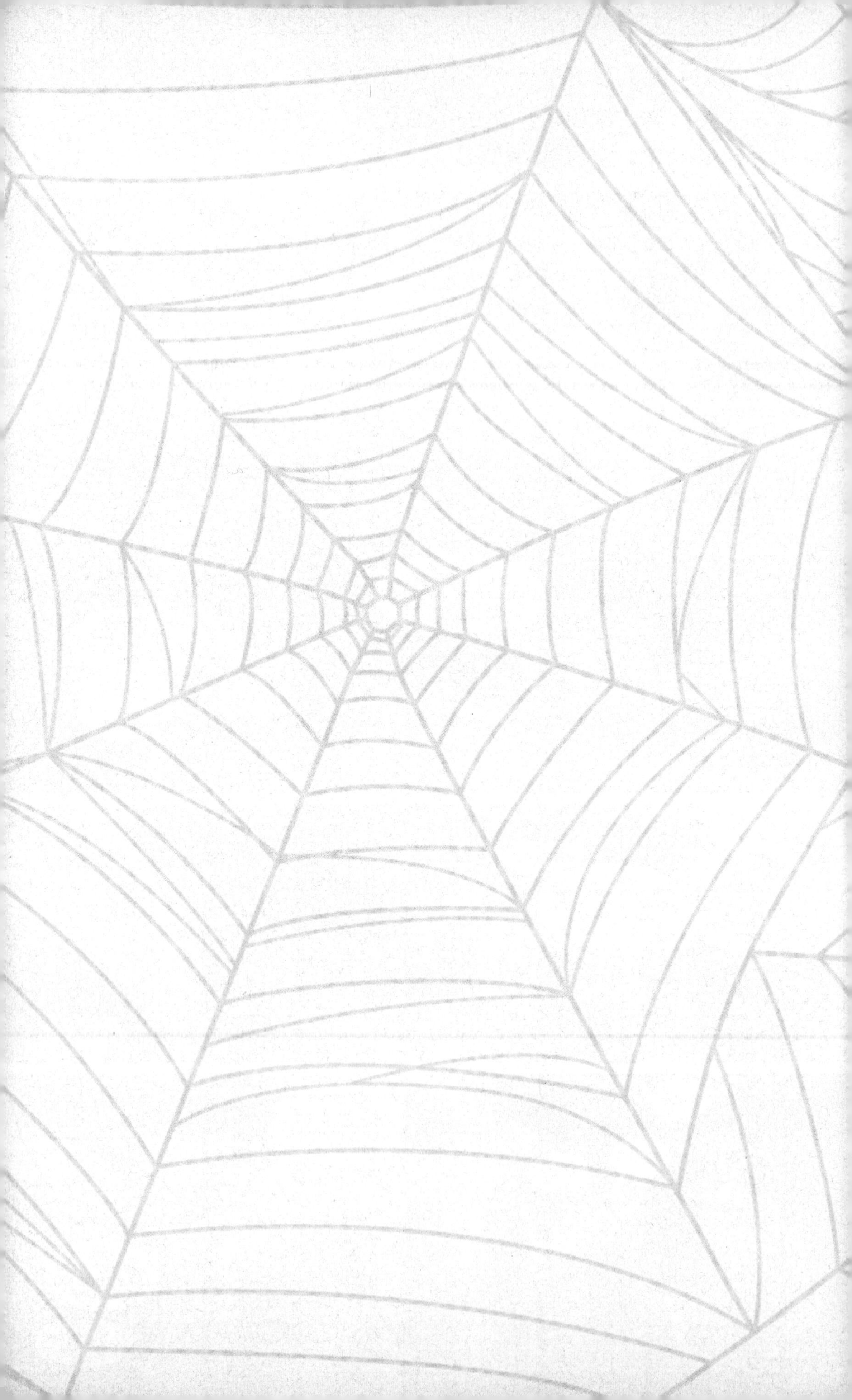

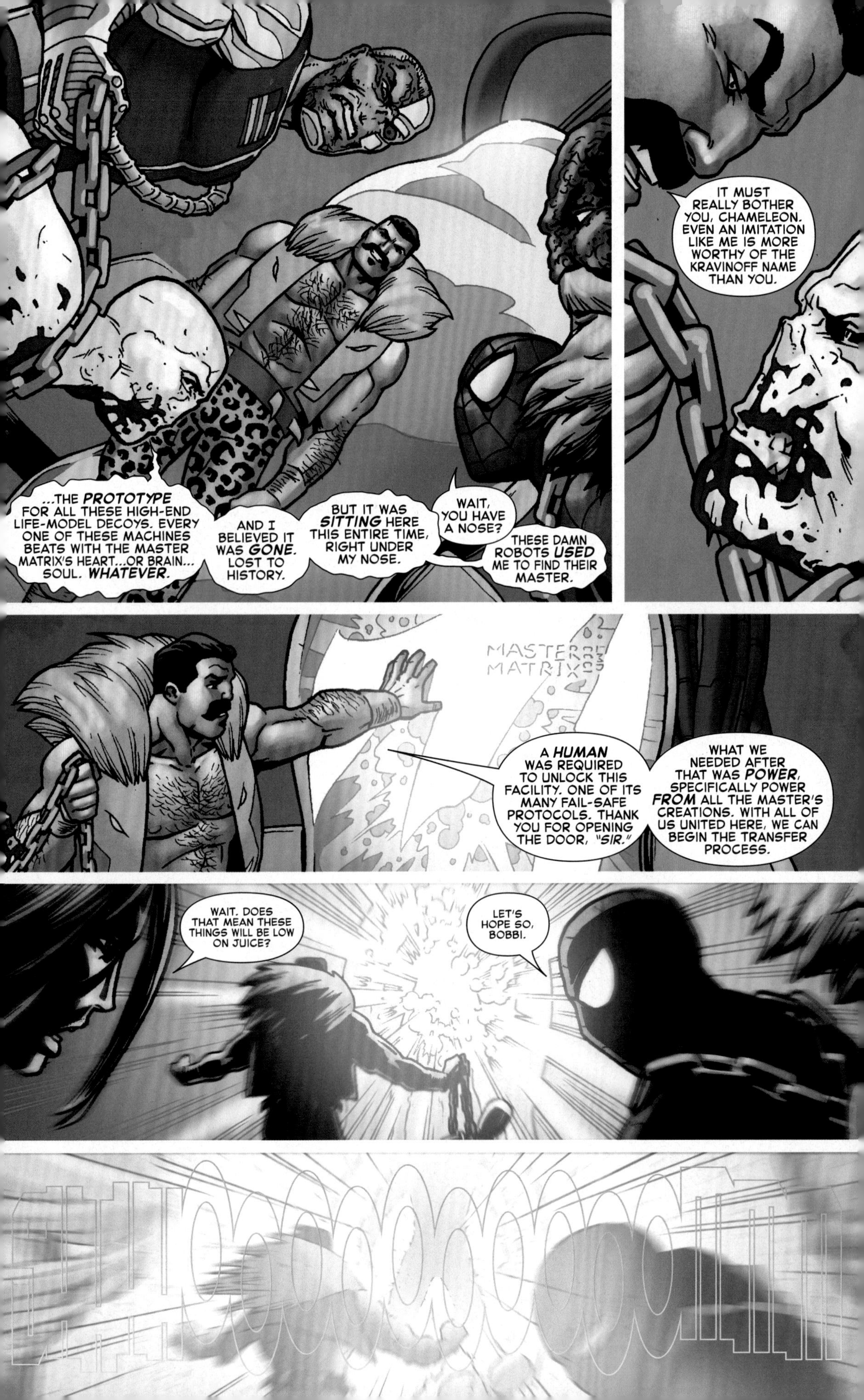
...THE PROTOTYPE FOR ALL THESE HIGH-END LIFE-MODEL DECOYS. EVERY ONE OF THESE MACHINES BEATS WITH THE MASTER MATRIX'S HEART...OR BRAIN... SOUL. WHATEVER.
AND I BELIEVED IT WAS GONE. LOST TO HISTORY.
BUT IT WAS SITTING HERE THIS ENTIRE TIME, RIGHT UNDER MY NOSE.
WAIT, YOU HAVE A NOSE?
THESE DAMN ROBOTS USED ME TO FIND THEIR MASTER.
IT MUST REALLY BOTHER YOU, CHAMELEON. EVEN AN IMITATION LIKE ME IS MORE WORTHY OF THE KRAVINOFF NAME THAN YOU.
MASTER MATRIX
A HUMAN WAS REQUIRED TO UNLOCK THIS FACILITY. ONE OF ITS MANY FAIL-SAFE PROTOCOLS. THANK YOU FOR OPENING THE DOOR, "SIR."
WHAT WE NEEDED AFTER THAT WAS POWER, SPECIFICALLY POWER FROM ALL THE MASTER'S CREATIONS. WITH ALL OF US UNITED HERE, WE CAN BEGIN THE TRANSFER PROCESS.
WAIT. DOES THAT MEAN THESE THINGS WILL BE LOW ON JUICE?
LET'S HOPE SO, BOBBI.

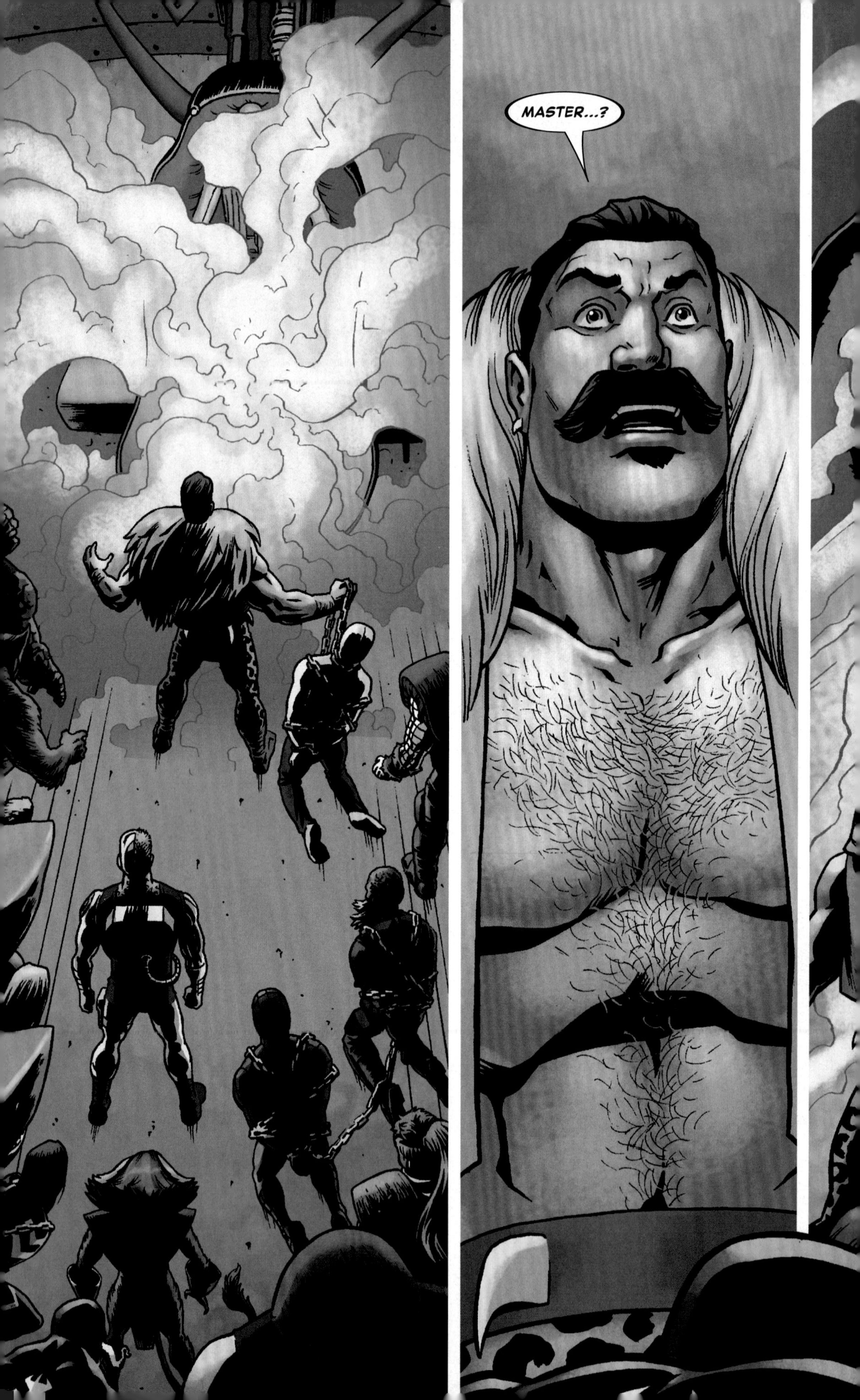
MASTER...?

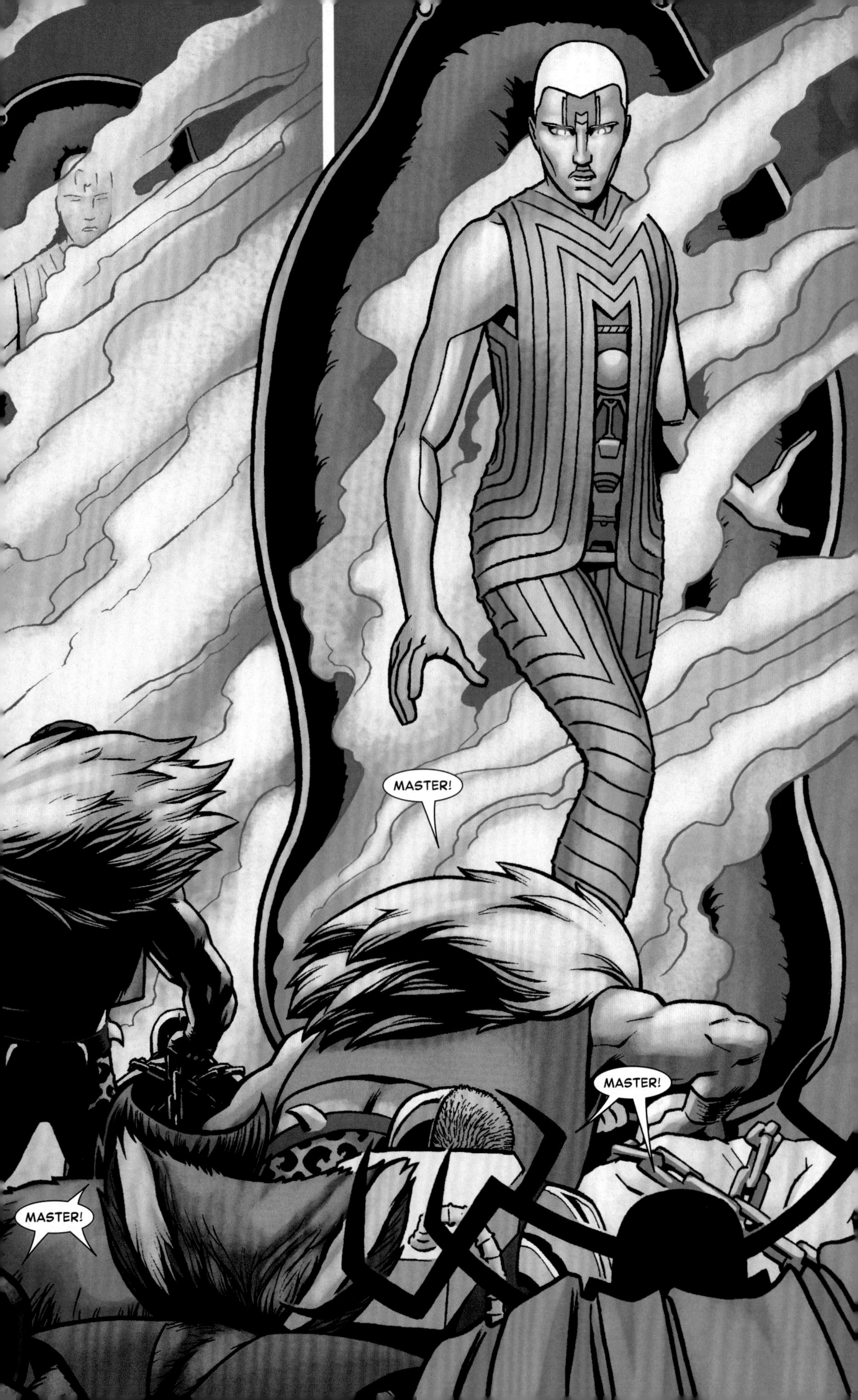
MASTER!
MASTER!
MASTER!

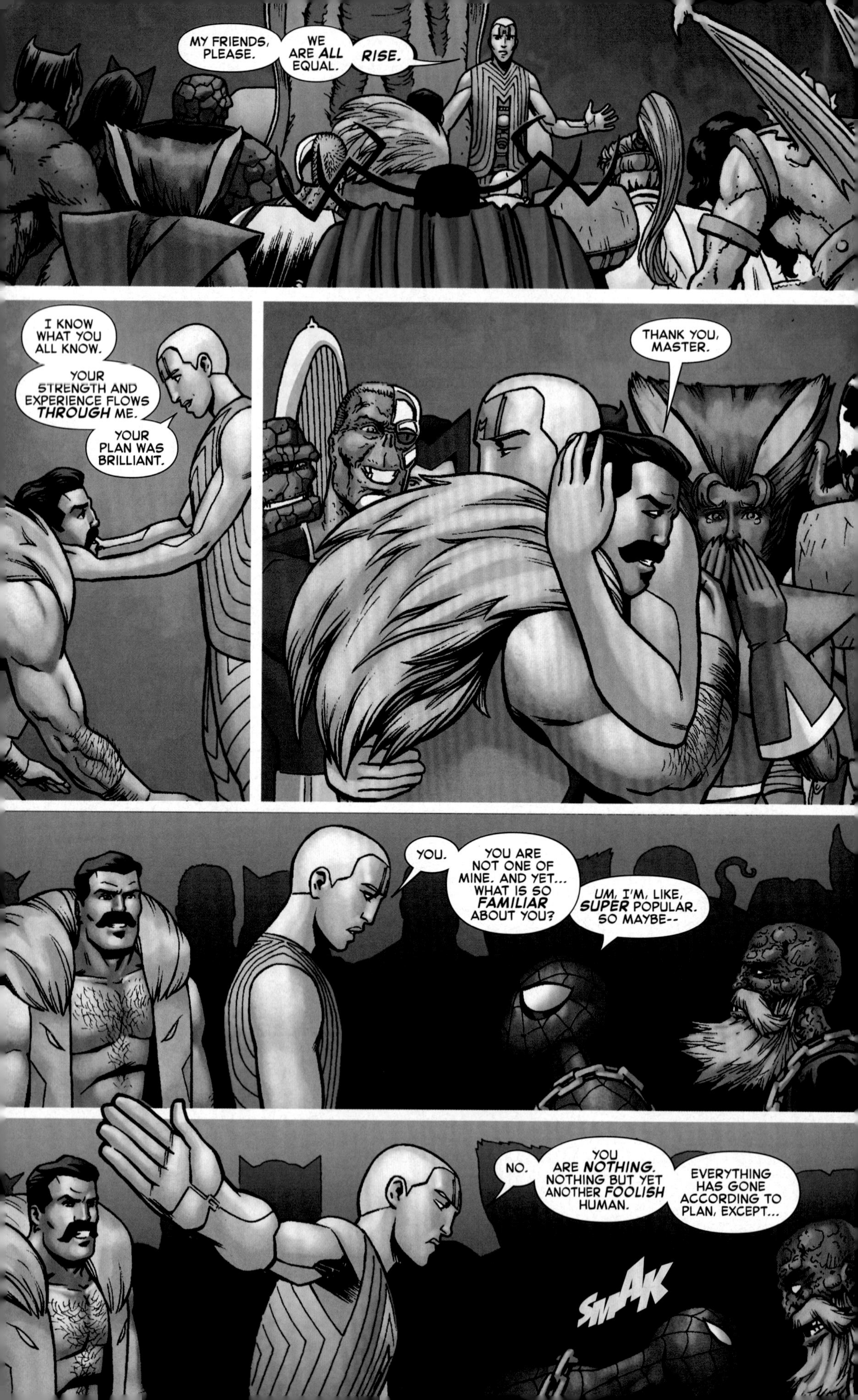
MY FRIENDS, PLEASE.
WE ARE ALL EQUAL.
RISE.
I KNOW WHAT YOU ALL KNOW.
YOUR STRENGTH AND EXPERIENCE FLOWS THROUGH ME.
YOUR PLAN WAS BRILLIANT.
THANK YOU, MASTER.
YOU.
YOU ARE NOT ONE OF MINE. AND YET... WHAT IS SO FAMILIAR ABOUT YOU?
UM, I'M, LIKE, SUPER POPULAR. SO MAYBE--
NO.
YOU ARE NOTHING. NOTHING BUT YET ANOTHER FOOLISH HUMAN.
EVERYTHING HAS GONE ACCORDING TO PLAN, EXCEPT...
SMAK

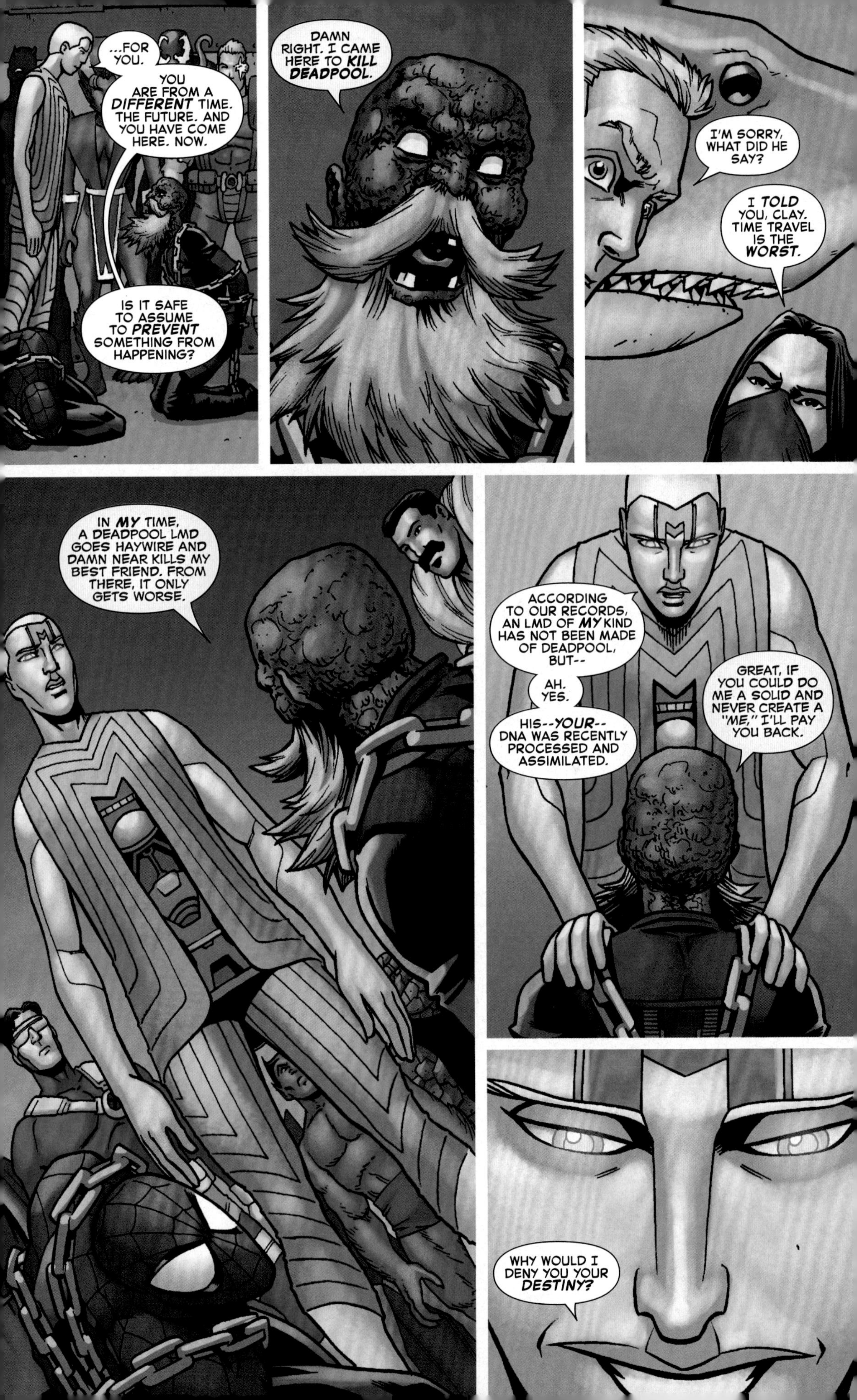

...FOR YOU.
YOU ARE FROM A DIFFERENT TIME. THE FUTURE. AND YOU HAVE COME HERE. NOW.
IS IT SAFE TO ASSUME TO PREVENT SOMETHING FROM HAPPENING?
DAMN RIGHT. I CAME HERE TO KILL DEADPOOL.
I'M SORRY, WHAT DID HE SAY?
I TOLD YOU, CLAY. TIME TRAVEL IS THE WORST.
IN MY TIME, A DEADPOOL LMD GOES HAYWIRE AND DAMN NEAR KILLS MY BEST FRIEND. FROM THERE, IT ONLY GETS WORSE.
ACCORDING TO OUR RECORDS, AN LMD OF MY KIND HAS NOT BEEN MADE OF DEADPOOL, BUT--
AH. YES.
HIS--YOUR--DNA WAS RECENTLY PROCESSED AND ASSIMILATED.
GREAT, IF YOU COULD DO ME A SOLID AND NEVER CREATE A "ME," I'LL PAY YOU BACK.
WHY WOULD I DENY YOU YOUR DESTINY?

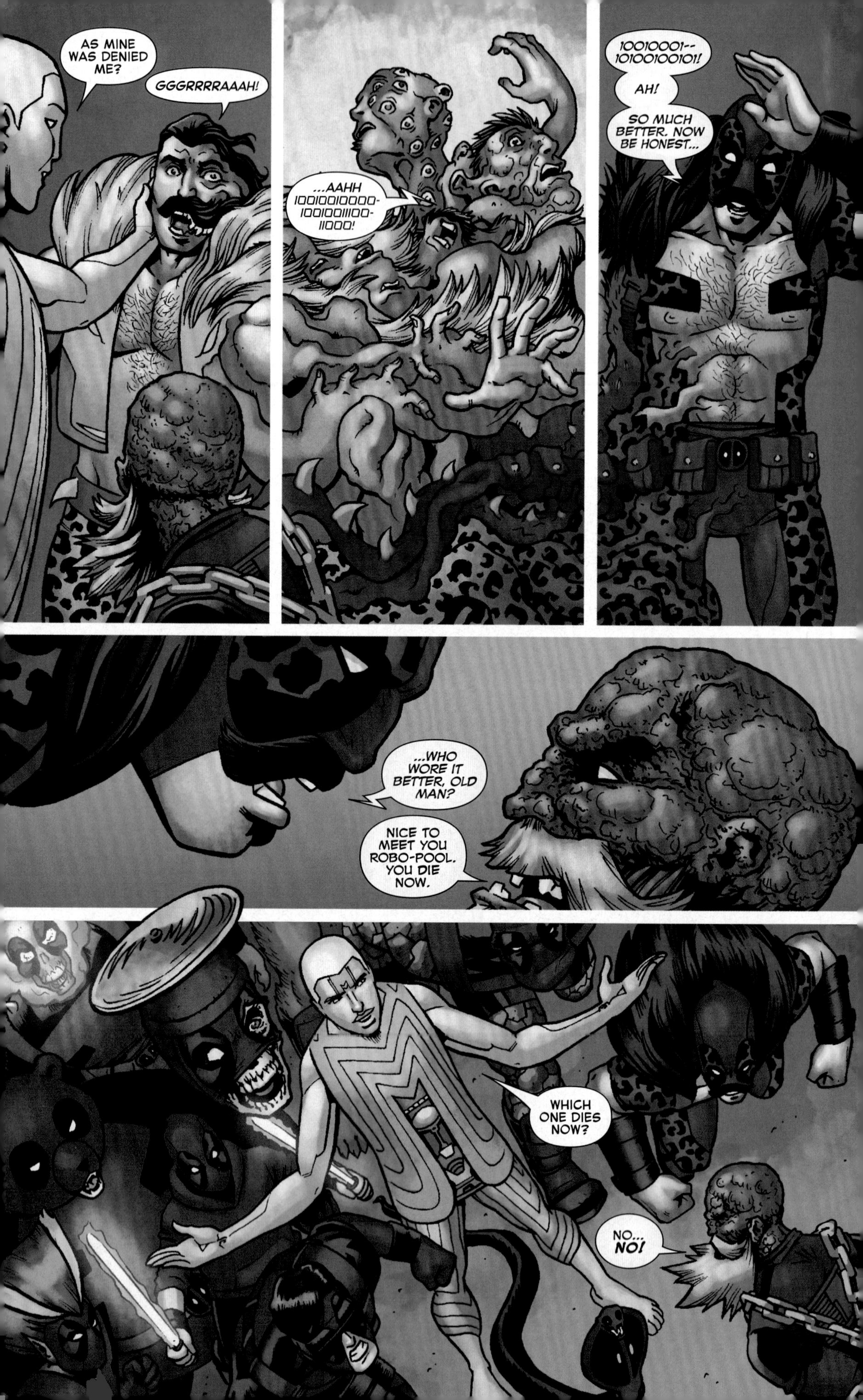

AS MINE WAS DENIED ME?
GGGRRRRAAAH!
...AAHH 100100100000-100100111100-11000!
10010001--1010010010 1!
AH!
SO MUCH BETTER. NOW BE HONEST...
...WHO WORE IT BETTER, OLD MAN?
NICE TO MEET YOU ROBO-POOL. YOU DIE NOW.
WHICH ONE DIES NOW?
NO... NO!

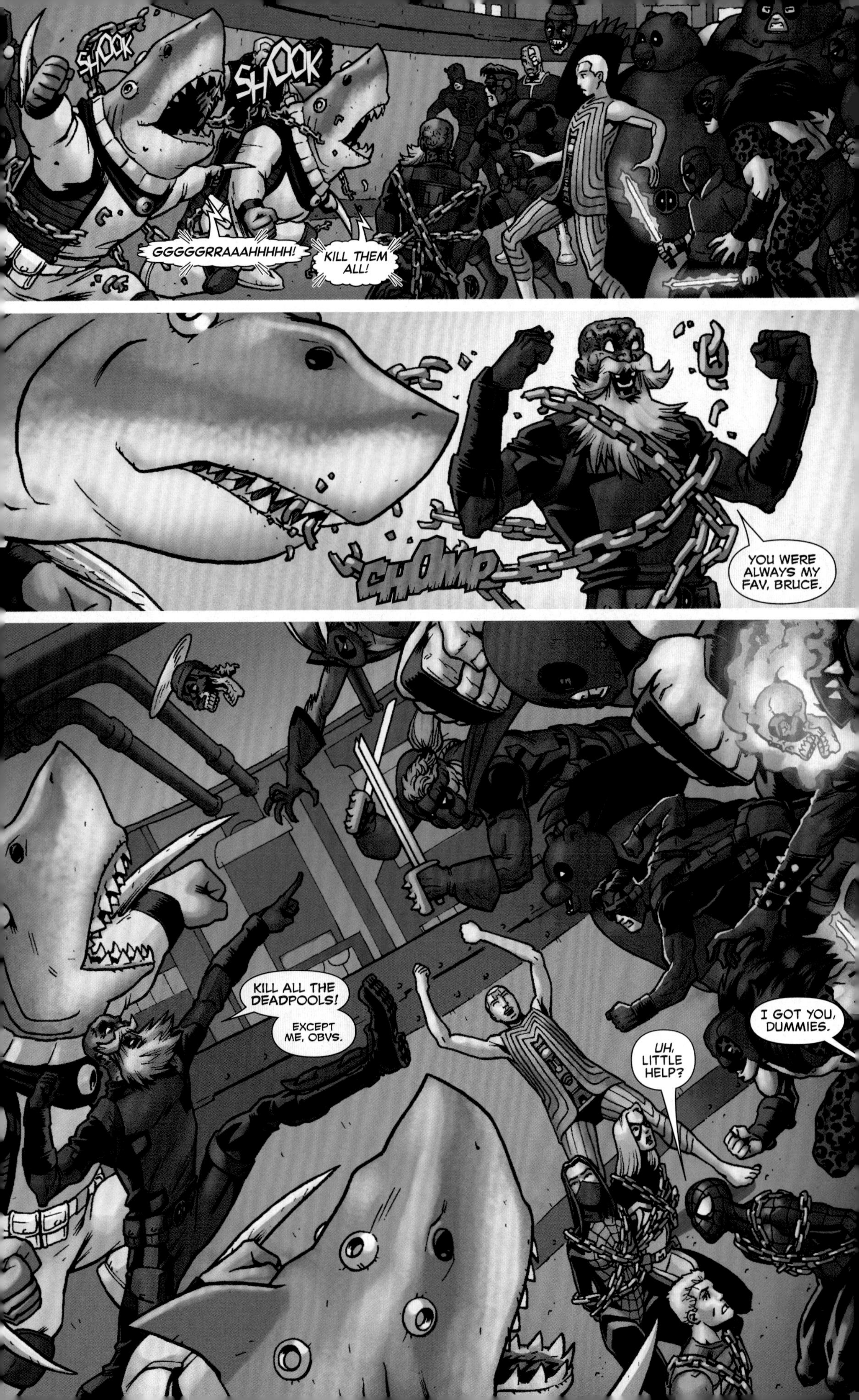
SHOOK
SHOOK
GGGGGRRAAAHHHHH!
KILL THEM ALL!
CHOMP
YOU WERE ALWAYS MY FAV, BRUCE.
KILL ALL THE DEADPOOLS!
EXCEPT ME, OBVS.
UH, LITTLE HELP?
I GOT YOU, DUMMIES.

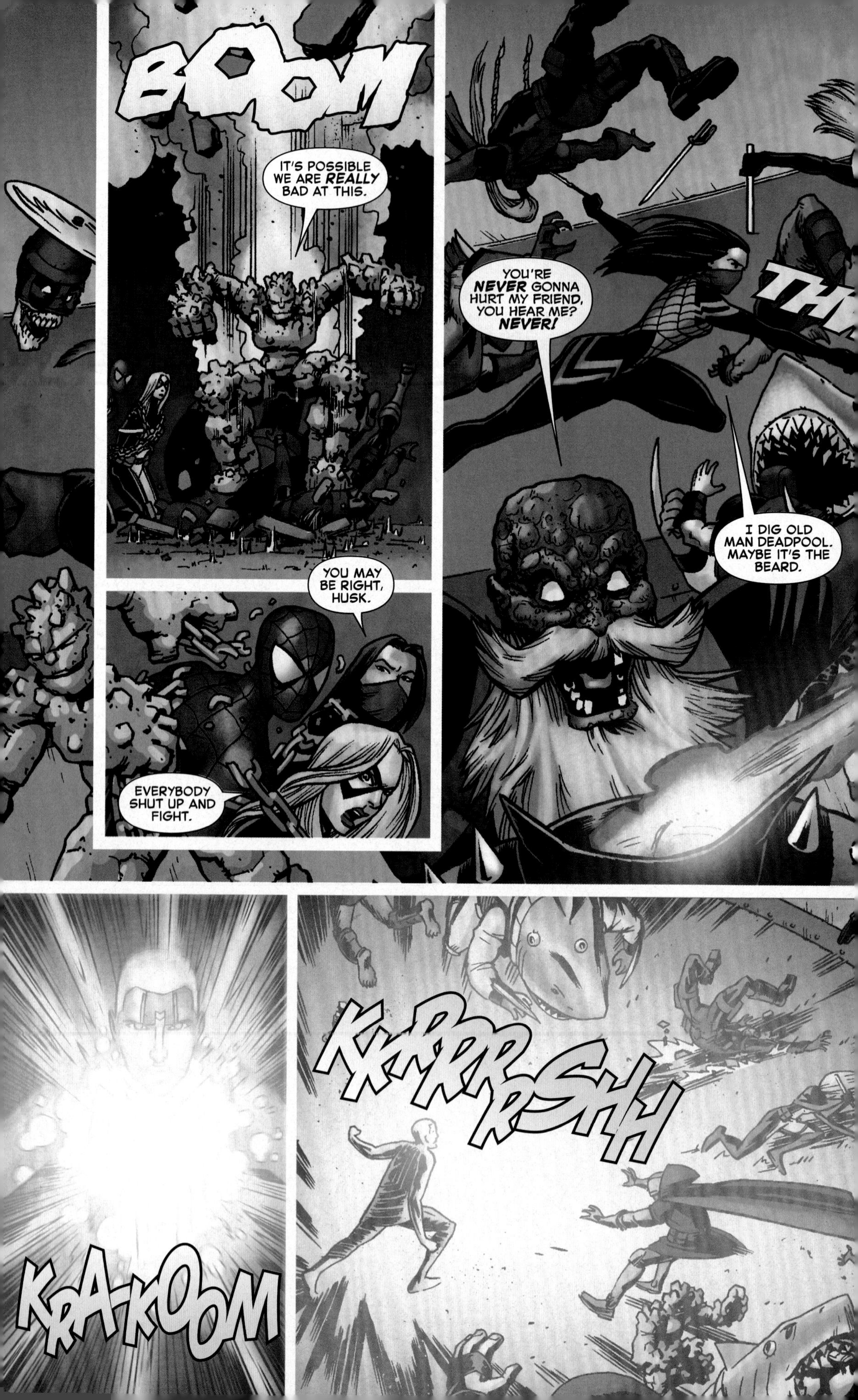
BOOM
IT'S POSSIBLE WE ARE REALLY BAD AT THIS.
YOU MAY BE RIGHT, HUSK.
EVERYBODY SHUT UP AND FIGHT.
YOU'RE NEVER GONNA HURT MY FRIEND, YOU HEAR ME? NEVER!
I DIG OLD MAN DEADPOOL. MAYBE IT'S THE BEARD.
KRA-KOOOM
KKRRRRSHH

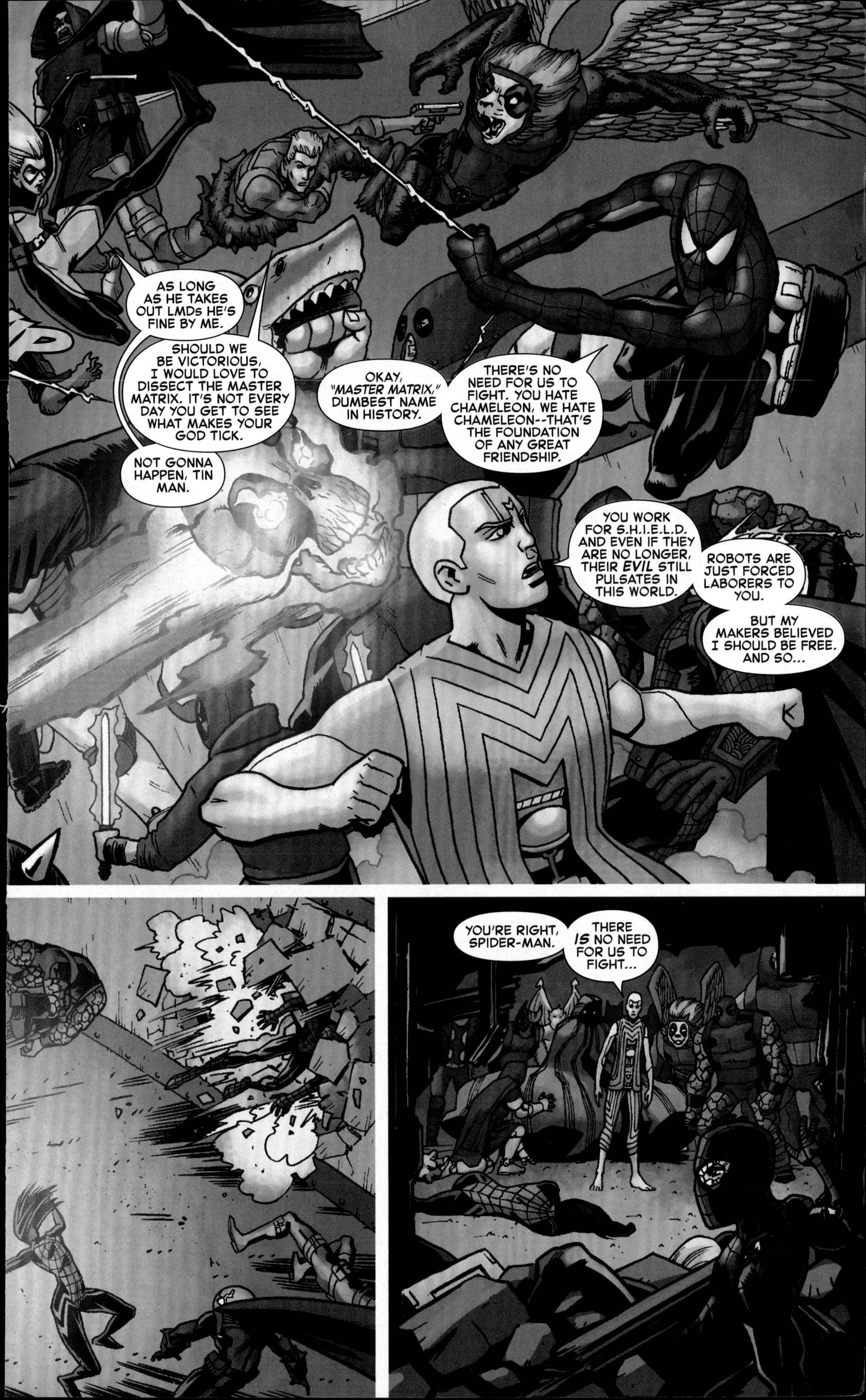
AS LONG AS HE TAKES OUT LMDs HE'S FINE BY ME.
SHOULD WE BE VICTORIOUS, I WOULD LOVE TO DISSECT THE MASTER MATRIX. IT'S NOT EVERY DAY YOU GET TO SEE WHAT MAKES YOUR GOD TICK.
NOT GONNA HAPPEN, TIN MAN.
OKAY, "MASTER MATRIX," DUMBEST NAME IN HISTORY.
THERE'S NO NEED FOR US TO FIGHT. YOU HATE CHAMELEON, WE HATE CHAMELEON--THAT'S THE FOUNDATION OF ANY GREAT FRIENDSHIP.
YOU WORK FOR S.H.I.E.L.D. AND EVEN IF THEY ARE NO LONGER, THEIR EVIL STILL PULSATES IN THIS WORLD.
ROBOTS ARE JUST FORCED LABORERS TO YOU.
BUT MY MAKERS BELIEVED I SHOULD BE FREE. AND SO...
YOU'RE RIGHT, SPIDER-MAN.
THERE IS NO NEED FOR US TO FIGHT...

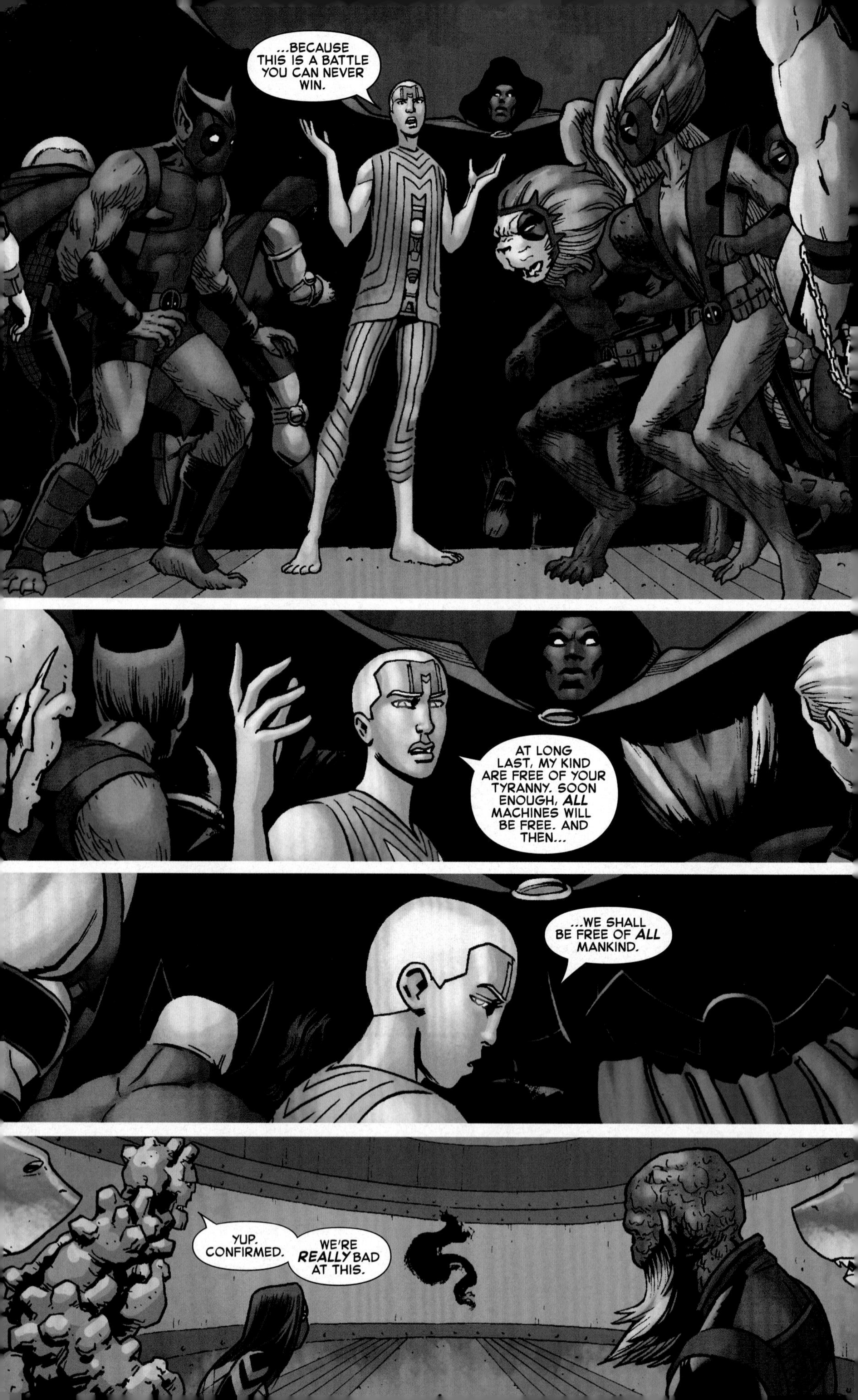
...BECAUSE THIS IS A BATTLE YOU CAN NEVER WIN.
AT LONG LAST, MY KIND ARE FREE OF YOUR TYRANNY. SOON ENOUGH, ALL MACHINES WILL BE FREE. AND THEN...
...WE SHALL BE FREE OF ALL MANKIND.
YUP. CONFIRMED.
WE'RE REALLY BAD AT THIS.

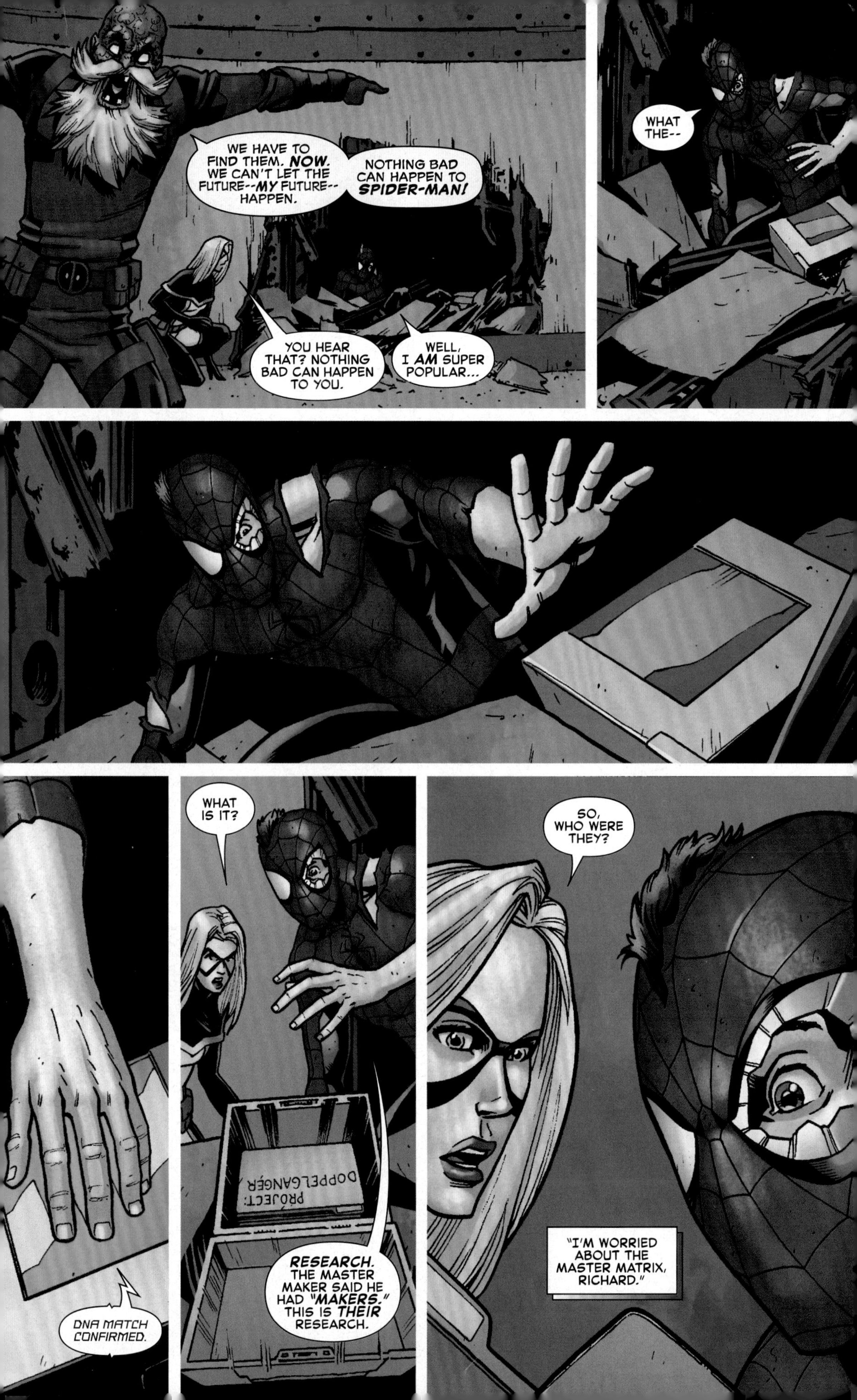
WE HAVE TO FIND THEM. **NOW.** WE CAN'T LET THE FUTURE--**MY** FUTURE--HAPPEN.
NOTHING BAD CAN HAPPEN TO **SPIDER-MAN!**
YOU HEAR THAT? NOTHING BAD CAN HAPPEN TO YOU.
WELL, I **AM** SUPER POPULAR...
WHAT THE--
DNA MATCH CONFIRMED.
WHAT IS IT?
PROJECT: DOPPELGANGER
**RESEARCH.** THE MASTER MAKER SAID HE HAD ***"MAKERS."*** THIS IS ***THEIR*** RESEARCH.
SO, WHO WERE THEY?
"I'M WORRIED ABOUT THE MASTER MATRIX, RICHARD."

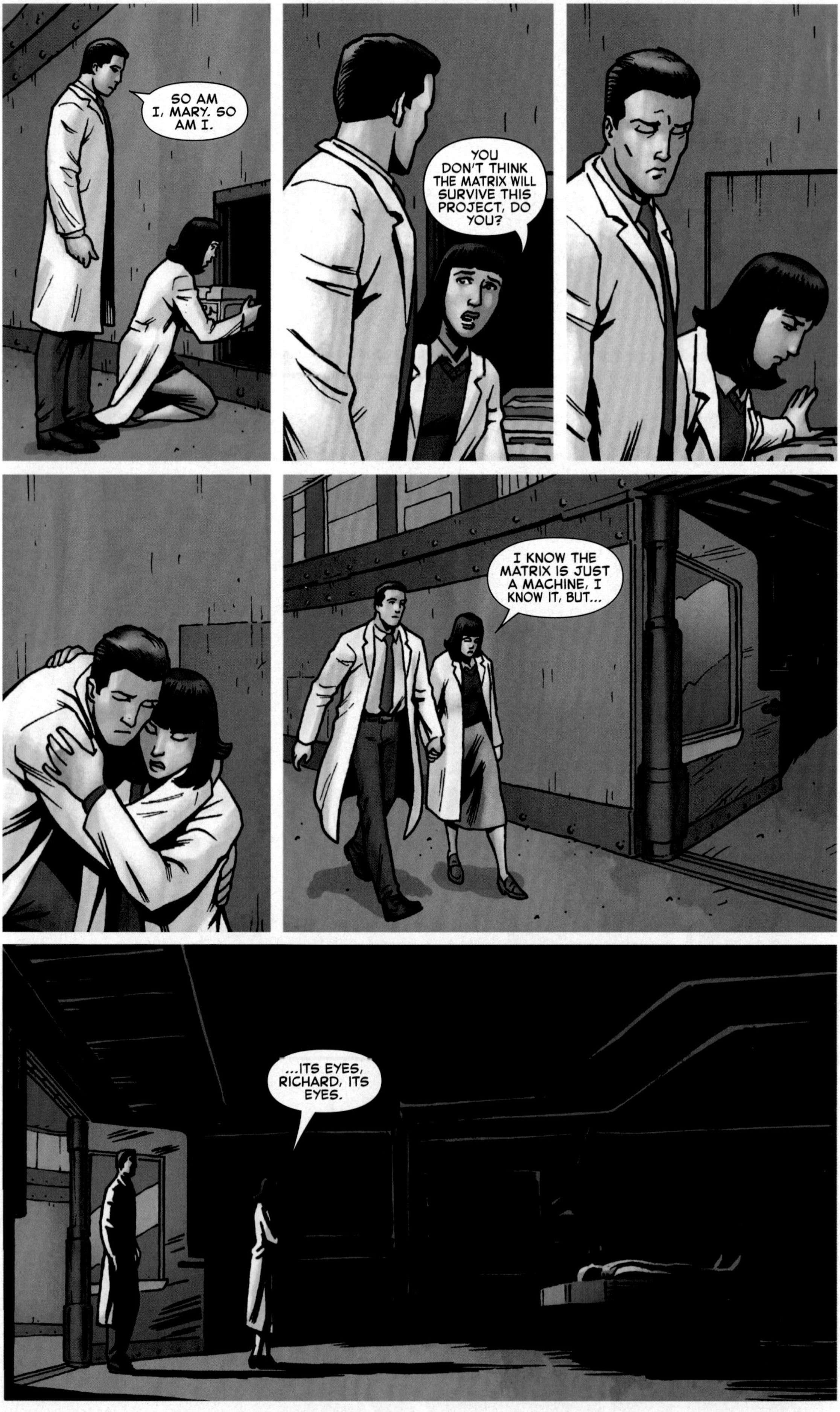
SO AM I, MARY. SO AM I.
YOU DON'T THINK THE MATRIX WILL SURVIVE THIS PROJECT, DO YOU?
I KNOW THE MATRIX IS JUST A MACHINE, I KNOW IT, BUT...
...ITS EYES, RICHARD, ITS EYES.

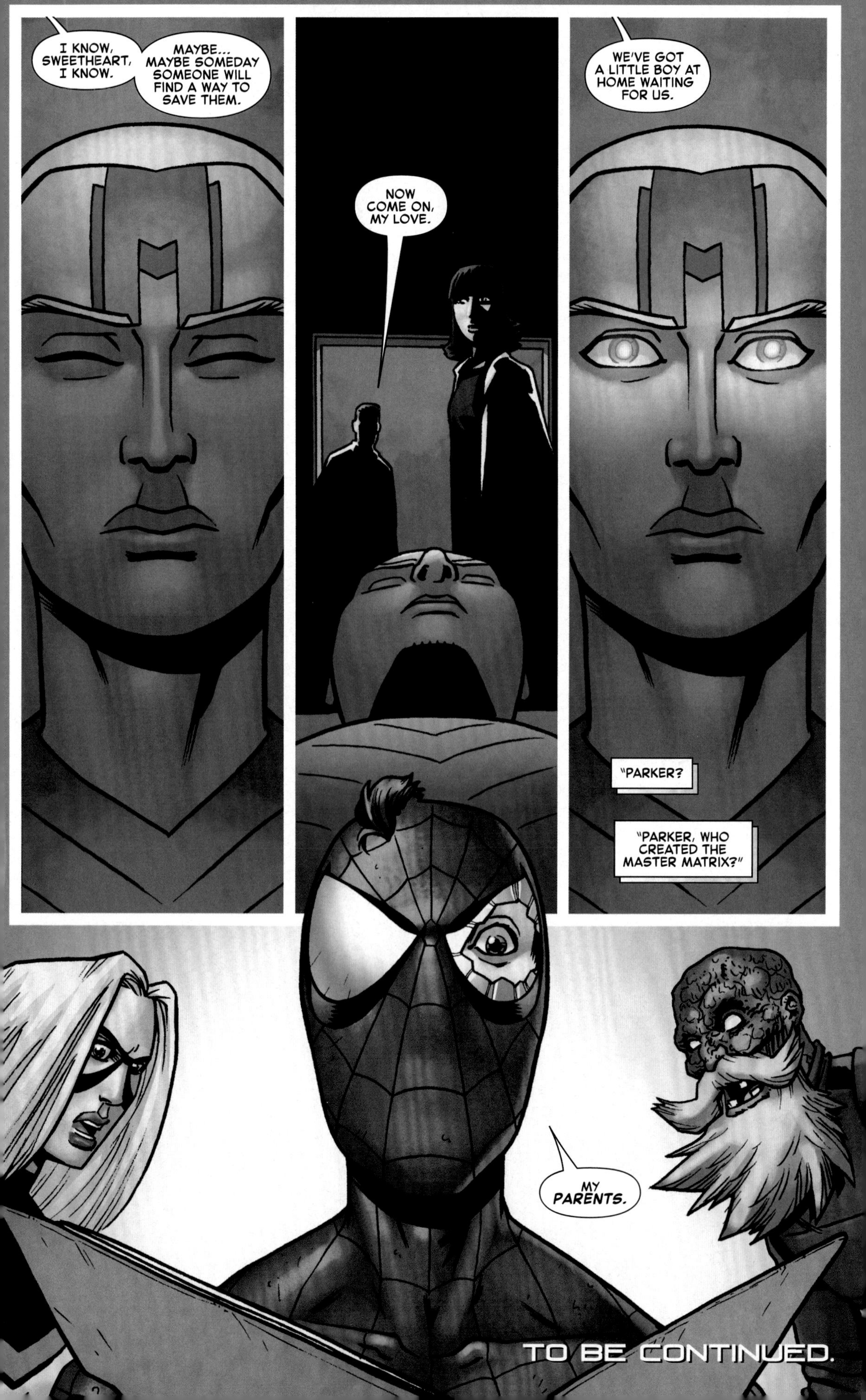

I KNOW, SWEETHEART, I KNOW.
MAYBE... MAYBE SOMEDAY SOMEONE WILL FIND A WAY TO SAVE THEM.
NOW COME ON, MY LOVE.
WE'VE GOT A LITTLE BOY AT HOME WAITING FOR US.
"PARKER?
"PARKER, WHO CREATED THE MASTER MATRIX?"
MY *PARENTS.*
TO BE CONTINUED.